Browning's Voices in *The Ring and the Book*

UNIVERSITY OF TORONTO PRESS

Browning's Voices in *The Ring and the Book*

A Study of Method and Meaning

Mary Rose Sullivan

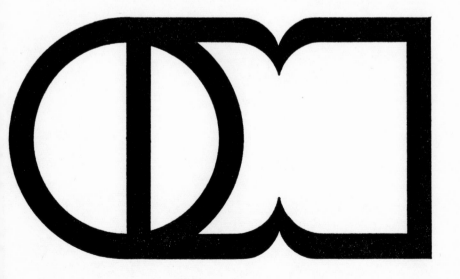

Copyright Canada 1969 by
University of Toronto Press
Printed in Canada

SBN 8020 5205 3

Acknowledgments

THIS STUDY WAS ORIGINALLY PREPARED, in somewhat different form, as a doctoral dissertation at Boston University. I should like to express my thanks to Professor Kingsbury M. Badger who supervised its preparation for the graduate school and gave generously of his time to provide helpful critical direction. I should also like to acknowledge my indebtedness to the late Professor David Bonnell Green who read and criticized the manuscript and whose advice and encouragement helped make possible its publication. The members of the Boston Browning Society, to whom I read portions of the manuscript while it was in preparation, stimulated me to a deeper study of *The Ring and the Book* by their warm interest and lively discussion and, most of all, by their genuine love for Robert Browning's poetry. Chapter 1 of this study has appeared, by kind permission of my publishers, in a special issue of *Victorian Poetry* marking the centenary of the publication of *The Ring and the Book*. Others to whom I owe thanks are Miss Rosemary Kehoe for help with clerical details in the preparation of the manuscript, and Professor Meredith B. Raymond of the University of Massachusetts who read the manuscript and offered critical advice and encouragement of inestimable value. I should also like to acknowledge with gratitude the financial support from the Publications Fund of the University of Toronto Press. Finally, I am indebted to Miss Francess G. Halpenny, Managing Editor of the University of Toronto Press, for her helpful suggestions and careful reading of the manuscript.

M.R.S.
University of Colorado Denver Center

Contents

Introduction

BROWNING'S *The Ring and the Book* is, in its length and scope, the most monumental poem of the Victorian period. That its unique style should have made it one of the least read of important nineteenth-century poetic statements is an irony which Browning would have appreciated. Today students of Victorian poetry are likely to be familiar with it, if at all, through anthologized "selected monologues" – usually those of Pompilia and the Pope – which, divorced from context, lose much of their significance and beauty and hence serve more as a deterrent than an encouragement to approaching the poem as a whole.

Not that *The Ring and the Book* has lacked for critical attention completely. Particularly since the publication of Charles Hodell's translation of *The Old Yellow Book* (1911), scholars have been busy with the question of the relationship between the poem and actual fact as found in the source document.[1] Even before Hodell's time, the

1/The most recent of these studies is Beatrice Corrigan, *Curious Annals: New Documents Relating to Browning's Roman Murder Story* (1956), which uses newly discovered documents concerning the Franceschini case (documents unknown to Browning) to prove conclusively that "Just as Pompilia was not the

poem was widely discussed for its ethical "message," its reflection of the Victorian ethos, and its demonstration of Browning's myth-making tendencies.[2] In more recent times, critical attention has shifted to a more aesthetic appreciation of the poem's structure as a unified work of art, the most notable contribution in this area being B. R. McElderry's tabular analysis of the plot which painstakingly disentangles the tightly woven threads of Browning's narrative.[3] But even such studies of form have taken a somewhat defensive tone (acutely conscious, no doubt, of Santayana's famous strictures on the poem's lack of architectonics[4]) and have been content to explain why so much repetition is necessary and to note how Browning has managed to find ingenious ways to say the same things again and again – a kind of criticism not calculated to win more enthusiastic interest from readers.

The repetitive nature of the poem, inevitably involved in Browning's scheme of having one event related from ten different points of view, is unquestionably the major obstacle to enjoying *The Ring and the Book* – more so than its length, formidable as that is at over 21,000 lines, or its notorious obscurity. The latter difficulty was effectively diminished by A. K. Cook's *Commentary upon Browning's "The Ring and the Book"* (1920), with its invaluable annotation of abstruse allusions and elucidation of more complicated syntactical constructions. The basic difficulty is less easily overcome. If, as the narrative structure indicates, we are not to read the poem for its plot, to find out "what happens," to what do we look for that interest which will carry us through the twelve books of repetitious narrative? Certainly not to the characterization alone: although recent studies of Browning's dramatic monologues have highlighted his mastery of character-portraying devices,[5] they would not attempt to

saint, so Guido was not the subtle villain of Browning's conception ..." (p. xlix). A summary of other influences and sources is given by William C. DeVane, *A Browning Handbook*, 2nd ed. rev. (1955), pp. 325–46. See also chapter VIII, n. 24.

2/The earliest critical opinions were summarized by B. R. McElderry, Jr. in 1939 in "Victorian Evaluation of *The Ring and the Book*." Later critical opinion, from 1910 to 1950, was summarized by W. O. Raymond in the first edition of *The Infinite Moment and Other Essays in Robert Browning* (1950), pp. 209–24.

3/"The Narrative Structure of Browning's *The Ring and the Book*" (1943), pp. 193–233.

4/He claimed that the "twelve monstrous soliloquies" were a "singular mechanical division" and that the poem had "no structure." "The Poetry of Barbarism," *Interpretations of Poetry and Religion* (1927), pp. 208, 211.

5/See, for example, Roma A. King, Jr., *The Bow and the Lyre* (1957) and Park Honan, *Browning's Characters: A Study in Poetic Technique* (1961).

claim that filling a portrait-gallery with eccentric characters is Browning's sole or even primary aim here. Neither do recent examinations of the rich figurative and symbolic texture of Browning's poetry – an approach given impetus by C. Willard Smith's full-length study, *Browning's Star-Imagery: The Study of a Detail in Poetic Design* (1941) – account fully for the peculiar structure: important as is the use of imagery to link monologues and reinforce dominant themes in *The Ring and the Book*, it is always a means to an end and not an end in itself.

Actually, the poet himself points the direction we are to look by emphasizing in Book i the *voices* the reader is to listen to and judge. He directs us to join him in weighing the conflicting testimony offered by the various speakers to determine the extent of their distortion and to extract the residue of fact from each reading or misreading of the case. The poem is not, he makes clear, simply about Pompilia, Caponsacchi, and Guido, but about the differing ways in which people interpret reality, the reasons why their interpretations disagree, and how we – with the poet's help – can penetrate to the fundamental truth beneath their confusion and find a meaning '*beyond the facts.*'

Obvious as is Browning's stress on the difference in the speaker's point of view in each monologue – the poet explicitly and repeatedly calls attention to this difference in the concluding lines of Book i – it has too often been overlooked or rejected by critics on the grounds that all the characters talk alike, that all talk like Browning, for that matter, and so the lack of variation vitiates any claim to distinctiveness or excitement in the individual speeches.[6] Only Arthur Symons of early admirers noticed that the apparent similarity between Browning's own expression and that of his characters in *The Ring and the Book* is merely "skin-deep" and insisted that closer examination would reveal sharp differences between speakers.[7] In point of

6/As soon as the poem was published, Browning had to face this complaint from his friend Julia Wedgwood who wrote: "... You never really vary the dialect. I shd have thought that very detachment of attention from sympathy wd have implied a filtering away of your own thoughts from your own representations, which is the very opposite of what I find with you." Richard Curle, ed., *Robert Browning and Julia Wedgwood: A Broken Friendship as Revealed by their Letters*, p. 157.

7/Symons said, "I have been astonished, in reading and re-reading the poem, at the variety, the difference, the wonderful individuality in each speaker's way of telling the same story; at the profound art with which the rhythm, the metaphors, the very details of language, no less than the broad distinctions of

fact, not only does such an examination indeed reveal these sharp differences, but it casts a bright light on Browning's dramatic method and tells us much about the manner and spirit in which he intended us to approach his *magnum opus*.

However, any attempt to apply the usual procedure for analysing a dramatic monologue to this poem meets with immediate obstacles. Many of the characteristics we expect in a Browning monologue are either not present here or are so muted or transformed as to be hardly recognizable. The speakers, for example, are not sharply individualized by philosophical attitude and historical moment. Many are representative, types rather than individuals, and all share the same historic and cultural milieu – late seventeenth-century Rome in the wake of a brutal and widely discussed murder. Hence, no sharp differentiation in vocabulary or localized allusions sets one speaker apart from another; not only are their backgrounds similar, but they are all concerned with the same primary subject, the murder trial, and with the same peripheral topics, such as the current Molinist heresy. None – with the doubtful exception of Guido – are caught in a moment of spiritual crisis or unconscious self-revelation; all, rather, direct and shape their utterances toward influencing a specific audience. Further, the unusually long speeches allow for a much more leisurely pace in development of interest, so that the broad strokes and economic presentation of the shorter, more familiar Browning monologues give way here to a gradual, at times barely perceptible, unfolding of perspective. Plenty of revealing clues to character are to be found, but they are subtly indicated, widely scattered, and must be carefully pieced together before the completed pattern emerges. And finally, the unique plan of linking several monologues to one central event indicates that the speeches must be treated not as separate entities but as interacting parts of a whole; the single adjustment of perspective involved in reading the simple dramatic monologue has to yield to a whole series of complex adjustments and re-adjustments, which must be stabilized by constant relation to one single, consistent, all-encompassing angle of vision.

What is called for here, then, is an intensive and comprehensive approach which can be applied to each of the books in turn, and will enable us to search out, examine rigorously, and assess all the ele-

character and the subtle indications of bias, are adapted and converted into harmony." *An Introduction to the Study of Browning* (1906), p. 21. Unfortunately, Symons contented himself with the general expression of this idea and supplied few examples to substantiate it.

ments that contribute to a given speaker's particular point of view – a kind of systematic method of reading which allows us to keep an eye on the more intricate details within a monologue, without becoming so distracted (or exhausted) by the endless variations on a single theme as to lose sight of the larger, unifying design of all the monologues taken together. To this end, the present study proposes a procedure aimed at spotlighting in each speech a series of some nine interlocking elements which lie at the heart of Browning's dramatic method and which operate as a primary means of controlling the reader's attention and response. All of these elements centre around the relationship between the speaker and his environment or, more simply, the functions of "voice and address."[8]

The initial elements to be isolated and identified are the three grammatical persons: (1) the *speaker*, the first person in any given speech, including profession, his relationship to the central event, and any details of personality, temperament, and interests that may be given; (2) the *addressee*, or audience, the second grammatical person, its number, definiteness of identity, and relation to the first person; and (3) the *third person*, the relative consciousness of some particular individual or individuals, not physically present but pressing upon the speaker's thoughts and influencing their direction. (The specific physical environment, that is, the actual locale and time of the speech, will be treated as part of the discussion of the addressee.) Other elements are: (4) the speaker's *motive*, the direct result (or cause) of the relationship between him and the second person (which motive may be expressed or unexpressed); (5) the corresponding *tension*, product of a more subtle relationship between the first and third persons which affects the speaker less consciously but markedly and which can best be determined by an analysis of the speaker's basic image or conspicuously recurrent phrases or allusions; (6) the *tone*, the way in which motive and tension are revealed in details of speech, such as diction, rhythm, sentence patterns, and all those verbal characteristics which may be said to reveal the speaker's attitude toward his audience and subject-matter; (7) the *mode of address*, closely allied to tone, but specifically denoting that manner of discourse which characterizes the speaker, including general speech habits such as irony, analogy, logical or dramatic development of

8/I have borrowed this term and adapted much of the terminology used in the description of the three grammatical elements from an article by J. C. LaDrière, "Voice and Address," *Dictionary of World Literature*, ed. Joseph T. Shipley (1953).

narrative, hyperbole – all those habitual usages which are influenced by the speaker's personality, profession, and general viewpoint. Finally, the results of all these interlocking relationships can be examined as the last two elements: (8) *facts revealed* and (9) *opinions expressed,* and this examination will show how all the converging influences discussed above work together to produce the meaning of the speech, i.e., it will reveal the particular selection, arrangement, emphasis, distortion, suppression, revelation, and interpretation of the basic narrative facts, noting wherever new information is introduced and previously revealed information denied or modified.

The process of examination is evaluative, then, as well as descriptive, involving not only the identification and analysis of the poetic devices used in the monologue, but the assessment of how well they are integrated to produce one consistent impression of the speaker's perspective. In chapter I, where this system is applied to Book I, the assumption is made that this first speech is intended to be a dramatic monologue, even though the speaker is Browning himself, and its role as introduction for the speeches to follow is explored. Chapter II applies the system to the books of the three Roman citizens and notes particularly their cumulative effect on the reader's judgment at this point. In subsequent chapters I have found it convenient to alter Browning's tripartite arrangement of the speeches to consider together the linked Pompilia-Caponsacchi monologues and to juxtapose the two Guido speeches for comparison. Far from treating the monologues as separate poems, however, a study of this kind must provide an insight into the relationship of each part to the whole – to show how the individual "meanings" together structure the poem and constitute the larger, single meaning. Chapter VII, then, attempts to evaluate the relationship of the monologues to each other and to the first and last books, touching on the question of Browning's selection, arrangement, and balancing of the different perspectives within the over-all design.

The results of such a procedure are illuminating. They demonstrate that in *The Ring and the Book* Browning is making his most elaborate and sustained statement about a question that concerned him from the time of his earliest work – the poet's function as God's agent appointed to share his vision of truth with other men – and is here expressing his further conviction that the most effective method the poet can use to carry out this function is the dramatic monologue.[9] He has presented these views in an impressive work of art that fuses matter and manner into a single element. My hope is that by highlighting those clues that the poet has supplied so precisely, so liberally, but so subtly, this study can help to increase the reader's awareness and appreciation of Browning's purpose and his artistic achievement.

No single work, most especially his masterpiece, can be read in isolation from the total body of a poet's work, of course. Since *The Ring and the Book* represents the culmination of a moral and aesthetic philosophy that Browning developed over decades of creative effort, it has seemed appropriate to add a last chapter to this study, tracing the evolution of some of the ideas and techniques used in his masterpiece. Such a survey helps to explain why Browning saw his re-creation of Pompilia's story as the statement of a universal truth, what he regarded as '*the glory and good of Art.*'

All quotations from Browning's work are from *The Works of Robert Browning* (London, 1912), edited with introductions by Frederick G. Kenyon – the Centenary Edition which preserves the original system of numbering half-lines as whole units. Citations in the first seven chapters are all to volumes v and vi of this edition, the volumes in which *The Ring and the Book* appears, and the *line* numbers are given in the text. In the last chapter, where other Browning poems are cited, volume and *page* number are given in the text after each citation, including those from *The Ring and the Book*. Full bibliographical information for critical works referred to in the text or in footnotes may be found in the list of "Works Cited" at the end of the text.

9/Browning's concept of the nature and function of poetry is discussed in some detail by Robert Langbaum in *The Poetry of Experience: The Dramatic Monologue in Modern Literary Tradition* (1957); he sees *The Ring and the Book* as a "relativist poem" embodying the new nineteenth-century theory of poetry as one in which the poet as "resuscitator" works, through history and psychology, "toward greater concreteness and not, as in traditional poetic theory, toward general truths" (p. 134). For a further discussion of Browning's aesthetic theory, see chapter viii.

The most recent extensive account of Browning's intention and accomplishment in the poem is *Browning's Roman Murder Story: A Reading of "The Ring and the Book"* (1968) by Richard D. Altick and James F. Loucks ii, published too late for comment in this book; it covers some of the same material as my study but from a somewhat different perspective.

Browning's Voices in *The Ring and the Book*

Chapter I

The Ring and the Book

THE VOICE SPEAKING in Book I is that of a nineteenth-century poet who, some four years previously, has discovered an old quarto volume containing documents of a seventeenth-century Italian murder trial. Immensely excited by the unexpected find in a Florence book-stall, he describes how he uncovered the book, how its subject gripped him, and how in his imagination he has since re-created every moment of the trial of Count Guido Franceschini which took place in the courts of Rome in January and February of 1698. He pictures himself as a kind of master craftsman who will fashion a poem out of the raw stuff of his old documents. Introducing the actors in the original case, he offers to 'resuscitate' or bring them back to life through a poetic reproduction of their voices. He concludes with an invocation to his 'lyric Love' for help in accomplishing his self-imposed task.

The setting for his monologue is apparently London; he says, 'The Book! I turn its medicinable leaves / In London now.'[1] He is perhaps in a sitting-room of house or club, since he refers to a near-by fireplace – 'Yonder's a fire, into it goes my book' (375). Brief topical references (to Roman Catholic churchmen like Wiseman, Newman,

1/Lines 774–5. All references in this chapter are to Book I.

and Manning) place the time at somewhere near the mid-century, but otherwise the date is not particularized.[2] The identity of the speaker's audience is also indicated obliquely: it is plural – the poet uses expressions like *'none of you'* and *'yourselves'* – it is English – he twice addresses his hearers as *'British Public'* and once as *'you London folk,'* and he takes pains to explain foreign phrases and customs to them: *'I found this book, / Gave a lira for it, eightpence English just'* (38–9). In the process, he incidentally identifies himself with his British audience: the priest was punished *'By relegation, – exile, we should say'* (1039); explaining the Roman legal system, he notes that there were no courts in Rome *'as we conceive of courts'* (158). The only other clearly established point about this audience is that the listeners are physically present in the company of the speaker. Far from being merely rhetorical, his numerous questions and directions are sharply pointed at some actual presence: *'Do you see this square old yellow Book, I toss / I' the air, and catch again, and twirl about ... ?'* (33–4), and *'Examine it yourselves!'* (38). At one point, after handing the book to his listeners for examination, he even exclaims, *'Give it me back!'* (89).

The speaker's intimate relationship with his audience is strongly emphasized by the repeated use of the 'I' subject in juxtaposition with second person references, as in (377–82)

> *You know the tale already: I may ask*
> *Rather than think to tell you, more thereof, –*
> *Ask you not merely who were he and she,*
> *Husband and wife, what manner of mankind,*
> *But how you hold concerning this and that*
> *Other yet un-named actor in the piece.*

Here the poet involves his listeners by referring to their knowledge of the case; elsewhere he frequently asks their opinion or calls on them to render a judgment: *'Then comes the all but end, the ultimate / Judgment save yours'* (1220–1), and, at one point (1105–16), he makes his first person reference plural, subtly including his audience in the process of re-creating the drama:

> *Then, since a Trial ensued, a touch o' the same*
> *To sober us, flustered with frothy talk,*
> *And teach our common sense its helplessness.*

2/Twice the poet speaks of the *'two centuries since'* the events of the trial (37, 88); at another point, he speaks of *'The passage of a century or so,/Decads thrice five'* (418–19).

For why deal simply with divining-rod,
Scrape where we fancy secret sources flow, ...
Let us make that grave mystery turn one wheel,
Give you a single grind of law at least!

In addition, he constantly calls attention to his source-book, its physical appearance, and the points of interest it reveals, as in: *'Here where the print ends, – see the pen and ink'* (258), and he prefaces almost every one of his frequent references to the book with the demonstrative *'this'*. *'Do you see this square old yellow Book ... ?'* (33); *'I found this book'* (38); *'I picked this book'* (75); *'Here it is, this I toss'* (84). The immediacy of his speech, the physical presence of his listeners and, especially, the actual existence of the source-book itself are thus underscored. The repetition of words like *'here'* and *'now'* in this connection produces the same effect, as when the poet says, *'The trial / Itself, to all intents, being then as now / Here in the book and nowise out of it'* (152–4), or, describing the court discussion, *'Nor ever was, except i' the brains of men, / More noise by word of mouth than you hear now'* (243–4).[3] The book in this way is made to serve as a tangible link with the past, a constant and concrete reminder that yesterday's dead drama lies ready for re-creation in the hand of the poet today: (86–8)

A book in shape, but, really, pure crude fact
Secreted from man's life when hearts beat hard,
And brains, high-blooded, ticked two centuries since.

The two direct addresses to the *'British Public'* (a title to which the poet both times adds the significant phrase, *'Ye who like me not'*) provide a clue as to the nature of the 'third person' of the speech, as well as to the speaker's motive. His present audience is a representative segment of the contemporary reading public which has not received the poet's previous work well, but for whom he continues to *'labour'* and to whom he looks now for support in his most ambitious venture. He can wryly joke about his lack of success in the past – suggesting that at times his audience consisted solely of himself – but his defensive remarks cannot conceal the intense desire, and in fact determination, to produce a significant artistic creation out of the materials that have fallen to his hand. Something of his tremendous absorption in the task is conveyed when he describes the impact of that first discovery: *'bit by bit I dug / The lingot truth, ... Assayed and knew my piecemeal gain was gold, ... I fused my live*

3/See also 140, 143, 167, 364, 688–95 for further examples.

soul and that inert stuff' (458–69). Most notable evidence of the seriousness of his purpose is the prayer to his *'lyric Love'* to shed some grace of help on his *'bent head and beseeching hand'* and the allusion to his *'song'* as his *'due / To God'* (1403–5); they suggest that the "third person" of his consciousness is his own artistic conscience, symbolized by the memory of the woman who was once his poetic inspiration. He is deeply committed to the concept of the poetic function as a high office, and intends to use the present occasion to demonstrate the artistic process and achievement.

The wryness of the references to his past unpopularity shows a kind of anxiety in the speaker at the reading public's demand for lucidity and simplicity in its poetic fare. In the past he has simply refused to compromise his artistic integrity to please a larger audience, but now he admits the care he has expended to make the meaning of his poem clear to the *'British Public'*: (1381–5)

> *Perchance more careful whoso runs may read*
> *Than erst when all, it seemed, could read who ran, –*
> *Perchance more careless whoso reads may praise*
> *Than late when he who praised and read and wrote*
> *Was apt to find himself the self-same me, – ...*

But the real tension of the speech springs from quite another source: the excitement of his find conflicts with the intensity of his purpose and the need to maintain artistic perspective. The tone of the monologue clearly reveals his failure to remain the detached and impersonal observer to the drama. It is a tone exultant most often, although frequently indignant and even at times horrified, as he relives the moment of the murder – but it remains always at a high emotional pitch. He recreates graphically the thrill of the June day at the Florence book-stalls, and shows that the earlier excitement was no less than what he feels now, four years later, as he handles the precious book: (774–8)

> *The Book! I turn its medicinable leaves*
> *In London now till, as in Florence erst,*
> *A spirit laughs and leaps through every limb,*
> *And lights my eye, and lifts me by the hair,*
> *Letting me have my will again with these. ...*

His high spirits show, moreover, in a series of nervous and excited gestures and phrases: in the repeated tossing of the book in the air; in the frequent jokes and puns – he quotes advice to get *'manned by*

Manning and new-manned / By Newman' (444–5); in the hyperbole of descriptions (215–20)

> That was a firebrand at each fox's tail
> Unleashed in a cornfield: soon spread flare enough,
> As hurtled thither and there heaped themselves
> From earth's four corners, all authority
> And precedent for putting wives to death,
> Or letting wives live, ...

even in the self-depreciating remarks about his poetical abilities, as when he recalls the Roman authorities asking him if there was an actual murder or 'don't you deal in poetry, make-believe, / And the white lies it sounds like?' (455–6), or when he concludes a passage on his poetic inspiration with the homely simile: 'Yet heaven my fancy lifts to, ladder-like, – / As Jack reached, holpen of his beanstalk-rungs!' (1346–7).

The lengthy, richly detailed account of his discovery of the treasure on the Florence book-stall particularly suggests the intensity of his excitement. Every circumstance touching on the uncovering of the precious document is as vividly before him now as it was on that June day four years ago. The blazing noon-time sun, the crowded palace steps in the midst of the bustling Lorenzo square, the market-men, the vendors, the lounging knaves, the girls who brimmed the cans of copper at the fountain, the odds and ends of worthless bric-à-brac that spilled over the stalls: the images pour out of his teeming brain as he relishes every memory of that unforgettable day.

Not only is he excited about the opportunity the book affords him to exercise his creative powers, but the incidents of the story he has to tell arouse his deepest emotions – notwithstanding the fact that he has lived with every detail of it for years and has repeated it many times: 'I used to tell the tale, turned gay to grave, / But lacked a listener seldom' (680–1). He cannot relive in his imagination the events of that fateful December night of Guido's attack without interjecting a cry of horror at the approach of the assassins, who came like bloodthirsty werewolves down on the villa where Pompilia lay inside: (616–19)

> While an inch outside were those blood-bright eyes,
> And black lips wrinkling o'er the flash of teeth,
> And tongues that lolled – Oh God that madest man!
> They parleyed in their language.

The highly emotive language, the picturing of the killers as ferocious animals, accentuate the speaker's involvement in the drama. At the climactic moment of the attack, he can only cry, *'Close eyes!'* (627), as though his powers of description had failed in the face of such horror. Throughout this passage he refers to Guido as rapacious, wolf-like, and to Pompilia as helpless, lamb-like; Arezzo is her *'trap and cage and torture-place,'* Guido's brothers are *'Two obscure goblin creatures, fox-faced, ... Cat-clawed'* and they have a *'grey mother with a monkey-mien,'* to complete the *'satyr-family'* (502–71). He is never the detached, impartial observer, giving all sides to the story (except for one brief passage of narrative summary, to be noted later), but the horrified onlooker to a crime which has left him profoundly affected and determined to communicate the intensity of his reaction to the audience.

These prominent elements of the poet's monologue, then, the sense of involvement and immediacy conveyed by the speaker–listener relationship, and the emotional, excited manner of speaking, merge to produce the impression of a strong, passionate personality, whose mind is already made up in regard to the respective guilt and innocence of the principals in the murder case, and who is anxious to persuade his hearers to the same verdict. Perhaps the single most dominating quality which his speech conveys, however, is a confidence in his poetic ability to reconstruct the events of the murder trial in such a way that his audience will be able to decide for itself who was telling the truth and who was not. He is proud of his discovery of the records, anxious to share the insights they afford, and conscious of the difficulties involved in his chosen task, but he is emphatically clear that it is only through *his* retelling of the facts that his listeners can experience *'the truth'* which the book holds in the form of *'crude fact.'* He insists – repeatedly – that the facts in the old yellow book *become* truth only after he, the poet, in his creative function, *'resuscitates'* them and gives voice to the dead principals who cannot speak through the written word of the records.

His concept of the unique power of the poet is striking in its scope and certitude. Initially, he describes the day of his discovery as one of direct inspiration; he found the book, he says, '(*Mark the predestination!) when a Hand, / Always above my shoulder, pushed me once'* (40–1). Then he compares himself first to Faust and next to Elisha who, with God's help, raised the dead to life again. He, the artist (717–29)

Repeats God's process in man's due degree,
Attaining man's proportionate result, –
Creates, no, but resuscitates, perhaps.
Inalienable, the arch-prerogative
Which turns thought, act – conceives, expresses too!
No less, man, bounded, yearning to be free,
May so project his surplusage of soul
In search of body, so add self to self
By owning what lay ownerless before, –
So find, so fill full, so appropriate forms –
That, although nothing which had never life
Shall get life from him, be, not having been,
Yet, something dead may get to live again. ...

He quotes the *'mage,'* in obvious reference to himself, to show that his own surplusage of soul and his special skill and perception enable him to perform this *'mimic creation'* – not creating out of nothing, but revivifying dead matter: (746–50)

"*Yet by a special gift, an art of arts,*
"*More insight and more outsight and much more*
"*Will to use both of these than boast my mates,*
"*I can detach from me, commission forth*
"*Half of my soul ...*"

Entering among the dry bones of the dead, he, the poet, breathes upon them and leads them forth into new life.

The speaker's stress on the significance and power of the creative process is most clearly demonstrated in his dominant metaphor – that of the beautiful rounded ring he fashions from the raw gold of the facts in the source-book. As poet, he is the skilled artisan who shapes the metal (*'fact'*), made malleable by the addition of an alloy (*'fancy'*) – he must *'Prime nature with an added artistry'* (29) – until with the removal of the alloy (withdrawal of the poet's own detectable personality), the ring stands *'justifiably golden,'* the completed work of art. He chooses the involved ring figure with deliberate care, calls attention to its use, extends the metaphor at some length, reverts to it at intervals throughout the monologue, and finally concludes with a last reference to it. ' *'Tis a figure, a symbol, say'* (31), he announces first, and then explains that *'the thing signified'* is the poem. Later, he reminds his listeners of the meaning: *'(beseech you, hold that figure fast!)'* (142). Next, he refers to his summary of the mass of factual material as '*The untempered gold ... The mere ring-metal ere the ring be made!*' (365–6). Then, expanding on the creative process, he describes how he '*dug*' the gold from the book, and hardened it for moulding by adding '*Something*' of his which, '*mixed up with the mass, / Made it bear hammer and be firm to file*' (462–3). In this step, he adds, '*I fused my live soul and that inert stuff, / Before attempting smithcraft*' (469–70) on the night when, the book read and laid aside, he began recreating the narrative in his own imagination. It is this process – described in lines 497–678, where he repeats the phrase '*I saw*' to show how the scenes took shape before his eyes – that fashioned the ring, by supplying the alloy: (682–6)

> Such substance of me interfused the gold
> Which, wrought into a shapely ring therewith,
> Hammered and filed, fingered and favoured, last
> Lay ready for the renovating wash
> O' the water. ...

But what is '*the water,*' the spirt of chemical which removes the alloy and leaves the gold in a pristine state? The answer comes obliquely; the poet's immediate comment is: '*I disappeared; the book grew all in all*' (687), implying that it is with the withdrawal of his own fashioning hand, his own identifiable personality,[4] that the truth emerges, through the separate voices of the characters in the drama. At this point, he turns away, for the first time, from the first-person narrative to introduce the actors – '*Here are the voices presently shall sound / In due succession*' (838–9) – and only after he has placed each one in his individual setting does he return to personal allusions, to the poet's function, and the ring metaphor. But this time – at the end of his "summoning up" of the cast of his drama – he speaks of

4/I am aware that this interpretation of the word "alloy" to mean the poet's "personality" is not the one usually accepted, but I feel that the context justifies such an interpretation. The poet himself, although he calls the alloy his "fancy," indicates in other references that he means it to signify something far more essential than the creating of mental images, or "imagination" as it is usually interpreted. He refers to it as the power by which the poet '*May so project his surplusage of soul / In search of body, so add self to self*' as to revivify dead matter (723–4); again, he says, '*I fused my live soul and that inert stuff*' (469) in the process of adding the alloy. He speaks of detaching from himself '*Half of my soul*' and interfusing the gold with '*motions of mine / That quickened*' (701–2). It is such a distinctive, vital, life-giving quality that I think it can best be approximated by the word "personality," meaning the totality of his individual characteristics, of which "imagination" is only a part.

the ring as now repurified: it has apparently already felt the *'reno-vating wash,'* because he says (1386-9)

> *Such labour had such issue, so I wrought*
> *This arc, by furtherance of such alloy,*
> *And so, by one spirt, take away its trace*
> *Till, justifiably golden, rounds my ring.*

Hence, he is saying that it was the conjuring up of the dead principals of the drama, by giving voice to them, that constituted the act of repristination.[5] He now presents to his audience the finished golden ring of the poem – the voices which speak out in the monologues of the next ten books, without further intervening comment by the poet. The recurrent characterization of himself as master craftsman and restorer of life to the dead prepares the way for the invocation of the final lines in which he promises that, although he began his *'song'* with *'bent head and beseeching hand,'* he will conclude by *'raising hand and head'* and *'blessing back'* the help he received. Thus the last note struck in the poet's speech is one of prayerful confidence in the success of his artistry.

In short, the overwhelming effect of the tone, diction, and imagery of the speaker in Book 1 is to emphasize the significant power and achievement involved in the poetic function and in the poet's role as "resuscitator" of dead voices. The somewhat complex mode of address serves to reinforce this impression. The whole speech is structured around the poet's description of the creative process by which he brought the old yellow book to life, and the most prominent speech pattern, even more notable than the ring metaphor, is the recurrent use of the first-person pronoun in conjunction with a strong verb form. The first 520 lines outline the steps he followed: *'I found ... I picked ... I leaned ... I find ... I read ... I took ... I dug ... I fused ... I fared ... I found'* – the verbs are all brief, forceful, emphasizing the productive quality of the process, and the constant repetition of *'I'* builds up the sense of individualized creative activity. At line 523, this form changes to the less projective, more receptive phrase, *'I saw'*; here the poet is describing the re-creation in his mind's eye of the scenes preceding the trial. These scenes take on the quality of a pageant, moving slowly before his eyes: he even uses the phrase *'the stage where the priest played his part'* (503) and refers to *'The tragic piece'* which *'Acted itself over again once more'* (522-3). Seven

5/See note at end of chapter.

times he repeats the phrase '*I saw,*' then after the murder scene –
briefly passed over with the exclamation '*Close eyes!*' – he changes
to the more conclusive form, '*I knew.*' The long '*I saw*' passage, with
its all-encompassing, almost Olympian viewpoint, might have conveyed a sense of omniscience and impersonality on the part of the
watcher, were it not for the highly coloured language (as in the were-
wolf images discussed above) which reaches a crescendo of emotion
when he describes the Franceschini treatment of Pompilia at Arezzo
and Caponsacchi's intervention: (580–8)

> ... *all was sure,*
> *Fire laid and cauldron set, the obscene ring traced,*
> *The victim stripped and prostrate: what of God?*
> *The cleaving of a cloud, a cry, a crash,*
> *Quenched lay their cauldron, cowered i' the dust the crew,*
> *As, in a glory of armour like Saint George,*
> *Out again sprang the young good beauteous priest*
> *Bearing away the lady in his arms,*
> *Saved for a splendid minute and no more.*

The speaker here is no detached observer, but a passionate partisan
of Pompilia and the priest, and a fierce condemner of the Franceschini.

   After this elaborate imaginative re-creation, the speaker resumes
the 'I–verb' structure – '*I kicked ... turned ... recognized ... could calculate ... I mixed ... I find ... I spell and speak*' – and, quoting the
'*mage,*' in oblique reference to himself: '*I raise ... I enter ... put old
powers to play, / Push lines out to the limit, lead forth last*' (744–56).
Now comes a brief passage of factual summary (780–823), noticeably
impersonal and unemotional (for example, he says that husband and
wife lived '*Unhappy lives, whatever curse the cause,*' until Guido
'*killed the three, / Aged, they, seventy each, and she, seventeen, /
And, two weeks since, the mother of his babe*'). This summary is
followed by an extended introductory section where he presents the
'*voices*' soon to sound in '*due succession.*' The poet's voice is unob-
trusive here: there are almost no first-person references until after
the last speaker, Guido in his cell, is introduced, and then the '*I*'
resumes the narrative, emphasizing his close relationship to the '*you*'
addressee – '*I led you ... I point you ... let me slope you back ... land
you on mother-earth.*' Thus the poet's role is pictured as having been
up to this point one of guide or master of ceremonies, leading and
directing the audience. Now he changes the emphasis slightly, with

a cluster of second-person references that signifies a shift in the creative process from the poet's role to that of the audience. *'See it for yourselves,'* he says of Guido's act, *'changeable because alive!'* (1364–5) – it *'shoots you dark for bright,'* and baffles *'Your sentence absolute'*; you see *'Your good men and your bad men'* from another side and *'you rub your eyes'* in confusion (1371–8). The speaker's task, then, is done, and his last words change to past tense – *'I yet have laboured ... I wrought this arc'* – as the audience is called on to listen and judge for itself of the voices to speak.

It becomes apparent that Browning has been concerned to establish the poet's dominance in Book I as craftsman, "resuscitator," guide, but some questions remain about the poet's mode of address. Why, as so many critics have asked, when the reader is to be given nine versions of the same story in the monologues to come, should he have to hear it no less than three times over from the poet himself in the first book? In view of the stress in Book I on the poetic method, some sort of deliberate plan may reasonably be sought in the narrative repetitions. The first time the poet gives a summary of the incidents leading up to the murder of 1698, it is as a paraphrase of the trial records in his old yellow book – what he calls the *'pure crude fact.'* Lest his listeners overlook this point, that he is presenting the CASE AS IT APPEARS IN THE PRINTED RECORD, the poet points again and again to the WRITTEN nature of his source material: he reads the title-page, *'Word for word'* as it is written *'in a Latin cramp ... interfilleted with Italian streaks'* (132–8); he describes how the Fisc *'Pleaded (and since he only spoke in print / The printed voice of him lives now as then)'* (166–7). After paraphrasing some of the trial arguments, he remarks, *'Thus paper second followed paper first'* (198), and then concludes, *'Thus wrangled, brangled, jangled they a month / Only on paper, pleadings all in print'* (241–2). Making another point, the poet is careful to remind his audience: *'I learn this from epistles which begin / Here where the print ends, – see the pen and ink'* (257–8), and again he notes of the last legal opinion: *'So said, so done – / Rather so writ, for the old Pope bade this, / I find, with his particular chirograph'* (344–6). Once more the qualification is immediate, pointed.

Throughout this section he continues scrupulously to acknowledge his source, by interjecting phrases like *'my writer adds'* or *'so I learn.'* This extraordinary insistence on the written character of his source materials serves to emphasize the fact that the poet is only at the stage of gathering his raw material: the pure crude fact of the old yellow book is still simply dead, dry documentation – '*The mere ring-metal ere the ring be made*' (366), as he calls it at the end of this summary. He might at this point throw his book into the fire – '*You know the tale already*' (377) – unless he, as poet, can *add* something to the tale, add, that is, the alloy of his '*fancy*' or vital powers. The SECOND summary does just that: it is an imaginative re-creation of the events leading to the trial (hence the '*I saw*' construction, the highly coloured language, the emotional pitch of the passage); at its conclusion he announces that the raw material is now '*wrought into a shapely ring*' and waits only the removal of the alloy to complete it. Now follows the THIRD summary – the forty lines of factual narrative presenting in bare outline the whole story, without interpretation or editorial comment. This summary represents a kind of prologue to the next, most important stage of the poetic process, which is the introduction of the individual voices of the monologues.

In this last, important section (838–1329), the poet is giving a preview of the procedure by which he withdraws the alloy – withdraws, in effect, his personality – and allows the actors to speak for themselves in dramatic monologue rather than present them himself in narrative. At this point in his "preview" he must still describe, of course, but he signals the nature of the change to come by dropping the "written word" allusions and first-person references to focus on the individual VOICES, their setting, their characteristics, their conclusions. The '*I*' truly disappears and the '*you*' (the audience) is called to the fore to hear (rather than see) the actors in the drama. The poet's tone becomes imperative, his verbs constantly stressing the listeners' auditory role, as he presents '*First, the world's outcry*' in the person of Half-Rome; next he directs, '*listen how, to the other half of Rome*' it all seemed; then, '*Hear a fresh speaker!*' (Tertium Quid). The principals follow: '*First you hear Count Guido's voice,*' now his '*tones subdued,*' now '*his tongue ... Incisive, nigh satiric.*' Then '*hear Caponsacchi who comes next,*' as he '*speaks rapidly, angrily, speech that smites,*' followed by Pompilia whose '*soul sighs its lowest and its last / After the loud ones.*' The lawers are preparing written arguments, but the poet invites the audience to LISTEN to them: Arcangeli, who '*Wheezes out law-phrase, whiffles Latin forth*' with his classical puns '*A-bubble in the larynx while he laughs,*' and Bottini, practising aloud – the poet exclaims, '*Ah, but you miss the very tones o' the voice. ...*' Similarly, the Pope although alone reads aloud and lets his thoughts flow '*Likewise aloud, for respite and relief.*' Finally, '*Then must speak Guido yet a second time*' from prison; '*the tiger-cat screams now, that whined before.*' The audience is thus forcefully reminded that these are the speakers whose voices will dominate henceforth, and is asked to take note of the particular perspective from which they speak, as well as their speech idiosyncrasies, their revealing inflections, intonations, nuances.

At the conclusion of this introductory passage, the poet announces, significantly: '*So I wrought / This arc, by furtherance of such alloy, / And so, by one spirt, take away its trace*' (1386–8). He means the breathing of life and voice into the characters of the old yellow book, then, to represent his pure ring of art; the three narrative summaries were necessary to highlight the progressive steps involved in fashioning the ring – first, the preparation of the crude material (finding and studying the written record); second, the moulding of it by mixing in a firmer, more malleable material (his emotional and imaginative re-creating of the scenes leading up to the trial); and third, the purifying of the shaped ring by the withdrawal of the alloy (suppression of his own personality in the dramatization of the events surrounding the trial).

This long, last section of Book I brings out another, less significant but still noteworthy, role of the poet-speaker, as one who establishes the circumstances under which each of the monologues is to be given. He takes pains not merely to characterize the voice by describing speech habits, but also to fasten it to a particular time and place, indicating its temporal relationship to the commission of the murder and to the delivery of the other monologues. In this way, the poet builds the framework within which the speeches are to become dramatic, sets the scene, so to speak, for a smaller drama of emotional reactions within the larger scheme of the objective events which took place in Arezzo, Castelnuovo, and Rome between 1695 and 1697. The "internal drama" takes place entirely in Rome, in street, palace, hospital, court-room, and prison, during the first two months of 1698; it begins AFTER the murderous attack, and ends with Guido's execution. The poet notes, for example, that the first speaker is describing the '*threefold murder of the day before*' as he lounges opposite the Church of San Lorenzo; that we must '*yet another day let come and go*' between the second and third speakers in marketplace and card salon, respectively; that Guido addresses the court before Pompilia dies in the house of Santa Anna, and he is followed by Caponsacchi the next day; that the lawyers and the Pope pore over the trial records in the six weeks' interval that follows; and, finally, that Guido speaks his last words in *'the doubtful dawn'* that follows by hours the Pope's decision.

The advantages to such a procedure are clear: the audience gets an immediate over-all view of the entire action which the monologues constitute, can picture the speaker's setting and relate it to the time of the murder, and feel a sense of present dramatic development, rather than continued narrative. The one obvious disadvantage to the procedure is the loss of suspense it involves, in anticipating the audience's verdict on each speaker. If the audience is to be called upon to make a judgment of each monologue, why does the poet conclude his introduction by indicating his own opinion about which speaker is wrong and which right? An interesting point bearing on the answer to this question emerges from an examination of the one issue which the poet does not clarify in his introduction of the voices: the motive for each speech.

The importance of the reasons why a speaker takes the perspective he does toward events is obvious. At first glance, this information does indeed seem to be included in the poet's summary – when he remarks upon each observer's failure to see the whole truth – but a closer examination indicates that these remarks are not omniscient or conclusive observations at all, but merely hazarded guesses on the poet's part. Half-Rome, he says, is *'Honest enough,'* but has some *'hidden germ of failure'* (848–50) in him: he swerves from the truth, but *'Who shall say how, who shall say why?'* (862). In point of fact, the reader can say how and why when he hears Half-Rome speak. Other Half-Rome, says the poet, happens on the truth but only through a *'fancy-fit,'* pure chance, or luck, or whim: *'Doubtless for some such reason'* (892) he made his choice. Other Half-Rome will refute the charge that his choice is pure whim when he speaks out. Tertium Quid, on the other hand, the poet sees as giving *'a reasoned statement of the case'* (920); he is *'no gossip-guess'* (926). But every word of Tertium Quid's reveals him as more interested in amusing his gossip-loving friends than in reasoning to a fair conclusion. Even Guido's ultimate responsibility is not clearly established; the poet's long disquisition on the evils of torture blurs the question of the murderer's motives. Caponsacchi's conflict is hinted at – *'Man and priest – could you comprehend the coil!'* (1017) – but is not examined. Pompilia's motive is attributed, by report, to the desire to defend herself, an interpretation not borne out by the subsequent monologue. Arcangeli's surface interests are named – *'Paternity at smiling strife with law'* (1146) – but the deeper ironic significance of his argument is not indicated. Bottini is credited *'With special end to prove Pompilia pure'* (1218); his actual speech shows this to be far from his aim. The poet depicts the Pope as deeply thoughtful, but gives no hint of the doubt and discouragement that rack the old man's soliloquy. And he sees in Guido's last speech only the *'bristling fury'* of a tiger-cat, not the bleating sheep revealed by the last monologue.

What this shows is that the poet's interpretation of the basic motives accounting for the different perspectives of his nine speakers is deficient in some way – either uncertain, or incomplete, or mistaken. It is quite true that most of these deficiencies are not apparent to the reader at this point in Book 1; they emerge only in retrospect after each monologue has revealed the true motivation. Nevertheless, enough hint is given to the reader that the poet's view lacks at this point a most significant dimension, a dimension which can only be provided by the speakers themselves. The poet, for example, will pose questions which the source-book leaves unanswered: Caponsacchi's *'strange course / I' the matter, was it right or wrong or both?'* (387–8); the Comparini's killing, *'What say you to the right or wrong of that ... ?'*(392). He does not answer them because the answers can only come from the speakers. Motives, then, are what we are to watch for, measure, and judge as we listen to the voices. The poet has already passed sentence on Guido, found him guilty and condemned him to death; he has thus disposed of any distracting concerns which might divert us from our single appointed task of determining, not who was right and who wrong in the original action, but why the objective reality appears so different to so many different eyes.

This examination of Book 1 for elements such as speaker, addressee, diction, tone, and mode of address points to some rather significant aspects of Browning's purpose in using dramatic monologues to structure his poem. Book 1 is an explanation, even a justification, for re-telling the story of the old yellow book in poetic form. It is concerned with making the poet-speaker dominant, dynamic, even exalted, a kind of *'mimic'* creator, who possesses a special power to see truth and make it known, to delve beneath the surface facts and bring out the meaning hidden from men. Although the poet is not omniscient, his knowledge extends far beyond that of the ordinary man. He sees the truth in an intuitive flash, but by his willingness to follow the visionary experience with patient, careful probing of individual motivations, he makes it possible for others less gifted to share his bright light of truth. The poet could have chosen merely to narrate his experience – could have stopped, that is, with the imaginative re-creation of the story – but had he gone only this far, he would not have persuaded us of the rightness of HIS interpretation: his would be simply one more voice added to the babel of contradictory opinions. Instead, by devoted use of his poetic powers of "resuscitation," he lets the actors in the original drama come before us to speak for themselves, revealing their motives consciously or unconsciously, but completely and irrevocably. This way, we actually participate in the process of judgment and end by reaching finally the same verdict the poet had come to instantly.

We can see now what Browning is doing in Book I. It might, after all, have been merely a prose argument to the poem, if its sole purpose was to introduce the ring of linked speeches, but it has been made a DRAMATIC monologue like those to follow. Browning is taking pains to make us see the poet (who is, of course, himself) in a concrete, actualized situation, in order to focus our attention on the actual process of poetic creation. What at first had seemed like identifiable "personal" touches in the book – references to his Florence find, the four years' work, his poetic unpopularity, his lyric Love invocation – are all used for dramatic purposes, less to tell us about the individual writer Robert Browning than to make us more vividly aware of what a poet does in making a poem. We are made to hear his voice, see his gestures, feel his emotion, so as to get the full contrast between the present, alive, inspired creative artist and the inert, misleading historical records, which he will transform before our eyes. Furthermore, we need to feel the full weight of his presence and personality in order to appreciate the achievement of his withdrawal, that necessary last step in the artistic process by which the poet immolates himself in his creations in order to let other men see what he has seen so gloriously. In other words, the real hero of *The Ring and the Book* is the poet, and to indicate that he is using himself as a type of the creative artist, Browning presents himself as a character – the leading character – in the drama by which old fact becomes new truth. But since the very essence of the poetic act is to restore life and voice to dead forms, letting the reader judge what he hears for himself, the poet's voice will not be heard again until Book XII.

THE RING AND THE BOOK / 19

Most critics have concluded that the ring metaphor is unworkable. A. K. Cook, in *A Commentary upon Browning's "The Ring and the Book"* (1920), for example, feels that "Perhaps the admirable metaphor was pressed too hard" (p. 2) and William C. DeVane, *A Browning Handbook* (1955), is even more positive, saying "Browning presses his figure too far" (p. 330). They base their objections on Browning's claim to have removed his alloy from the finished product, an obvious impossibility if alloy means imagination. However, Paul A. Cundiff in "The Clarity of Browning's Ring Metaphor," (1948) defends the figure on the grounds that Browning knew enough about metal craft to realize that the spirt of acid which cleanses the finished object only removes part of the alloy – the removal of all of it would make the metal shapeless and unmanageable – and leaves a film of pure gold on the surface only. Hence, he concludes, Browning meant that "he similarly removed himself from the FACE of the poem" (p. 1279). As George Wasserman points out in "The Meaning of Browning's Ring-Figure" (1961), Cundiff is right but does not go far enough, and "overlooks a more important distinction implicit in his own interpretation, that be-tween a 'fancy' which fused itself with the facts of *The Old Yellow Book* and an 'I' which disappeared from this fusion, a distinction between a subjective alter ego which identified itself with the life behind the fact and an objective alter ego which recorded that life" (p. 424). My own opinion is that, perceptive as his remarks are, Wasserman in turn does not go far enough in seeing the implications of his own statement; he concludes simply that "The jeweler's repristination of the amalgamated ring is, then, only an approximate analogy of the creative process of the poet. The poet's fancy is actually not separated from the poem; moreover, what repristina-tion that does occur, in a roughly equivalent way, occurs before the poem is written down" (p. 426). But the poet says that the repristination occurs, not in the early imaginative re-creative stage, where only the alloy-mixing takes place (*'I fused my live soul and that inert stuff, / Before attempting smithcraft'*; 469–70, emphasis mine, but rather after he has fused some-thing of himself into the design and the ring stands, complete and rounded, waiting only for the removal of the *'something.'* Then he says, *'so I wrought / This arc, by furtherance of such alloy,'* implying by the past tense that the ring is finished in design and shape, and adds, *And so, by one spirt, take away its trace'* with the present tense implying that the removal, the repristination, is only now taking place. The heavy emphasis on the *'I'* mode of address throughout most of Book I until its sudden conspicuous disappearance in the "voice" section demonstrates this "remo-val" in action, as it signals the change from narrative to dramatic form to come in the next books. Complex as this whole ring figure is, then, it seems to me not only a workable device but a remarkably apt and rich vehicle for conveying Browning's concept of the poetic method. At least one critic has come to something of this same conclusion: A. G. Drachmann, "Alloy and Gold" (1925), sees the gold as "the truth about the motives" and the alloy as the poet's "fancy," but he interprets the repristination as "the fact that Browning in the poem (Books II–XI) refrains from speaking in his own person ... leaving it to ourselves to find out the *truth*" (p. 423).

Chapter II

Half-Rome, The Other Half-Rome, Tertium Quid

I

FROM BOOK II WE LEARN that the first person, or speaker, is Half-Rome, who has just come from viewing the bodies of the slain Comparini on the steps leading to the altar of the Church of San Lorenzo. A married man who takes the side of the husband in the pending murder trial of Guido Franceschini, he represents, as his name indicates, the sentiments of a large segment of the Roman citizenry. Through various speech habits and mannerisms, he reveals himself as frank, highly opinionated, self-confident, sure both of the rightness of his convictions and of the accuracy of his knowledge of the case. He is cynical about women, especially suspicious of wives, callous in describing the slaying, and apparently enjoys a kind of vicarious thrill in studying the murder technique and weapon. He is inordinately conscious of money and of the importance of a man's 'honour.'

The second person, or addressee, is a friend he meets, either by chance or by design, in the crowd outside the church and to whom he decides to give the "true" facts of the case. The friend is not given a name, is addressed merely as 'Sir.' His cousin has told him that Guido was to blame for the terrible murder, so the speaker feels he must "set him right." It is at dusk on January 3, the day after the attack, but the crowd which has thronged San Lorenzo since the bodies were laid out at dawn is still present. The speaker therefore leads his hearer aside a short way, out of the jostling mob, across the street by the Palace Ruspoli, where they can carry on their discussion while watching the excitement of the coming and going on the church steps opposite.

The listener remains completely silent during the speaker's discourse, but his presence is clearly suggested throughout. Besides the direct address with which the speaker introduces each new idea (he calls his hearer 'Sir' twelve times in the course of 1500 lines), he also draws him into the talk by the use of questions, parenthetical remarks, or responses to some implied gesture or comment. For example, after describing Guido's pathetic situation, he says:

> You, Sir, who listen but interpose no word,
> Ask yourself, had you borne a baiting thus?
> Was it enough to make a wise man mad?
> Oh, but I'll have your verdict at the end![1]

The last line indicates that he has waved off the proffered reply with a gesture. Again, he seems directly to invite an answer when he says, 'Is this your view?' (603) or, 'I want your word now: what do you say to this?' (1385), but the answer is always forestalled as he rushes on, either to supply it himself in the next words (' 'Twas Guido's anyhow') or to add another question to the last ('What would say little Arezzo and great Rome, / And what did God say and the devil say ... ?'). He seems to be aware of occasional gestures of impatience on the part of the other: 'Somehow or other, – how, all in good time! / By a trick, a sleight of hand you are to hear' (225–6); or, 'Then was the story told, I'll cut you short' (929); or, 'I see the comment ready on your lip' (526). Many of his comments and questions seem more than merely rhetorical, even when he proceeds to supply his own answers, indicating perhaps a smile or other facial expression which he accepts as agreement on the part of his listener, as in (1213–15)

> ... Now, am I fair or no
> In what I utter? Do I state the facts,
> Having forechosen a side? I promised you!

1/Lines 1260–3. All references in this section of the chapter are to Book II unless otherwise indicated.

or (1428–30)

> *And had a harmless man tripped you by chance,*
> *How would you wait him, stand or step aside,*
> *When next you heard he rolled your way? Enough.*

The effect of such remarks is to keep the relationship between speaker and audience always to the forefront, and to increase the sense of an unfolding action, by making the speech conspicuously an occurrence in present time rather than a mere recital of past events.

The "third person" in the monologue could be said to be the *'certain cousin'* of the listener, since it is the consciousness of the cousin's relationship to his own wife that dominates the speaker's attention throughout. He refers to this cousin again and again, ostensibly for the purpose of correcting his errors of fact – *'A certain cousin of yours has told you so? / Exactly! Here's a friend shall set you right'* (190–1) – but actually for the purpose of issuing a thinly veiled warning to this cousin who is paying too much attention to Half-Rome's wife. It is not clear that Half-Rome has arranged this present meeting deliberately, but he is glad to see this particular man and anxious to hold him – *'(Just the man I'd meet)'* (1); *'(The right man, and I hold him)'* (16). The reader does not learn the full significance of the man's identity until the last lines, when Half-Rome defends the use of violence by a deceived husband with the pointed conclusion: (1542–7)

> *... a matter I commend*
> *To the notice, during Carnival that's near,*
> *Of a certain what's-his-name and jackanapes*
> *Somewhat too civil of eves with lute and song*
> *About a house here, where I keep a wife.*
> *(You, being his cousin, may go tell him so.)*

But there have been sufficient hints before that to point to the role of the cousin in Half-Rome's consciousness. *'There's more to come / More that will shake your confidence in things / Your cousin tells you, – may I be so bold?* (619–21), he says at one point, and again, speaking of one who is *'A cousin of Guido's and might play a prank,'* he breaks off (936–7) to insert the parenthetical question *'Have not you too a cousin that's a wag?'*

Frequent references to the forthcoming Carnival, which is not directly connected with the murder story at all, seem to show that it is linked in Half-Rome's mind to his own wife and this cavalier cousin, suggesting as it does freedom from restraint and opportunities for licence. He mockingly asks, for instance, of Caponsacchi, *'who so fit / To figure in the coming Carnival?'* (1452–3) and says of him and Pompilia that he *'threw comfits at the theatre / Into her lap, – what harm in Carnival?'* (801–2), the last remark heavy with irony. These references are picked up and made more pointed in the last speech of warning (*'a matter I commend / To the notice, during Carnival that's near ...'*). The recurrence of these two ideas, the cousin and the Carnival, at intervals throughout his narrative signals the fact that, for Half-Rome, the cause of all the present trouble is the social environment in which Guido's crime took place, a society which allows husbands to be publicly betrayed and held up to scorn, while depriving them of the right to take personal vengeance and thus forcing them to rely on the ministrations of an inadequate legal system: (1470–6)

> *If the law seeks to find them guilty, Sir,*
> *Master or men – touch one hair of the five,*
> *Then I say in the name of all that's left*
> *Of honour in Rome, civility i' the world*
> *Whereof Rome boasts herself the central source, –*
> *There's an end to all hope of justice more.*
> *Astraea's gone indeed, let hope go too!*

His idea that society is to blame – and the cousin's activity therefore is a symptom of this society's weakness – is conveyed quite clearly by the manner in which Half-Rome not only identifies his situation with that of Guido, but attempts to universalize the situation to include his listener and all the husbands of Rome. Moving from the singular form which he has been using to the plural form, he says: (1479–83)

> *What, are we blind? How can we fail to learn*
> *This crowd of miseries make the man a mark,*
> *Accumulate on one devoted head*
> *For our example? – yours and mine who read*
> *Its lesson thus –*

and later: (1537–9)

> *All which is the worse for Guido, but, be frank –*
> *The better for you and me and all the world,*
> *Husbands of wives, especially in Rome.*

Another presence or influence that plays a part in Half-Rome's motivation, though perhaps less consciously, is that of the pair whose mangled corpses lie on the altar steps opposite where he now stands discussing them. The sight of the dead Comparini seems to have had a significant impact on Half-Rome, although he indicates it is not an uncommon sight, that he is, indeed, something of an expert on such displays and can assess the attention to detail on the part of the persons responsible for this one: (100–5)

> Yet they did manage matters, to be just,
> A little at this Lorenzo. Body o' me!
> I saw a body exposed once ... never mind!
> Enough that here the bodies had their due.
> No stinginess in wax, a row all round,
> And one big taper at each head and foot.

Nevertheless, an extraordinary interest in this particular display is shown by the fact that he remains, after many hours at the scene, 'From dawn till now that it is growing dusk' (88), and that he frequently interrupts his narrative to revert to the topic of the corpses, the only interruptions in an otherwise straightforward recitation of events. In Book i, the poet has stated that Half-Rome lingered at the scene to 'perhaps prolong thereby / The not-unpleasant flutter at the breast' (i, 871–2) produced by the spectacle at San Lorenzo. There is more than that element of morbid curiosity which brings so many other Romans to the scene in the fascinated attention Half-Rome gives to the condition of the bodies, especially Violante's. He relates with apparent relish how he examined the stab-wounds and can now report that it only appears that Violante has more than Pietro because hers are all about the face; she is 'punished thus solely for honour's sake,' he explains, and elaborates: (30–5)

> A delicacy there is, our gallants hold,
> When you avenge your honour and only then,
> That you disfigure the subject, fray the face,
> Not just take life and end, in clownish guise.
> It was Violante gave the first offence,
> Got therefore the conspicuous punishment

and he tells of the playful speculation he and others enjoyed – 'We fancied even, free as you please' (38) – about the traces of resentment and indignation they could detect on the face of Pietro even now. He reports, with obvious satisfaction, the rumour that Pietro's body had actually turned and rolled away from that of his wife when they had laid it *'loving-husband-like'* beside it. He describes how he learned from old Luca Cini that the peculiar cuts were made by a special Genoese blade, ' *"Armed with those little hook-teeth on the edge"* / *"To open in the flesh nor shut again"* ' (148–9). Moving on to the story of Pompilia's adoption and marriage, he pauses twice more to comment further on the spectacle before them. He can express the extent of their deception of Guido best by just pointing: (613–16)

> *But that who likes may look upon the pair*
> *Exposed in yonder church, and show his skill*
> *By saying which is eye and which is mouth*
> *Thro' those stabs thick and threefold, –. ...*

He rises to an unusual pitch of passion in describing the murder scene: (1433–7)

> *Vengeance, you know, burst, like a mountain-wave*
> *That holds a monster in it, over the house,*
> *And wiped its filthy four walls free at last*
> *With a wash of hell-fire, – father, mother, wife,*
> *Killed them all, bathed his name clean in their blood,*

and he concludes his tale, with ill-concealed satisfaction: (1442–6)

> *Of how the old couple come to lie in state*
> *Though hacked to pieces, – never, the expert say,*
> *So thorough a study of stabbing – while the wife*
> *(Viper-like, very difficult to slay)*
> *Writhes still through every ring of her, poor wretch.*

The intensity of such lines indicates something more than mere callousness in the face of all too common violence; it points to a sense on Half-Rome's part (of which he may be only dimly aware) of personal involvement in, even of identification with, the situation of Guido, the deceived husband who committed the bloody murders and is even now awaiting sentence in a cell in New Prison. This personal involvement – or sense of it, since Half-Rome is merely a bystander and there is no evidence that he is actually acquainted with Guido – emerges most sharply in his conception of Violante's role in the events leading up to the murder. From these first lines in which he gloats over her disfigurement, until the end when he shifts most of the blame to Pompilia, it is evident that for Half-Rome woman is the villain of the piece, the direct cause of the tragedy. Twice he applies the 'Eve' figure – once to Violante, once to Pompilia – to indicate the woman's deceiving of an unsuspecting husband. Of Violante, he says she added lie to lie: (253–6)

> ... lest Eve's rule decline
> Over this Adam of hers, whose cabbage-plot
> Throve dubiously since turned fools'-paradise,
> Spite of a nightingale on every stump.

He describes Caponsacchi as a 'Lucifer / I' the garden where Pompilia, Eve-like, lured / Her Adam Guido to his fault and fall' (167–9). Violante is the chief object of his attack: 'It was Violante gave the first offence' (34); 'She who had caught one fish, could make that catch / A bigger still, in angler's policy' (270–1); 'Here was all lie, no touch of truth at all, / All the lie hers' (555–6). But when she leaves the scene and the spotlight turns to Pompilia, the language is hardly distinguishable – 'Oh, the wife knew the appropriate warfare well, / The way to put suspicion to the blush!' (867–8) – from that used for Violante, who could (75–8)

> Ply the wife's trade, play off the sex's trick
> And, alternating worry with quiet qualms,
> Bravado with submissiveness, prettily fool
> Her Pietro into patience. ...[2]

Everything that he says about these two projects the depth of the bitterness poisoning Half-Rome's thoughts. The relationship between him and the 'certain cousin' (expressed indirectly through the listener) is simply an occasion for revealing the tension that affects his whole discourse and inevitably influences his judgment of the participants in the murder case. The tension comes from a passionate and deep-seated jealousy of his wife and a fear of betrayal by her, which make it impossible for him to see anything of the present case objectively. Guido's situation is, he fears, too much like his own. This anxiety is something which goes far beyond even the acknowledged private motive – to warn the cousin away – and colours every aspect of the issue for him, flashing forth in signs like the fascinated interest in the murder weapon and the vilification of Violante, in an impassioned attack on the law's inadequacies, and an almost irra-

2/See also 247, 533.

tional defence of violence for the sake of *'honour.'* Had Guido murdered his wife, he cries, when he first found her in flight, the world would understand it was only *'natural law'*; had he (1491–7)

> *... exacted his just debt*
> *By aid of what first mattock, pitchfork, axe*
> *Came to hand in the helpful stable-yard,*
> *And with that axe, if providence so pleased,*
> *Cloven each head, by some Rolando-stroke,*
> *In one clean cut from crown to clavicle,*
> *— Slain the priest-gallant, the wife-paramour,*

then, he adds, *'the world had praised the man'* (1503).

Half-Rome's attitude, subconscious or otherwise, is revealed most tellingly by the tone of his discourse. Certain details of speech are so constantly used as to constitute an habitual or characteristic mode of speaking, in which he unknowingly gives away something of his feelings, but there are other mannerisms which he seems to employ consciously, for a desired effect. The most characteristic elements of his diction are the use of colloquialisms and slang, and of epithets and undignified descriptive words, and the refusal to treat the Comparini seriously – devices which shrink everything he touches on and at the same time contribute to the appearance of self-assured cleverness on his part. Pompilia he describes as *'Plaything at once and prop ... A fiddlepin's end!'* (228–30); he laughs contemptuously at Pietro crawling on *'all-fours with his baby pick-a-back'* (259), and at the efforts of the old man and his wife to *'realize the stuff and nonsense long / A-simmer in their noddles'* (434–5) and to make Girolamo *'leave his mumps'* (493) and *'go buzz'* (502).

The belittling effect of this kind of language is most apparent in the treatment of Pompilia's escape with Caponsacchi; Half-Rome reduces it to the level of the ludicrous by a deliberate selection of demeaning or ironic expressions. Caponsacchi is *'The man with the aureole, sympathy made flesh'* (782), who poses as an *'Apollo'* (794), while Pompilia tries to deny that she *'so much as peeped at him / Between her fingers while she prayed in church'* (901–2). The flight itself is described in gay, mocking terms. *'One merry April morning,'* a carriage draws up, and *'In jumps Pompilia, after her the priest,'* and soon the pair is *'jollily / Jaunting it Rome-ward'* (889–948). They feel safe when they reach Castelnuovo, (1005–9)

> *So, in the inn-yard, bold as 'twere Troy-town,*
> *There strutted Paris in correct costume,*

> *Cloak, cap and feather, no appointment missed,*
> *Even to a wicked-looking sword at side,*
> *He seemed to find and feel familiar at.*

When Pompilia seizes Guido's sword at the most dramatic moment of the encounter, Half-Rome says that she *'pinked her man / Prettily'* (1038–9). He summarizes the whole incident in terms of a farcical performance: (1052–6)

> *Here was a priest found out in masquerade,*
> *A wife caught playing truant if no more;*
> *While the Count, mortified in mien enough,*
> *And, nose to face, an added palm in length,*
> *Was plain writ "husband" every piece of him.*

He had earlier applied the term *'farce'* to the Pompilia-Guido alliance – *'This makes the first act of the farce'* (622) – and his version of the story, with further allusions to the *'madcap Caponsacchi'* (1245) and the *'spitfire'* Pompilia (1254), maintains it at that level.

Less jaunty and more biting are the words Half-Rome uses to describe the Comparini, especially Violante, revealing the depth of his feeling against the scheming wife. Pietro is *'the old murdered fool'* (21), Violante his *'wretched wife'* (22) or his *'bad wife'* (56). The husband is a man in his dotage who shuts *'his fool's-eyes'* (215) to live in a *'fools-paradise'* (255). With Violante, duplicity is stressed: the words *'lie,' 'cheat,'* and *'trick'* recur again and again in descriptions of her actions. *'Linking a new victim to the lie'* (64) with Pompilia's marriage, she passed her off as her own *'By a trick, a sleight of hand'* (226), in order to *'cheat the rightful heirs'* (580). The first two of the three words emphasized here are each used seven times and the third four times, always with reference to Violante; coming as they do all in the first half of the monologue, the closely spaced repetitions (shown typographically below) increase the sense of scorn and righteous wrath: (249–52)

> *She, whose trick brought the babe into the world,*
> *She it was, when the babe was grown a girl,*
> *Judged a new trick should reinforce the old,*
> *Send vigour to the lie now somewhat spent*

and: (588–90)

> *One sees a reason for the cheat: one sees*
> *A reason for a cheat in owning cheat*
> *Where no cheat had been. ...*

The only other kind of epithet Half-Rome ever uses for the Comparini is ironic: Violante is *'discreet'* (373) when engineering the marriage, and *'sage'* (547) when confessing her sin at the right time; they both are *'the kindly ones'* (653) and *'pleasant'* (1267) when they abandon Pompilia and turn on Guido.

By comparison, the descriptions of Guido are complimentary. He is *'honest'* and a *'man of birth'* (69–70); he holds his head aloft, *'Bravely although bespattered'* (669) and *'Manlike'* (1300) meets the foe in public court. The only time he is treated with anything like the mocking tone of the other descriptions is in the passage showing how he failed to kill his wife and the Canon on the spot when overtaking them; this failure draws forth Half-Rome's most scornful remarks: (1060–5)

> Taken to Rome they were;
> The husband trooping after, piteously,
> Tail between legs, no talk of triumph now –
> No honour set firm on its feet once more
> On two dead bodies of the guilty, – nay,
> No dubious salve to honour's broken pate. ...

All the lines about Guido are interlaced with references to *'poison'* – the poison that he suffers – and the recurrence of this idea, sometimes used figuratively, sometimes literally, works to build up a subtle kind of sympathy for the Count more effectively than direct pleading for his cause. The notion of marrying Pompilia is presented as first occurring to him as a kind of healing balm after a life-time of frustration and disappointment: *'What if he gained thus much, / Wrung out this sweet drop from the bitter Past ... ?'* (325–6). This use of *'drop'* is echoed with sharply different overtones when Pompilia leaves him and the Comparini continue to plot against him: (1267–71)

> ... on Guido's wound
> Ever in due succession, drop by drop,
> Came slow distilment from the alembic here
> Set on to simmer by Canidian hate,
> Corrosives keeping the man's misery raw.

Later, speaking of the same plot, Half-Rome says: *'Let a scorpion nip, / And never mind till he contorts his tail! / But there was sting i' the creature; thus it struck'* (1305–7). The poison image becomes more than metaphor in the description of Pompilia's flight. She has been advised by her parents to put poison in Guido's cup and set fire to the house to cover all traces on the night she leaves; in point of fact, says the speaker, she *'Had simply put an opiate in the drink / Of the whole household overnight'* (905–6), thus delaying her husband's pursuit for several hours, until he could shake off *'the relics of his poison-drench'* (953). The final use of the figure recalls both the earlier ones, as Half-Rome says to his listener: (1373–7)

> *Come, here's the last drop does its worst to wound:*
> *Here's Guido poisoned to the bone, you say,*
> *Your boasted still's full strain and strength: not so!*
> *One master-squeeze from screw shall bring to birth*
> *The hoard i' the heart o' the toad, hell's quintessence.*

These lines – referring to the last blow, news of the birth of a son to Pompilia – bring back the use of *'drop'* as well as the scorpion image (in the toad) and serve to justify the ensuing violence: *'Why, the overburdened mind / Broke down ...'* (1389–90). It is in these moments, describing Count Guido as the injured husband with no resort but to the unsatisfactory justice of the courts, that Half-Rome abandons his light, colloquial tone and speaks most passionately and convincingly, as in the lines describing the murder scene (*'Vengeance ... burst like a mountain-wave ...'*) and in those giving the reasons for violence in the heat of revenge. His quarrel with the law and his belief in the prior claims of *'honour'* are powerfully expressed in lines decrying Guido's earlier hesitation; with the piling up of repetitions of the word *'law'* (typographically stressed here) the contemptuous indignation rings out in every phrase: (1505–18)

> *He hesitates, calls* law *forsooth to help.*
> *And* law, *distasteful to who calls in* law
> *When honour is beforehand and would serve,*
> *What wonder if* law *hesitate in turn,*
> *Plead her disuse to calls o' the kind, reply ...*
> *"You whose concern it was to grasp the thing,*
> *"Why must* law *gird herself and grapple with?*
> *"Law, alien to the actor whose warm blood*
> *"Asks heat from* law *whose veins run lukewarm milk, –*
> *"What you dealt lightly with, shall* law *make out*
> *"Heinous forsooth?"*

Half-Rome's most characteristic speech habit, which is in keeping with his cynical attitude and also incidentally helps to create a subtle kind of sympathy for Guido, is the use of animal imagery to describe the actors in the piece. The scorpion, toad, and even the viper-figures for Pompilia, linked with the poisoning of the victim Guido, comprise only one small part of a larger pattern of animal-like comparisons applied to every figure which contribute to the demeaning and dehumanizing effect already set up by the speaker's well-demonstrated callousness. The Franceschini are not exempt; Guido's brother is introduced (295–8) as

> ... a web-foot, free o' the wave,
> And no ambiguous dab-chick hatched to strut,
> Humbled by any fond attempt to swim
> When fiercer fowl usurped his dunghill top –

and their younger brother Girolamo is 'also a fledgling priest, / Beginning life in turn with callow beak / Agape for luck' (339–41). The period the Comparini spend with the Count at Arezzo is described as four months of 'Dog-snap and cat-claw' (505), and the suspicious Guido is shown as seeing Caponsacchi's actions in terms of the prowling fox: (821–5)

> Back to mind come those scratchings at the grange,
> Prints of the paw about the outhouse; rife
> In his head at once again are word and wink,
> Mum here and budget there, the smell o' the fox,
> The musk o' the gallant. ...

Guido's friends advise: (837–40)

> "... never dream,
> "Though he were fifty times the fox you fear,
> "He'd risk his brush for your particular chick,
> "When the wide town's his hen-roost!"

But the threatened husband cannot get the Canon to face him: 'The fox nor lies down sheep-like nor dares fight' (866). The persistent allusions to him as a fox imbue the figure of the priest with disagreeable overtones of furtiveness and treachery, while Guido seems, as a result, the harassed and preyed-upon.

But the most effective dehumanizing device that Half-Rome employs throughout his monologue is the pervasive 'angler' figure in which each time Violante plays the scheming and skilled caster, Pompilia the helpless bait, and Guido the unsuspecting victim. He makes use of this figure of speech consciously, well aware of the ultimate effect, as manifested by the careful manner in which he weaves it into the narrative at periodic intervals and by the way he subtly draws his listener's attention to its use. He introduces the analogy immediately after picturing Violante in terms of Eve ruling her Adam in their 'fools'-paradise' where Pietro is incapable of planning for the future with the necessary guile: (268–74)

> And who must but Violante cast about,
> Contrive and task that head of hers again?
> She who had caught one fish, could make that catch
> A bigger still, in angler's policy:
> So, with an angler's mercy for the bait,
> Her minnow was set wriggling on its barb
> And tossed to mid-stream. ...

A few lines later, he picks up the same figure with deliberation: (321–3)

> Who but Violante suddenly spied her prey
> (Where was I with that angler-simile?)
> And threw her bait, Pompilia, where he sulked –

and then, after presenting Guido's reasoning about what he might expect from such an alliance, he concludes: 'Such were the pinks and greys about the bait / Persuaded Guido gulp down hook and all' (342–3). Once more he invites attention to the cleverness and aptness of the simile when he returns to it to depict the last treachery of the Comparini: (1354–60)

> ... yes, the pair
> Who, as I told you, first had baited hook
> With this poor gilded fly Pompilia-thing,
> Then caught the fish, pulled Guido to the shore
> And gutted him, – now found a further use
> For the bait, would trail the gauze wings yet again
> I' the way of what new swimmer passed their stand.

Besides emphasizing the craftiness and practised duplicity of Violante, and the victimization of Guido, this kind of figure works further to present Pompilia as an unthinking pawn in the hands of the angler, first as a minnow 'wriggling on the barb,' and then as a 'gilded fly' set to trail wings before a new swimmer; she is seen as a thing, less than human. Although this concept is inconsistent with other images of her as a *'Helen'* (1003), a wife who *'knew the appropriate warfare well'* (867), Half-Rome uses it whenever he wishes to play especially upon the hearer's sympathy for Guido; the other images of the scheming wife, useful in their place, put the Count too clearly in a ridiculous light and so are avoided where sympathy is the object. He increases the dehumanizing of the girl-wife when, in the comparison of Caponsacchi to an Apollo, he adds, *'while the snake / Pompilia writhed transfixed through all her spires'* (794–5). Whenever he uses the *'lamb'* figure, employed in Book 1 to contrast the innocent Pompilia with the wolf-like Count, he does so ironically: *'This lamb-like innocent of fifteen years'* (903) had simply put an opiate in the drink of the whole household. He refers sardonically to the court's deliberations: (1087–90)

> *What else shall glad our gaze*
> *When once authority has knit the brow*
> *And set the brain behind it to decide*
> *Between the wolf and sheep turned litigants?*

The conscious manipulating of the angler simile is allied to other devices which distinguish Half-Rome's particular mode of address. As indicated by his choice of words, his attitude is cynical and callous, and this attitude is further conveyed by his most typical speech patterns, that is, by his general treatment of a subject, going beyond simply the choice of words to the selection and arrangement of details of the narrative and to the manner in which the whole is presented. For Half-Rome this manner can be summed up as one of exaggeration and insinuation. Much of the effect of ridicule and belittling that is evident in his description of Caponsacchi and Pompilia in the inn encounter is equally evident in his paraphrased summary of the court's findings in the divorce suit. He deliberately exaggerates the couple's protestations of innocence: (1109–13)

> *"The accused declare that in thought, word and deed,*
> *"Innocent were they both from first to last*
> *"As male-babe haply laid by female-babe*
> *"At church on edge of the baptismal font*
> *"Together for a minute, perfect-pure.*

In the lines referring to the alleged letter-exchange, the piling up of outraged verbs has the same effect of weakening their defence by overstatement of the case: (1130–2)

> "The accused, both in a tale, protest, disclaim,
> "Abominate the horror: 'Not my hand'
> "Asserts the friend – 'Nor mine' chimes in the wife. ...

So with the repetition of the sceptical judgment, ' "strange may yet be true" ' (1107), and ' "Difficult to believe, yet possible" ' (1114, 1125). Always the hyperbole of the argument Half-Rome presents results in a casting of doubt over the statement, as in this denial of meetings with the exchange of letters: (1154–7)

> "Why, she who penned them, since he never saw
> "Save for one minute the mere face of her,
> "Since never had there been the interchange
> "Of word with word between them all their life ...

where the calculated use of extreme terms like 'never,' 'mere,' 'all their life,' signals the speaker's intention to suggest just the opposite of what he is saying. It is similar to the kind of thing he does in telling how Guido's enemies responded to his treatment; their reaction is presented in heightened and exaggerated language, so as to make them seem both coarse and faintly ridiculous. 'Did not they shout, did not the town resound!' (485) he says, as Pietro 'trumpeting huge wrongs / At church and market-place, pillar and post' joined Violante in protesting 'In whatsoever pair of ears would perk / From goody, gossip, cater-cousin and sib' (507–13), even while Pompilia was 'shrieking all her wrongs forth' (881).

Some of this exaggeration, with its consequent effect of debasing whatever it is aimed at, takes the form of sarcasm or irony; Half-Rome will say, for instance, that 'Thus minded then, two parties mean to meet / And make each other happy' (462–3), after he has brought out the scheming and fraud behind the meeting of the Count and the Comparini. But the most deadly effect comes from insinuation, of which Half-Rome is past-master. Here he is more subtle, sometimes obscuring the distinction between fact alleged and fact proved, at other times throwing out in parentheses a sly hint as to motivation. An example of the first can be found in his quoting of Pompilia's denial that she can read and write, when he adds, with studied ambiguity, 'she read no more than wrote, / And kept no more than read' (1137–8), and of the second, when he says that she won her freedom from the Convertites (1332–5)

> By intervention of her pitying friends
> Or perhaps lovers – (beauty in distress,

> *Beauty whose tale is the town-talk beside,*
> *Never lacks friendship's arm about her neck). ...*

This kind of treatment pervades the whole of the court summary (1083–1215) and becomes the dominant note in any reference to Caponsacchi – described, for example (910–15), as

> *... the Canon who, Lord's love,*
> *What with his daily duty at the church,*
> *Nightly devoir where ladies congregate,*
> *Had something else to mind, assure yourself,*
> *Beside Pompilia, paragon though she be,*
> *Or notice if her nose were sharp or blunt!*

Allied to these mannerisms, which have the secondary effect of implying a superiority on the speaker's part, is Half-Rome's emphasis upon the correctness and completeness of his knowledge of all the facts in the case. It becomes increasingly obvious, after his initial pronouncements on the details of the corpses' condition, that he takes enormous pride in his intimacy with every circumstance of the affair. He knowingly hints at the identity of a certain *'personage'* who has visited San Lorenzo that day, and with little or no urging reveals it to be the Cardinal; he positively informs his hearers of the matter involved in Pompilia's confession; and he initiates his narrative with the sweeping assurance (183–7) that

> *Case could not well be simpler, – mapped, as it were,*
> *We follow the murder's maze from source to sea,*
> *By the red line, past mistake: one sees indeed*
> *Not only how all was and must have been,*
> *But cannot other than be to the end of time.*

He assumes the role of an experienced guide, a cicerone, not only in recounting the story, but even in issuing directions to his listener: (2–4)

> *Be ruled by me and have a care o' the crowd:*
> *This way, while fresh folk go and get their gaze:*
> *I'll tell you like a book and save your shins.*

He instructs, *'Turn out here by the Ruspoli! ... Here's a friend shall set you right, / Let him but have the handsel of your ear'* (188–92). Even narrating, his tone is authoritative: *'Leave it thus, and now revert ...'* (759); *'Admire the man's simplicity'* (862); *'– look me in the face!'* (1469); *'take the old way trod when men were men!'*

(1524). The verbs are imperative and insistent, demanding attention.[3] Just as insistent is his conviction of rightness, of having all the
facts and only the facts. Almost as though suspecting a lapse in his
hearer's confidence at one point, he says sternly (719–21)

> Fact this, and not a dream o' the devil, Sir!
> And more than this, a fact none dare dispute,
> Word for word, such a letter did she write

or he corrects him brusquely: 'This you expect? Indeed, then, much
you err' (997). Again, he repeats (1049–51)

> But facts are facts and flinch not; stubborn things,
> And the question "Prithee, friend, how comes my purse
> "I' the poke of you?" – admits of no reply.

He asserts his objectivity emphatically: 'God knows I'll not prejudge
the case' (680); and, finally, triumphantly (1213–15)

> Now, am I fair or no
> In what I utter? Do I state the facts,
> Having forechosen a side? I promised you!

Apparently his audience accepts this claim with no demur, in spite
of its obvious inaccuracy.

For all his insistence on the facts of the case in the face of his
biased interpretation, Half-Rome is still a good story-teller and presents the events in chronological order in a swiftly moving narrative
that holds the interest. After the initial discourse on the mutilated
corpses and the day's events, he goes straight to the narrative and
does not digress (except for the aforementioned expostulations on
the exposed bodies at intervals throughout), in spite of an obvious
relish for gossip which his first remarks reveal. He is very conscious
of his role as narrator (partly, no doubt, because of his pressing
awareness of his audience's relationship to the 'certain what's-his-
name' he fears), and he takes pains to make each point clear while
arousing his listener's attention and curiosity with such remarks as
'For I should tell you' (656), 'I presently shall show' (1002), 'Then
was the story told, I'll cut you short' (929). He pays close attention
to details of time and place, and increases the excitement of the
account of the flight by stressing the passage of time: Guido woke
'After the cuckoo, so late, near noonday' (890), to find the couple had
left, robbing him. Half-Rome notes of the flight, 'This was eight

3/See also 15, 17, 883, 885.

hours since' (951), and then graphically pictures (952–69) the deserted husband's reaction:

> *Guido heard all, swore the befitting oaths,*
> *Shook off the relics of his poison-drench,*
> *Got horse, was fairly started in pursuit*
> *With never a friend to follow, found the track*
> *Fast enough, 'twas the straight Perugia way,*
> *Trod soon upon their very heels, too late*
> *By a minute only at Camoscia, at*
> *Chiusi, Foligno, ever the fugitives*
> *Just ahead, just out as he galloped in,*
> *Getting the good news ever fresh and fresh,*
> *Till, lo, at the last stage of all, last post*
> *Before Rome, – as we say, in sight of Rome*
> *And safety (there's impunity at Rome*
> *For priests, you know) at – what's the little place? –*
> *What some call Castelnuovo, some just call*
> *The Osteria, because o' the post-house inn,*
> *There at the journey's all but end, it seems,*
> *Triumph deceived them and undid them both. ...*

These lines illustrate his ability to carry his audience along with him: their very tempo echoes the rush and speed of the desperate Guido, the effect being increased by the piled-up verbs of motion and the omission of connectives (even the parenthetical remark is less a digression than a stressing of the need for haste); the attention to place-names, the effort to distinguish the exact location, reinforce the sense of accurate and intimate knowledge. The couple had halted *'at early evening,'* he says; now ' *'twas day-break'* and as they rested in ease at the *'trifling four-hours'-running'* left to Rome, *'So gained they six hours, so were lost thereby'* (972–82).

This attention to detail and to chronological order, along with the various devices for building suspense and sustaining interest, makes Half-Rome's narrative superficially convincing in regard to the facts revealed and almost succeeds in balancing the heavy bias of the attacks on Violante and the defence of Guido; however, where he clearly deviates from facts to outright interpretation of motive, his narrative loses whatever conviction of truth it had seemed to hold. The opinions revealed can be detected, first of all, by their divergence from what the poet-speaker set forth in Book 1 (where we have already been given an outline of the action and an indication of relative guilt and innocence with the Comparini largely excused and Guido condemned) and, secondly, by the curiously heavy and indeed almost overwhelming emphasis that Half-Rome puts on *money* as the motivating factor for all the evil done in the tale. This unexplained preoccupation with the pervasive influence of greed, which is not even mentioned in the poet's earlier summary, is so prevalent throughout the speaker's narrative that it becomes almost as obsessive as the hatred of women and by virtue of its weight and reiteration arouses a similar suspicion in the reader's mind about Half-Rome's understanding of the true meaning of the tragedy. Over and over again words like *'buy,' 'purchase,' 'bargain,'* and *'wealth'* recur in his analysis of the Comparini's plotting, the marriage, the flight, the court's decision – every incident of the story. He begins by setting forth the picture of the old couple enjoying their considerable worldly goods: with only themselves to *'use the wealth for: wealthy is the word, / Since Pietro was possessed of house and land'* (200–1). He owned *'some usufruct, had moneys' use / Lifelong'* (211–12), but for the sake of an heir *'purchased'* Pompilia; she was *'bought, paid for'* (574). Half-Rome describes the marriage ceremony in terms of *'the price paid and manner of the sale,'* clandestinely performed by *'some priest-confederate / Properly paid to make short work and sure'* (355–62). Violante had given Guido time to think twice beforehand, that he *'Might count the cost before he sold himself / And try the clink of coin they paid him with'* (377–8). And now, says Half-Rome, *'coin paid, bargain struck and business done'* (379), all parties must make the best of this wholly commercial deal. As for Pompilia's part: (402–8)

> ... *she paid her own expense;*
> *No loss nor gain there: but the couple, you see,*
> *They, for their part, turned over first of all*
> *Their fortune in its rags and rottenness*
> *To Guido, fusion and confusion, he*
> *And his with them and theirs – whatever rag*
> *With coin residuary fell on floor*

since it was felt that the Abate (415–19)

> *Might play a good game with the creditor,*
> *Make up a moiety which, great or small,*
> *Should go to the common stock – if anything,*
> *Guido's, so far repayment of the cost*
> *About to be. ...*

In effect, to Half-Rome's mind money is the single motivating
factor for Violante, for Pompilia, for Caponsacchi, for everyone[4] –
and one of Guido's chief claims to sympathy is his poverty. He describes the Count *'Pinching and paring'* to furnish a *'frugal board,
bare sustenance, no more, / Till times, that could not well grow
worse, should mend'* (459–61). Guido (280–3) is head of *'an old
noble house'* but

> *Not over-rich, you can't have everything,*
> *But such a man as riches rub against,*
> *Readily stick to, – one with a right to them*
> *Born in the blood ...*

and his penury is the only reason why he is so quick to take Violante's bait. These conspicuous money images ultimately suggest a
special significance for Half-Rome's situation: they are all of a piece
with his deep-seated distrust of women and his insecurity in his own
marital affairs, and point to a further identification of himself with
the straitened circumstances of Guido. They also mark him as more
grasping and greedy than any he castigates, but mainly their constant reappearance serves to put the reader on guard about accepting
Half-Rome's assessment of any motive. Blinded by his pressing
personal fears and drives, his reading of the Franceschini case is not
to be trusted.

II

The first person, or speaker, of Book III is Other Half-Rome, a young
bachelor with a strong interest in both the artistic and the religious,
who has just come from the hospital of Santa Anna's where the girl-
wife Pompilia lies dying. He is deeply impressed by her beauty and
goodness and takes her side in the murder case, representing in this
position the other half of divided public opinion. His tone and diction
reveal him as idealistic and imaginative, with a tendency to romanti-
cize the sordid aspects of the case, less sure of himself and his convictions than Half-Rome, and more inclined to be tentative in his
conclusions, except on the one point of Pompilia's innocence.

His audience is only barely indicated as present and no indication
of the relation to the speaker is given, until the somewhat ambiguous
last lines which suggest a possible legal or business connection between the two men. The quiet, musing tone of the monologue sug-

4/See also 440–2, 520–1, 544–5, 711–13, 895–6, 942.

gests that it is addressed to an audience of one rather than to a group and that the one is probably a friend, since the speaker makes little attempt to attract or hold his attention, instead seeming to feel sure of a sympathetic response. He calls him 'Sir' only twice, and the first time does not come until some 1300 lines have gone by; this infrequency of address accounts in part for the indefiniteness of the hearer's identity. Also, the first mention of the setting is not made until after some 100 lines and it is not referred to again except for one indirect remark, so that the whole scene is less vividly pictured than the previous one. The over-all effect is of self-absorption on the speaker's part, suggesting that he is still under the spell of the sight of Pompilia on her deathbed; however, a close look at his manner of speaking reveals that he is conscious of the importance of his narrator's role and interested, although less conspicuously than Half-Rome, in holding his audience's attention. He makes use of pauses in the recital and introductory comments intended to arouse suspense, although again these devices are employed in a characteristically indirect or understated fashion: 'Will you go somewhat back to understand?'[5]; 'The court that also took – I told you, Sir –' (1335); 'Whither it leads is what remains to tell' (1418); and (788–91)

> Now begins
> The tenebrific passage of the tale:
> How hold a light, display the cavern's gorge?
> How, in this phase of the affair, show truth?[6]

In this way, the illusion of a present utterance is maintained, even in the absence of the implied comments and gestures that marked Half-Rome's discourse so prominently, but the speaker's words are made to seem less self-conscious and more thoughtful. The speaker seems to be more concerned with his subject-matter and less with the effect, and the relationship with the audience consequently appears relatively unimportant.

The setting of the monologue is indicated briefly. It is given on January 4, the day after Half-Rome's speech, on a Roman street near 'the long white lazar-house' of Santa Anna's which has been besieged by visitors for 'these two days' since the attack (35–6). The speaker and his companion stand in the sun in the market-place, near Bernini's fountain: he points to 'yon Triton's trump' (118). They are

5/Line 964. All references in this section of the chapter are to Book III unless otherwise indicated.
6/See also 737, 1236, 1338–9, 1642.

both aware of the two mutilated bodies laid out on the altar steps of San Lorenzo; Other Half-Rome adverts to them occasionally, because he remembers that the crowd there now is waiting for Pompilia's to join the other two, but he is far more conscious of the small cell where she lies in the hospital nearby: (221–8)

> For that same deed, now at Lorenzo's church,
> Both agents, conscious and inconscious, lie;
> While she, the deed was done to benefit,
> Lies also, the most lamentable of things,
> Yonder where curious people count her breaths,
> Calculate how long yet the little life
> Unspilt may serve their turn nor spoil the show,
> Give them their story, then the church its group.

They know that the trial of Guido Franceschini is pending but are less interested in it than in the fate of his wife, Pompilia. The speaker implies that execution for the murderer is inevitable: his conclusion is, 'Out with you / From the common light and air and life of man!' He dismisses the prisoner's present situation with a few words, returning as always to the victim still lingeringly alive; the pursuers, he says, overtook the assassins 'And brought them to the prison where they lie,' but more importantly, 'the wife lives yet by miracle' (1639–41).

The third person, not present but playing a part in the speaker's consciousness, seems to be Guido's brother, the Abate Paolo; at least his figure takes for Other Half-Rome the same dominating role that Violante's took for Half-Rome. Where the latter only mentioned him as one of the family Franceschini, an intermediary in the effecting of the marriage settlement, here he becomes the principal actor in the plot to marry Pompilia to the Count and the shadowy figure behind all the later events involving Pompilia's flight and the murder. It is true that he is not a part of the first of Violante's frauds, the adoption (which is treated with some sympathy as Other Half-Rome rationalizes her action and stresses the good to Pompilia from it), but he and not the Comparini makes the first move toward the alliance: 'one day brought a priest, / Smooth-mannered soft-speeched sleek-cheeked visitor' (250–1), and Other Half-Rome pictures him in a brilliantly conceived scene, pleading the family cause, holding forth the advantages for Pompilia's side in such a match. 'Our spokesman, Paolo, heard his fate' (436), even before Guido himself learns of Pietro's first refusal, and when the marriage finally takes

place, it is hinted that Paolo once again is instrumental: *'A priest –
perhaps Abate Paolo'* (455) performs the secret ceremony. (Half-
Rome had used the same occasion to guess that it was simply a paid
'priest-confederate.') Pietro must be mollified by *'Paolo's patron
friend,'* the Cardinal who offers to supervise the drafting of the
marriage articles, and when Guido protests the court's decision on
his marriage, his case is presented *'through the Abate's mouth'* (669).
Indeed, *'Cried Guido, or cried Paolo in his name'* (686), is the way the
speaker carefully puts it. It is the Abate who broadcasts the story of
Pompilia's letter setting forth the Comparini plot, the Abate who
prepares his brother's counterclaim after the flight – helped most
'At words when deeds were out of question' (1331) – the Abate who
brings *'To the arms of brother Guido'* the news that the Comparini
have instituted still another suit, and he who takes on the burden of
defence against it: (1465–72)

> *Brave Paolo bore up against it all –*
> *Battled it out, nor wanting to himself*
> *Nor Guido nor the House whose weight he bore*
> *Pillar-like, by no force of arm but brain.*
> *He knew his Rome, what wheels to set to work;*
> *Plied influential folk, pressed to the ear*
> *Of the efficacious purple, pushed his way*
> *To the old Pope's self, – past decency indeed, –*

until (1487–9)

> *All of a terrible moment came the blow*
> *That beat down Paolo's fence, ended the play*
> *O' the foil and brought mannaia on the stage.*

Even at this point, however, Paolo's role is not ended; he must pay
the costs for his brother of Pompilia's sojourn with the Convertites –
'So, Paolo dropped, as proxy, doit by doit / Like heart's blood'
(1498–9) – and then break the news to Guido of the birth of his heir.
With this, Other Half-Rome delicately hints that the fine hand of
Paolo is behind the murder; he quotes him writing to his brother:
*' "I shall have quitted Rome ere you arrive" / "To take the one step
left" '* (1540–1). Guido responds to the direction immediately, hast-
ening to Rome with his accomplices to occupy the vacancy *'Left them
by Paolo, the considerate man / Who, good as his word, disappeared
at once / As if to leave the stage free'* (1585–7).

All this extraordinary attention to Paolo's role points to the inescapable conclusion that for some reason, perhaps to imply a Church connection of Other Half-Rome which would account for his intimate knowledge of Paolo's activities and his severe condemnation of them, the speaker magnifies the part played by Guido's brother in the events leading up to the murder. This emphasis on Paolo's plotting also allows, of course, for further characterizing of the speaker as chivalrous and sentimental in his relatively sympathetic treatment of Violante. To condone or minimize her role, so enlarged by his predecessor, Other Half-Rome must provide an alternative explanation for the marriage machinations and domestic quarrels – and the Abate Paolo makes a rewarding substitute.

But in a truer sense the significant third person in the second monologue can best be described as Pompilia herself. She, more than anyone or anything else, is the focal point for all Other Half-Rome's attention. A distinction needs to be made here between her role in Book III and the role of Guido in Book II. In the latter, Guido functions merely as an actor in the narrative, albeit an important one and one with whom the speaker identifies himself, in his ACTIVE role in the killing, but he does not function outside the plot of Half-Rome's story; in other words, Guido the prisoner lying in his cell in New Prison does not dominate the consciousness of Half-Rome in any sense – only Count Guido Franceschini, the injured husband who wrought vengeance on his enemies in the PAST action. It is quite different with Other Half-Rome; Pompilia is not simply the heroine of his narrative, but in a very real sense she figures as the leading character in the present action, his unfolding of her story. Other Half-Rome's purpose in speaking is to defend her, to vindicate the reputation of the living Pompilia in whose actual presence he has so lately been and to preserve the memory when that presence fades from life.

This sense of her continuing presence and of the need to defend her innocence accounts for much in his presentation of her story. The first 115 lines are devoted to a description of her and the scene at her bedside in terms which characterize her explicitly as a saint – 'Thus saintship is effected probably' (111) – who is now living only by divine intervention – 'Alive i' the ruins. 'Tis a miracle' (7). After relating how she came to be adopted by Violante and Pietro, Other Half-Rome returns to the present, lingering not on the dead Comparini, but on the wounded Pompilia as she lies surrounded by curious onlookers who count her breaths, 'Calculate how long yet the little life / Unspilt may serve their turn' (226–7). When he comes to the marriage scene at San Lorenzo, he reminds his hearer that where the old couple lie now, she will lie soon. In recounting her sufferings at Arezzo, he interrupts the narrative to come back once again to the present: (792–5)

> Here is the dying wife who smiles and says
> "So it was, – so it was not, – how it was,
> "I never knew nor ever care to know –"
> Till they all weep, physician, man of law,

and even, he adds, the friar Celestino; here the speaker reports how the Augustinian had likened her to a harmless, trapped bird, adding his own question, 'But we, who hear no voice and have dry eyes, / Must ask, – we cannot else, absolving her' (812–13) – how much of a victim was the Canon then? This last comment of Other Half-Rome points up the fact that although he is no longer present in Pompilia's hospital cell, he still feels the spell of her presence; he also feels compelled to deny the extent of her influence and to attempt an impartial and dispassionate judgment of the case.

The main difficulty in this task he finds to be the role of Caponsacchi in the affair. 'You will find it hard' (824), he admits, measuring the Canon's emotions by his own, to persuade the mocking world that this priest was inspired by charity alone in his daring flight with the distressed wife. As he describes the Canon's background and the way in which he must have been attracted by the sight of the sad and beautiful Pompilia, once more he moves in time from then to the present, comparing the priest to all those who have been to see her on her deathbed and acknowledging again the power of her presence: (868–71)

> Half at the least are, call it how you please,
> In love with her – I don't except the priests
> Nor even the old confessor whose eyes run
> Over at what he styles his sister's voice. ...

Always, when giving her side of the argument, he quotes her as speaking in these placid dying moments (in sharp contrast to Half-Rome who pictured her 'shrieking' forth her wrongs), with emphasis on the credibility and calmness of her story; 'For her part, / Pompilia quietly constantly avers' (907–8), he will say, or, 'as she avers this with calm mouth/Dying, I do think "Credible!" you'd cry' (923–4). Giving her version of the night at the inn, he stresses the weakness and weariness she felt after the long journey and enhances the atmosphere of tranquillity and calm by using words like *'sleep'* and *'dream.'* She was so weary that speech became *'mere talking through a sleep'* and weak flesh *'fell like piled-up cards'* until finally, she says, *' "something like a huge white wave o' the sea" / "Broke o'er my brain and buried me in sleep" '* (1137–48). Then, Other Half-Rome concludes, she lay *'wax-white, dead asleep, deep beyond dream'* (1278) – the emphatic phrase calls to mind that Half-Rome had described this same scene as one where she *'still slept or feigned a sleep'* (II, 1026). Pompilia's defender evidently feels it important to stress her fatigue and confusion at this point in order to account for the discrepancy in times mentioned by her and Caponsacchi – she says they arrived at the inn at dawn, he places the time at sunset – but beyond this, there is a further gain in sympathy for the dying girl who seems to be speaking herself, even though at a remove, in these lines. The underlying tension in Other Half-Rome's situation emerges here: he feels compelled to capture the very spirit of the young wife whom he has idealized into a martyr and saint, and to tell her story as she might have told it, while explaining away every vestige of guilt or blame that her flight has aroused.

The tone of the monologue sets forth his attitude clearly. The rhythm and diction of the opening lines contrast markedly with the violent conclusion of the previous speech; the quiet and respectful, even tender, feeling is the result of the simplicity of adjectives (*'little,' 'patient,' 'poor,' 'flower-like,' 'quiet,' 'cool,' 'sad'*) combined with a profusion of verbs and nouns with spiritual or religious over-tones. In the first twenty-five lines we have *'miracle,' 'Madonna,' 'prayer,' 'confess,' 'absolved,' 'friar,' 'confession,' 'soul,' 'angels,'* and *'God.'* All subsequent references to Pompilia are couched in the same language of dignity, respect, sympathy. She of the *'harmless life'* and *'gentle face'* and *'girlish form'* (86–7) was like a *'fragile egg'* dropped by some careless wild bird and nourished till *'forth broke finch / Able to sing God praise'* (217–18). She lives yet, *'pure from first to last,'* like a saint not spared suffering, (105–8)

> *Though really it does seem as if she here,*
> *Pompilia, living so and dying thus,*
> *Has had undue experience how much crime*
> *A heart can hatch.*

He often compares her to a harmless captive bird, innocent victim of another's plot, and the comparisons recall Half-Rome's similar but less pleasant image of her as *'the wriggling bait'* on the angler's

hook. He quotes others to the same effect: the artist Maratta describes her face as ' "Shaped like a peacock's egg, the pure as pearl,"
/ "That hatches you anon a snow-white chick" ' (64–5). Fra Celestino likens her to the trapped bird who concludes: (809–11)

> "So I fluttered where a springe
> "Caught me: the springe did not contrive itself,
> "That I know: who contrived it, God forgive!"

Imagining her life at Arezzo, Other Half-Rome himself sees how
Guido would 'worry up and down' Pompilia, (778–84)

> The woman, hemmed in by her household-bars, –
> Chase her about the coop of daily life,
> Having first stopped each outlet thence save one
> Which, like bird with a ferret in her haunt,
> She needs must seize as sole way of escape
> Though there was tied and twittering a decoy
> To seem as if it tempted. ...

Carrying the bird image further (1533–8), Other Half-Rome depicts Pompilia's first impulse to flee in terms of the stirring of nature:

> So when the she-dove breeds, strange yearnings come
> For the unknown shelter by undreamed-of shores,
> And there is born a blood-pulse in her heart
> To fight if needs be, though with flap of wing
> For the wool-flock or the fur-tuft, though a hawk
> Contest the prize, – wherefore, she knows not yet.

This strikingly beautiful simile echoes the words he quotes (1121–4)
of Pompilia herself:

> She says, "God put it in my head to fly,
> "As when the martin migrates: autumn claps
> "Her hands, cries 'Winter's coming, will be here,
> " 'Off with you ere the white teeth overtake!' "

The ambiguity of the term 'white teeth,' apparently referring in
Pompilia's figure to the oncoming snow but with overtones of the
ominous pursuit by Guido, perhaps unrecognized by her but surely
clear to Other Half-Rome, adds to the pathos of the words.

Perhaps the speaker's most conspicuous verbal device for creating
and extending sympathy toward his heroine – and one that incidentally fosters the impression of his as a sensitive and imaginative

nature – is his recurrent use of the flower-image, which stands out in contrast to the sordid narrative. We hear first of the bruised *'flower-like'* body lying in the hospital, and then, when the strangely assorted visitors have come to gaze in admiration on Pompilia's beauty, the speaker picks up the image to castigate those who now admire but who four years ago ignored her as she leaned *'flower-like'* from her window to look for help. He says: (75–8)

> *'Tis just a flower's fate: past parterre we trip,*
> *Till peradventure someone plucks our sleeve –*
> *"Yon blossom at the briar's end, that's the rose*
> *"Two jealous people fought for yesterday. ..."*

He pictures the growth of the child, after her adoption by Violante and Pietro, as that of a delicately nurtured blossom (231–48); her parents are

> *Each, like a semicircle with stretched arms,*
> *Joining the other round her preciousness –*
> *Two walls that go about a garden-plot*

where a precious bloom

> *Year by year mounting, grade by grade surmounts*
> *The builded brick-work, yet is compassed still,*
> *Still hidden happily and shielded safe, –*

until, in her twelfth year,

> *The coping-stone was reached;*
> *Nay, above towered a light tuft of bloom*
> *To be toyed with by butterfly or bee,*
> *Done good to or else harm to from outside:*
> *Pompilia's root, stalk and a branch or two*
> *Home enclosed still, the rest would be the world's.*

The beauty and delicacy of this imagery is borne out in a generally gentle and sympathetic treatment of all the characters – with the notable exception of Guido – as opposed to the mocking scorn of Half-Rome's view of the same people. Not only is Pompilia pictured in dignified, reverent terms, but even Violante is seen as moved more by love of her child than by greed for herself. Pietro is treated not with contempt but with pity; we see him going to beg from door to door of his old friends after fleeing in desperation from Guido's cruelty, and we hear his voice speaking through Other Half-Rome, pathetically longing for Pompilia's return to them so that the three of them may be their *'old selves'* again. Unlike his predecessor, this speaker rarely uses slang or colloquialisms; the only such occasions seem to be when he is quoting someone else's words, as those of the disillusioned Pietro about the Count, *'the lout-lord, bully-beggar, braggart-sneak'* (637), or the ever-present crowd of unsympathetic friends who, as in Half-Rome's version, are always ready to offer rowdy but good-natured advice. The word *'fool'* – so omnipresent in the first speaker's vocabulary – is here used solely when quoting these *'friends'* who *'Heartily laughed'* in Pietro's *'fool's-face'* (396) or advised him against paying the dowry promised in *'first fool's-flurry'* (500). Similarly, irony is almost completely absent from Other Half-Rome's speech; on the rare occasions when it is used, it lacks the bite of Half-Rome's, as in this interpretation of the decision of the friar to whom Pompilia had appealed for help: (1027–34)

> The good friar
> Promised as much at the moment; but, alack,
> Night brings discretion: he was no one's friend,
> Yet presently found he could not turn about
> Nor take a step i' the case and fail to tread
> On some one's toes who either was a friend,
> Or a friend's friend, or friend's friend thrice-removed,
> And woe to friar by whom offences come!

A fundamental difference in attitude can be seen in Other Half-Rome's referring to an incident as *'the play's first act'* (1338) where Half-Rome had called it *'the first act of the farce'* (II, 622). Unlike his predecessor, he uses little or no sarcasm or humour, usually taking the serious approach, although the long passage describing the wily Paolo's visit to Violante is a masterpiece of subtle satire, catching every gesture and nuance in the Abate's well-studied argument, missing no detail of his appearance as he prepares to state his case: (264–9)

> So – giving now his great flap-hat a gloss
> With flat o' the hand between-whiles, soothing now
> The silk from out its crease o'er the calf,
> Setting the stocking clerical again,
> But never disengaging, once engaged,
> The thin clear grey hold of his eyes on her—

(this last line reminds us sharply whose brother this is, as it brings back the poet's presentation of Guido before the court in Book 1, 975–6: '*And never once does he detach his eye / From those ranged there to slay him or to save*'). The unrelenting severity and tinge of malice in this passage seem to be out of keeping with the generally idealized and less concrete and particularized manner of the rest of the monologue. It is almost entirely, for one thing, in indirect discourse, which captures the wheedling and insinuating tone of the visitor: '*He came to see; had spoken, he could no less – / (A final cherish of the stockinged calf) / If harm were, – well, the matter was off his mind*' (370–2). And it is punctuated with brief objective "stage directions" which penetrate the smooth façade with deadly effect: '*(here the hat was brushed)*' (300); '*(A certain purple gleam about the black)*' (375); he goes forth '*grandly, – as if the Pope came next*' (376), so that we are constantly reminded of the presence of a keen-eyed observer of the private scene being played out in Violante's chamber. A possible, though not very convincing, argument might be made for Other Half-Rome's artistic eye coming into play here to bring into sharp focus the wealth of detail he is capable of noticing, especially where his favourite target, the Abate, is concerned; certainly, however, he does not give evidence of this kind of vividly realized scene-setting and dramatization elsewhere, so that the overall effect is of a passage which, though one of his best, is somewhat out of character.

Much more typical of his mode of address is the passage with which he begins the narrative of events, where his penchant for imagistic expression and unheightened statement can be plainly seen. It calls to mind a similar passage in Half-Rome's speech where he sardonically stressed the Comparini's wealth and greed, ridiculing their situation with the ironic Adam and Eve allusions. Other Half-Rome, on the other hand, begins in his usual quiet fashion: (119–26)

> *What could they be but happy? – balanced so,*
> *Nor low i' the social scale nor yet too high,*
> *Nor poor nor richer than comports with ease,*
> *Nor bright and envied, nor obscure and scorned,*
> *Nor so young that their pleasures fell too thick,*
> *Nor old past catching pleasure when it fell,*
> *Nothing above, below the just degree,*
> *All at the mean where joy's components mix.*

The very rhythm and syntactical structure of these lines embody the balanced, moderate view they convey: the repetition of the word 'nor' at the beginning of consecutive lines, the weighing of the word 'low' against the word 'high' and 'poor' against 'richer,' the double adjective in the first half of the fourth line balanced in the second half with two adjectives opposite in meaning, this antithetical structure then widened to include a whole line set against another, with 'young' and 'old' both connected with 'pleasure' but linked by different verbs ('fell' with its sense of effortlessness and 'catching' with its idea of strain) – all summed up in the words 'just,' 'degree,' 'mean,' and 'mix' with their connotations of evenness and moderation that hark back to the original 'balanced' and 'scale.'

The following lines continue the same thought, speaking of 'adequate half' with 'half to match,' as each supplies the other's deficiency, both together making 'a whole that had all and lacked nought' (130). Indeed, by the time we come to the next lines with phrases such as 'round and sound,' 'composure,' 'union,' 'rightly mixed,' 'each element in equipoise,' we might begin to wonder if the speaker is using irony here to describe a couple who are, by the objective evidence, far from constituting such a perfection of marital union; however, the next thought comes in time to indicate that although the speaker may have been quite serious in his estimation of the Comparini match (as would be in keeping with his already demonstrated tendency to idealize), he is nevertheless not without an understanding of the basic weakness in their situation. 'A fatal germ lurked here,' he says, 'Out of the very ripeness of life's core / A worm was bred' (146–7) – their lack of an heir to share their worldly goods – and we are immediately reminded of Half-Rome's almost identical conclusion: 'here's the worm i' the core, the germ / O' the rottenness and ruin which arrived' (II, 209–10).

Again, when Other Half-Rome moves on to use the Eden-figure, naturally suggested by the idea of the worm in the apple breeding rottenness and ruin – 'Adam-like, Pietro sighed and said no more: / Eve saw the apple was fair and good to taste, / So, plucked it' (169–71) – we hear the echo of the earlier speaker who had used just such a metaphor but to an altogether different end: 'lest Eve's rule decline / Over this Adam of hers, whose cabbage-plot / Throve dubiously since turned fools'-paradise' (II, 253–5). In the earlier speaker's words, the emphasis was on woman's deceit; in the second, it is on woman's weakness and mistaken judgment. And where for Half-Rome greediness had been the prime motive for the Comparini in their adoption of the child, for Other Half-Rome it is only secondary; ' " 'Tis in a child, man and wife grow complete," / "One flesh:

God says so: let him do his work!" ' (153-4) is the very different way
he quotes them and then only as an afterthought does he admit,
indirectly through the figure of the mill-wheel wearing out and the
river sweeping on to grind some neighbour's corn, that the old couple
were also moved in their desire for a child by worldly considerations
for a legal heir.

Another point of contrast with the previous speaker comes in the
use of animal imagery which Other Half-Rome uses less pervasively
and more selectively. He compares only two characters – Guido and
Pompilia – to animals, each for a different end. Besides the bird
figure for her, he uses the image of the lamb to deepen sympathy
for her helpless position. The wolf–lamb contrast had been made
extensively by the poet in Book i, briefly by Half-Rome in an ironic
sense. Now the present speaker works toward the presentation of
Pompilia as pure, mild, harmless. The picture of the Abate and
Violante, for example, striking their bargain over the uncomprehending head of the girl is vividly drawn in these lines (462-8) which
show her playing

> *As brisk a part i' the bargain, as yon lamb,*
> *Brought forth from basket and set out for sale,*
> *Bears while they chaffer, wary market-man*
> *And voluble housewife, o'er it, – each in turn*
> *Patting the curly calm inconscious head,*
> *With the shambles ready round the corner there,*
> *When the talk's talked out and a bargain struck.*

Pietro picks up the image when he cries: ' *"Give us our lamb back,*
golden fleece and all," / "Let her creep in and warm our breasts
again!" ' (642-3). The speaker even puts it into the mouth of Guido:
(1300-6)

> *This was the froward child, "the restif lamb*
> *"Used to be cherished in his breast," he groaned –*
> *"Eat from his hand and drink from out his cup,*
> *"The while his fingers pushed their loving way*
> *"Through curl on curl of that soft coat – alas,*
> *"And she all silverly baaed gratitude*
> *"While meditating mischief!" – and so forth.*

The figure gains added pathos when Pietro juxtaposes it with an
animal image for Guido: ' *"Ay, let him taste the teeth o' the trap, this*
fox" ' (641); the expression applied by Guido's advocate to Capon-

sacchi is here applied to Guido himself. Other Half-Rome uses such images, usually of animals fierce, vicious, or skulking, to describe Pompilia's tormentor: *'Like an uncaged beast'* his cruelty sprang on her, and she prayed for help to take *'the claws from out her flesh'* (966–71). The frightened Comparini flee *'in the first roughness of surprise / At Guido's wolf-face whence the sheepskin fell'* (990–1), leaving him *'lord o' the prey, as the lion is'* (534). Guido, *'The beast below the beast in brutishness'* (1299), took himself to his own place, *'the wildcat's way'* (1324), after his plan at the inn failed, and the town talked to see *'how he ne'er showed teeth at all, / Whose bark had promised biting; but just sneaked / Back to his kennel'* (1459–61).

The most striking difference from the first speaker in mode of address is Other Half-Rome's lack of self-assurance in his conclusion – this, in spite of his conviction of Pompilia's innocence. Unlike Half-Rome, he often admits to doubt about the true version of disputed incidents, and this uncertainty is most apparent in his assessment of Caponsacchi's role. He admits that much stands in the way of excusing the Canon's rash action in intervening in Pompilia's marriage: (816–19)

> *We deal here with no innocent at least,*
> *No witless victim, – he's a man of the age*
> *And priest beside, – persuade the mocking world*
> *Mere charity boiled over in this sort!*

He concludes that *'You will find it hard'* (824). So he can only advise his hearer: *'Anyhow, / Here be facts, charactery; what they spell / Determine, and thence pick what sense you may!'* (836–8). At a loss to determine what exactly was Caponsacchi's motive, he leans to the belief that the Canon must have been in love with Pompilia, since he cannot see how it could be otherwise: (880–2)

> *Men are men: why then need I say one word*
> *More than that our mere man the Canon here*
> *Saw, pitied, loved Pompilia?*

Accepting the fact, then, he tries to find an explanation for why the priest was not more discreet in hiding the fact, why he should be (892–6)

> *But flirting flag-like i' the face o' the world*
> *This tell-tale kerchief, this conspicuous love*
> *For the lady, – oh, called innocent love, I know!*

> Only, such scarlet fiery innocence
> As most folk would try muffle up in shade. ...

He can only conclude wonderingly, ' 'Tis strange,' and admit his
bafflement at Caponsacchi's claim that he received letters from
Pompilia first: *'but the tale here frankly outsoars faith: / There must
be falsehood somewhere'* (906–7). He wavers constantly between
the desire to accept the priest's story and the need to reject its obvious contradictions of Pompilia's version, and his narrative at this
point ceases while he carries on a kind of dialogue with himself,
turning over the questions in his mind, musingly: (932–5)

> Why should this man, – mad to devote himself,
> Careless what comes of his own fame, the first, –
> Be studious thus to publish and declare
> Just what the lightest nature loves to hide,

until a sudden idea strikes him and he turns again to his hearer:
(948–52)

> Or what do you say to a touch of the devil's worst?
> Can it be that the husband, he who wrote
> The letter to his brother I told you of,
> I' the name of her it meant to criminate, –
> What if he wrote those letters to the priest?

Anticipating an objection to this version of what was obviously an
entirely accidental first meeting between the two, he provides an
answer based more on faith than on reason: *'– if this were thus? /
How do you say? It were improbable; / So is the legend of my
patron-saint'* (1049–51). And when he resumes the narrative, it is
without having reached any definite conclusion: (1052–61)

> Anyhow, whether, as Guido states the case,
> Pompilia, – like a starving wretch i' the street
> Who stops and rifles the first passenger
> In the great right of an excessive wrong, –
> Did somehow call this stranger and he came, –
> Or whether the strange sudden interview
> Blazed as when star and star must needs go close
> Till each hurts each and there is loss in heaven –
> Whatever way in this strange world it was, –
> Pompilia and Caponsacchi met. ...

The allowance for alternative explanations and the tendency to start, not with a conclusion, but with an effort to work it out in his own mind as he considers the facts aloud, make Other Half-Rome seem less importunate and self-assured than the speaker before him, and give the impression of one who responds intuitively rather than logically. This impression is borne out by the manner in which he develops the central points of his narrative. Although he treats the various events leading to the present crisis in generally chronological order, he does not present them as dramatically as Half-Rome; he interpolates passages of interpretative material and personal comment much more often and tends to take incidents as they strike him in importance; this sometimes necessitates repetition and clarification, as indicated by the use of phrases like *as I told you* and *to go somewhat back.*[7] He presents scenes from his imagination rather than from the direct narrative viewpoint, putting himself in the place of the actors and conceiving of what their emotions must have been in the given circumstances. *How I see Guido taking heart again!* (1281) he says, picturing the scene as the pursuing husband mounts the stairs of the inn where his wife lies, or, guessing at the feelings with which the Comparini fled the house at Arezzo: (535–9)

> *And, careless what came after, carried their wrongs*
> *To Rome, – I nothing doubt, with such remorse*
> *As folly feels, since pain can make it wise*
> *But crime, past wisdom, which is innocence,*
> *Needs not be plagued with till a later day.*

Not only the interpreting of the principals' feelings here, but the brief moralizing or philosophizing tag in the last quoted lines which follows in a natural way on the comment seem to be innate in the character of the speaker. Commenting on Pompilia's suffering, for instance, he will say: (111–14)

> *Thus saintship is effected probably;*
> *No sparing saints the process! – which the more*
> *Tends to the reconciling us, no saints,*
> *To sinnership, immunity and all.*

He does not hesitate to pause at the most critical moment of his recital, the murder scene, to consider at some length the deeper significance involved in the use of Caponsacchi's name as password: (1601–6)

7/See 964, 1002, 1290, 1335.

What? Had that name brought touch of guilt or taste
Of fear with it, aught to dash the present joy
With memory of the sorrow just at end, –
She, happy in her parents' arms at length
With the new blessing of the two-weeks' babe, –
How had that name's announcement moved the wife?

Other Half-Rome is a man who can refer to the legend of his patron saint in almost the same breath as he speaks of *'extemporized'* romance-books. Although he is careful to give the correct hour of the couple's arrival at the inn, in order to defend Pompilia's veracity, he does not show the same concern for details of time and place that his predecessor did; in fact, he makes an egregious error of time when he speaks at one point of Pompilia's being on her deathbed *'since four days'* (867), since it is only the second day after the attack when he speaks. When he gives her version of the encounter at the inn, all is a blur of noise and excitement, as she might have experienced it on awakening from the sleep, *'deep beyond dream'*: (1150–6)

"And where was I found but on a strange bed
"In a strange room like hell, roaring with noise,
"Ruddy with flame, and filled with men, in front
"Who but the man you call my husband? ay –
"Count Guido once more between heaven and me,
"For there my heaven stood, my salvation, yes –
"That Caponsacchi all my heaven of help, ... "

All this adds up to a picture of a man who is guided more by instinct or intuition in his understanding than by cold reasoning and explains why, despite his correct judgment of the respective guilt and innocence of Guido and Pompilia, he is wrong on other points, such as Caponsacchi's motivation; his is a *'swerve'* toward the side of truth, as the poet tells us in Book I, that meets with near-success. However, Other Half-Rome's speech reveals that the *'swerve'* is due less to a *'fancy-fit'* as the poet had claimed than to a characteristic intuitive reaching after the right answer by a sensitive and imaginative nature. Ironically, it is his affinity for Caponsacchi that causes him to misjudge the Canon and his adulation of Pompilia that blinds him to the true nature of Caponsacchi's feeling for her.

The facts he reveals are not many or new for the most part. He gives Fra Celestino's argument for the virtue of the dying wife, which Half-Rome did not mention; he directly contradicts the statement of the latter in regard to the notes that Pompilia was supposed to have written to the Abate Paolo; he casts doubt on the idea that she wrote to Caponsacchi at all, again contradicting the previous speaker; and he denies the story that she stole money and drugged her husband before she fled, imputing these charges to Guido's lies and implying instead that Guido feigned sleep to let her go. Another point, small in the narrative but significant in arousing sympathy for Pompilia's straits as a captive at Arezzo, is the revelation that she had even contemplated suicide in her desperation: she 'told how fierce temptation of release / By self-dealt death was busy with her soul' (1018–19).

Most of the opinions revealed have to do with the speaker's reading of Guido's motives for the killing. Far from touching on his honour, the birth of a child to Pompilia was a signal that the dowry money might slip through his fingers, thinks Other Half-Rome: (1546–52)

> By an heir's birth he was assured at once
> O' the main prize, all the money in dispute:
> Pompilia's dowry might revert to her
> Or stay with him as law's caprice should point, –
> But now – now – what was Pietro's shall be hers,
> What was hers shall remain her own, – if hers,
> Why then, – oh, not her husband's but – her heirs'!

He provides his own explanation for the problem of why the murderer used Caponsacchi's name to gain admission to the villa, attributing it to Guido's knowledge that the Canon was nowhere at hand to intervene. He scornfully dismisses the defendant's claim of injured honour, using his own situation as an example of its insufficiency, and expresses his belief that Guido will be condemned to die. Addressing him directly, he commands: (1692–4)

> If any law be imperative on us all,
> Of all are you the enemy: out with you
> From the common light and air and life of man!

III

Tertium Quid, the third speaker, is a member of the aristocracy who takes neither the husband's nor the wife's side but attempts to judge the case impartially from a standpoint superior to both. He is a friend of men in high places in government and in Church and seeks their favours by ingratiating himself through an exhibition of wit and knowledge. He is highly articulate, skilled in the uses of language, sophisticated and cynical, and has no personal feelings or sympathies in the present affair, except an attitude slightly more biased in favour of Guido as a near-aristocrat and against the Comparini because of their low social status. His only strong emotion is a scorn for the common man, whom he sees constituting the unreasoning mob of Rome.

His audience is plural, consisting primarily of a Cardinal and a Prince, although there are indications that occasionally other members of the card-playing circle leave their tables to drift by and listen to the talk or look up to eavesdrop for a moment – 'And here's the Marquis too!'[8] They have withdrawn from their game to a secluded window seat in the glittering mirror-panelled salon of a Roman palace. The time is evening on January 5, the third day after the murder, the bodies of the Comparini still lie exposed in San Lorenzo, and Pompilia lingers on her deathbed. The time for the start of the trial which has aroused the interest of all Rome fast approaches. In Tertium Quid's words (2–5), summing up the situation:

> Though she's not dead yet, she's as good as stretched
> Symmetrical beside the other two;
> Though he's not judged yet, he's the same as judged,
> So do the facts abound and superabound. ...

But the trial which 'begins next week,' says Tertium Quid, is really ' "end o' the Trial, last link of a chain" / "Whereof the first was forged three years ago" ' (21–3), and he proposes to explain to his audience how this came to be and to anticipate the court's decision. He addresses himself with unflagging attention and flattering concern to the high-placed personages who make up his audience, calling them by their respective titles, 'Excellency' and 'Prince,' no less than twenty-two times in the course of his speech, and at least a half-dozen other times by less specific titles, 'my wise friends,' 'Sirs,' and the like. He is extremely anxious to hold their interest and continually seeks their opinion on certain disputed or thorny points: 'Excellency, your ear! / Stoop to me, Highness, – listen and look yourselves!' (68–9); 'Your Excellency supplies aught left obscure?' (165); 'Highness, decide! Pronounce, Her Excellency!' (1113).[9] He

8/Line 57. All references in this section of the chapter are to Book IV unless otherwise indicated.

9/See also 227–32, 313–15, 631–5, 915–16, 1280, 1442–5.

indicates his acute awareness of their reactions by commenting on the slightest response – *'Here you smile'* (1125); *'In truth you look as puzzled as ere I preached!'* (1580) – or by imputing agreement – *'(I take the phrase out of your Highness' mouth)'* (1055). On at least two occasions his use of asides shows that the flattery cloaks the true feeling of contempt with which he views the pair: *'(That's for the Cardinal, and told, I think!)'* (1414) and his final comment, *'(You'll see, I have not so advanced myself, / After my teaching the two idiots here!)'*

The third person in this monologue is none of the people involved in the case at all, but *'the mob'* which crowds the streets below the palace discussing the murder and coming trial, and which is also constantly present in Tertium Quid's mind as a threat to *'justice,'* peace, and order. His contempt for this *'rabble's-brabble of dolts and fools / Who make up reasonless unreasoning Rome'* (10–11) breaks through his veneer of well-bred superiority time and again as he refers to them as *'simpletons,'* *'fools,'* or, most commonly, *'the mob.'*[10] He uses the last phrase scathingly to indicate the division between his present company, *'Qualified persons'* who can pronounce an *'authoritative word'* (8–9), and the vast numbers of the ignorant lower classes who presume now to pass judgment on the current legal action. Such a distinction is never far from his mind. He judges every individual in terms of his class: Pietro and Violante, for instance, he dismisses as *'cits'* who live almost as well as *'their betters'* (72), Guido is *'A burgess nearly an aristocrat'* (344) and therefore deserving of more interest. His social standing and not his wealth caused the Comparini to seek him out, says Tertium Quid; they were delighted to find *'the prize'* was *'Exorbitant for the suitor they should seek, / And social class should choose among, these cits'* (340–1). The Count was head of an old family in Arezzo, old *'To that degree they could afford be poor / Better than most'* (357–8) and his sisters had *'done well / And married men of reasonable rank'* (385–6). This class-conscious view Tertium Quid projects on Guido himself, having him protest the suing of the Cardinal for favours, since the prelate is beneath him socially: *' "a purple popinjay, whose feet I kiss" / "Knowing his father wiped the shoes of mine" '* (422–3). In the course of his monologue this speaker refers more than a dozen times to the lower class; he speaks variously of *'the plebs,'* *'the commonalty,'* *'the cits,'* *'burgesses,'* or simply *'the people,'* or *'the class,'* most often of *'the mob,'* to indicate his scorn for this troublesome segment of the Roman population.

10/See 15, 19, 43, 60, 62, 1620.

Part of this scorn seems ingrained and perhaps unconscious, so constant and ill-tempered are the references, but part of it may no doubt be attributed to Tertium Quid's motives for telling the story. He intends to entertain and amuse his listeners by regaling them with some of the intimate details of the case (which the mob could not be expected to be aware of); he will allow his illustrious audience the opportunity to match wits with the judges presently to be considering it, to reach their own immediate and perspicacious conclusion: (49–53)

> Why, Excellency, we and his Highness here
> Would settle the matter as sufficiently
> As ever will Advocate This and Fiscal That
> And Judge the Other, with even – a word and a wink –
> We well know who for ultimate arbiter.

The last remark, with its nudging reference to the Pope, signals another, unexpressed motive for the speech: to win the attention and approbation of his distinguished audience by his wit and cleverness and ultimately to advance himself through their favours. To this end, he flatters them outrageously by courting their opinions, and more subtly by consistently aligning them with himself in the group of 'qualified persons' who can speak on the matter; hence, another reason for the ever-present allusions to the unthinking mob. Hence also, perhaps, references to the Pope like that above and in the comparison of Pompilia's suitability for a Franceschini alliance – 'why, it suited, slipped as smooth / As the Pope's pantoufle does on the Pope's foot' (459–60) – where the easy familiarity of the simile will amuse his audience.

The game of judging that the three are to play requires that they maintain a superficial air of disinterestedness, so that they may not fall into the error of the common class who think the case 'Fused and confused past human finding out' (35). Tertium Quid points out that 'history, / Eusebius and the established fact' show how the dispassionate, intelligent observer can 'look through the crimson' of the first surprise and horror of the murder reports and 'trace lines' (40–2), and so he vows to present his hearers with nothing but the facts, unflavoured by human prejudices and emotions. He says: (58–61)

> Indulge me but a moment: if I fail
> – Favoured with such an audience, understand! –
> To set things right, why, class me with the mob
> As understander of the mind of man!

But although he is unfeeling as far as the individuals in the affair are concerned, seeing them all as simply representative of their respective classes or of the follies of some human types, he finds it difficult to maintain the complete impartiality he affects. Part of the difficulty springs from the fact that Count Guido Franceschini represents a higher social class than Pompilia's parents and the consciousness of this superiority, coupled with the dislike of the mob which he fears may side with the Comparini, causes in Tertium Quid a "swerving" toward the husband's side of which he is hardly aware. Initially, the bias is not apparent as he gives first one side and then the other in his presentation of the story, but it becomes evident near the end when the slightly longer and more strongly stated arguments for Guido's side loom larger emotionally as well as spatially. The tension resulting from this struggle between the desire to be impartial and the fear of the mob is increased by his secondary motive, to be witty and amusing for the benefit of his audience. In this effort to impress them with his rhetorical skill and cleverness, he sometimes must sacrifice fidelity to his "equal time" allotment; he will compromise his objectivity, for example, when he sees the opportunity to make a telling point or to bring in an entertaining piece of gossip or bright remark as commentary or illustration. His scandalous story of a court lady whose downfall was the result of her husband's tolerance is told mainly for the purpose of titillating his audience with gossip, as shown by the emphasis on the illustrious identity of his subject and by the reiterated 'we': (872–6)

> Look now, – last week, the lady we all love, –
> Daughter o' the couple we all venerate,
> Wife of the husband we all cap before,
> Mother of the babes we all breathe blessings on, –
> Was caught in converse with a negro page.

The ultimate effect of this anecdote, however, is to cast more doubt on Pompilia's argument than on Guido's, linked as it is with the Eve image which implies a cynical pseudo-tolerant view of the woman's penchant for blaming her husband; Eve's daughters ever since, concludes Tertium Quid, 'prefer to urge / "Adam so starved me I was fain accept" / "The apple any serpent pushed my way" ' (857–9).

The speaker's tone accurately reflects the attitude of the supercilious, callous observer of human foibles and follies, but it also reflects a deliberateness of style, a careful choice of words, and a concern with effect so great as to mark him as more concerned with the manner of the telling than with the story itself. Showing the *silvery and selectest phrase* that the poet had ascribed to him in Book I, he employs the choicest Latin expressions and quotations to make a point, interrupting himself at one point (30–2) to ponder aloud the best translation:

> "*Crammed to the edge with cargo – or passengers?*
> " 'Trecentos inseris: ohe, jam satis est!
> " 'Huc appelle!' – *passengers, the word must be.*"

Of Violante, he says: '*She meditates the tenure of the Trust,* / Fidei commissum *is the lawyer-phrase*' (134–5), to impress the listeners with his knowledge of the legal terminology, and his attentive little remark, '*I take the phrase out of your Highness' mouth,*' refers to his own 'Cui Profuerint!' (1054), which he imputes to the Prince. He quotes Paolo as saying, ' "Notum tonsoribus! *To the Tonsor then!*" ' on the visit to the wig-maker. (437) He uses the lawyer's phrase again to describe Violante as '*first* / *Author of all his wrongs,* fons et origo / Malorum' (1576–8).

When on occasion he descends to using slang, it is for purpose of making an effect, as in '*a cur-cast mongrel, a drab's brat,* / *A beggar's bye-blow*' (611–12), where the crude language is supposed to be a quotation of Guido repudiating Pompilia after learning of her parents' deceit and serves to convey vividly the extent of the husband's anger and frustration. At other times, this kind of language merely expresses the amused superiority of the unconcerned: (898–902)

> *We must not want all this elaborate work*
> *To solve the problem why young Fancy-and-flesh*
> *Slips from the dull side of a spouse in years,*
> *Betakes it to the breast of Brisk-and-bold*
> *Whose love-scrapes furnish talk for all the town!*

Similarly, his frequent use of imagery seems less an inadvertent revelation of a slant of mind, as with Other Half-Rome and his dominant flower-image, or a deliberate attempt to weight the case as with Half-Rome's angler simile, but rather a concern with the most striking way of expressing himself, regardless of the ultimate effect on the parties involved or on the course of the narrative. Tertium Quid uses imagery with the sure hand of a practised rhetorician, playing with a basic image to see how many twists and turns he can give it before reluctantly letting it go to turn to something novel and different. He begins with the story of the Comparini, for instance, by saying that they fed their own lamp only to come to age fifty and find the wick full to the depth, ready to moulder out and lie a prize for any passerby; now that the dark *'begins to creep on day,'* they fear their lack of an heir, for (104–7)

> *Let the lamp fall, no heir at hand to catch –*
> *Why, being childless, there's a spilth i' the street*
> *O' the remnant, there's a scramble for the dregs*
> *By the stranger. ...*

Having wrung out the last drop of meaning from the lamp figure, he passes on to toy with the flower-image that comes so naturally to mind in connection with Pompilia. Here he employs it because of the rich opportunities for ironic use of biblical and classical allusions. He first speaks of *'the sudden existence, dewy-dear, / O' the rose above the dung heap'* (246–7), in order to justify for the moment Violante's fraud – *'Why, moralist, the sin has saved a soul!'* (255) – and then (323–9) sees the child growing

> *Lily-like out o' the cleft i' the sun-smit rock*
> *To bow its white miraculous birth of buds*
> *I' the way of wandering Joseph and his spouse, –*
> *So painters fancy: here it was a fact.*
> *And this their lily, – could they but transplant*
> *And set in vase to stand by Solomon's porch*
> *'Twixt lion and lion!*

When he uses images of animals, the figure again is usually less consistent or effective than with earlier speakers, reflecting more of the speaker than of the object described. Violante is a *'poor sheep'* because she seems a harmless household creature, but then she has *'great teeth / Fit to crunch up and swallow a good round crime'* (130–3). He sees Pompilia as a lamb, as other speakers had, but there is neither Half-Rome's biting sarcasm nor Other Half-Rome's genuine pity for the creature over whose *'curly, calm, inconscious head'* the fateful bargain was struck; instead Tertium Quid cynically pictures her as the lure set out to draw the victim and then abandoned: (665–7; 675–7)

> *A pet lamb they have left in reach outside,*
> *Whose first bleat, when he plucks the wool away,*
> *Will strike the grinners grave.*

> *These fools forgot their pet lamb, fed with flowers,*
> *Then 'ticed as usual by the bit of cake*
> *Out of the bower into the butchery.*

Once, depicting the attack on Pompilia, he uses the bird-image that his predecessor had used so effectively to portray her helplessness: *'And last, Pompilia rushes here and there / Like a dove among the lightnings in her brake'*; but the pathos these lines might have held is lost with the next caustic remark that Guido's *'last husband's-act'* is to determine that she is really dead ' *"at last"* ' and with a *'deep satisfied breath'* to throw down *'the burden on dead Pietro's knees'* (1382–90).

Tertium Quid compares Guido to a bull with full consciousness that the simile is not an appropriate one, but too clever to surrender. Criticizing the Count's delay in the execution of the murder, he asks: (1559–64)

> *"Does the furious bull*
> *"Pick out four help-mates from the grazing herd*
> *"And journey with them over hill and dale*
> *"Till he find his enemy?"*
> > *What rejoinder? save*
> *That friends accept our bull-similitude.*

This weak *'rejoinder'* allows him the opportunity to play with the comparison, to demonstrate cleverly all the ways in which Guido's friends might find him to be indeed like the bull: (1565–70)

> *Bull-like, – the indiscriminate slaughter, rude*
> *And reckless aggravation of revenge,*
> *Were all i' the way o' the brute who never once*
> *Ceases, amid all provocation more,*
> *To bear in mind the first tormentor, first*
> *Giver o' the wound that goaded him to fight. ...*

He strains the image all the way to his conclusion, *'So Guido rushed against Violante. ... Do you blame a bull?'* (1576–9). To make it work at all, the last part has to be attributed to Guido's partisans, but his audience must appreciate Tertium Quid's resourcefulness and ingenuity anyway.

Inevitably, this connoisseur of fine phrases finds eventual reason to employ as well Half-Rome's favourite angler figure for the marriage negotiations; in his hands, however, it is merely a passing reference, aimed at dismissing the claims of both parties to the argument: (708–11)

> They baited their own hook to catch a fish
> With this poor worm, failed o' the prize, and then
> Sought how to unbait tackle, let worm float
> Or sink, amuse the monster while they 'scaped.

The fact is that this rhetorician rather surprisingly makes less use of imagery than either of the two previous speakers, relying much more heavily on other stylistic devices such as paradox, analogy, antithesis, and anecdote and illustration.[11] All these devices are part of his love of intellectual byplay, as well as a potential source of delight to his audience. Most of his witty remarks are in the nature of sardonic references to Guido's unlucky efforts to pursue an ecclesiastical career (a topic his hearers will appreciate): 'he clipped / His top-hair and thus far affected Christ' but that was not enough for promotion and at forty-six years of age he was 'worn threadbare of soul' (404–8). So he was 'thus left, – with a youth spent in vain / And not a penny in purse to show for it' (416–17). The moral to be drawn from the story of the head of the police force catching his death of cold in his pursuit of the killers is pithily expressed: (1411–13)

> A warning to the over-vigilant,
> – Virtue in a chafe should change her linen quick,
> Lest pleurisy get start of providence.

Of Pompilia's prayer that she might live to make the truth known, he remarks caustically that this 'seems to have been about the single prayer / She ever put up, that was granted her' (1431–2), and summarizes her final ordeal thus: (1435–7)

> She bore the stabbing to a certain pitch
> Without a useless cry, was flung for dead
> On Pietro's lap, and so attained her point.

11/Park Honan, in Browning's Characters: A Study in Poetic Technique (1961), notes that Tertium Quid's attempt to convince his auditors of the "neat and discriminating balance of his mind" causes his lines to be filled with "phonetic, verbal and syntactical parallels" of which he gives many examples (pp. 278–9).

Tertium Quid's love of paradox can be seen in comments like the following (350–4) on the reversal of the Comparini's plans to arrange the marriage:

> Alack, were it but one of such as these
> So like the real thing that they pass for it,
> All had gone well! Unluckily, poor souls,
> It proved to be the impossible thing itself,
> Truth and not sham: hence ruin to them all.

His pleasure in relating gossip appears in the recounting of Violante's visit to the mother of Pompilia, with its wealth of intimate detail – the little lane behind San Lorenzo and the labyrinth of dwellings, the certain blind house with the blinking candle in the top casement, the cord on the wall to guide one up the filthy stairs to the door ajar in the dark. This description, like that of Paolo's visit to the peruke-woman, with its atmosphere of easy-living, intrigue-ridden Rome, is introduced as much to show off Tertium Quid's inside knowledge of the seamy side of lower Roman life as to add anything substantial to the narrative. And so with the anecdote about the 'lady we all love.'

These long passages are more than digressions, however. A significant element in the speaker's mode of address is his use of anology; many of his descriptive passages make a telling point by bringing out an unexpected likeness between the situation of his titled listeners and that of the actors in the sordid drama he unfolds. For example, when stressing that a good end came from Violante's deceitful act – passing off Pompilia as the Comparini's own did, after all, rescue her from a life of disease and vice – he points to the pearl hanging about the neck of a noble lady sitting nearby and reminds his hearers that the rich jewel was formed about nothing more than 'a grain of grit'; nevertheless, the pearl could hardly be called 'worthless for the worthless core' (310–11). Another time he breaks off his narrative for the same purpose of justifying Violante's fraud and points suddenly to the 'marvelous gem' the Cardinal wears on his finger, repeating the story he has heard that its present owner found it accidentally on a pathway in a vineyard – well, he shrugs, does that hurt the 'five clowns' of the vine-dresser's family who lost it? – or, as he adds scornfully, does it matter in the least that not one of these clowns 'keeps it in his goatskin pouch / To do flint's-service with the tinder-box?' (266–7). The answer, he can be confident, will be a "no" from the startled Cardinal who unexpectedly finds himself a part of the argument, on Violante's side, for the *'harmless cheat.'*

One of Tertium Quid's cleverest analogies likens the present drama to a puppet show (1289–94), in which the husband and wife trade blows as the crowd claps or hisses according to its disposition until,

> *... by the time the mob is on the move,*
> *With something like a judgment* pro *and* con, –
> *There's a whistle, up again the actors pop*
> *In t'other tatter with fresh-tinseled staves,*
> *To re-engage in one last worst fight more*
> *Shall show, what you thought tragedy was farce.*

The last word here recalls the similar judgment of Half-Rome, and contrasts with the serious view of Other Half-Rome, but it stands apart from both by virtue of its belittling of *both* sides of the argument and its reducing the tragedy to the level of an entertainment for the noisy, thoughtless crowd. An ostentatious impartiality is, in essence, the speaker's general approach in balancing the opposing arguments for his audience – the balancing act itself being what engages him, rather than any merits of the respective arguments. He seems to be trying to be equally unfair to both sides, if such is possible. The basic structure of his monologue is the debate, with the speaker presenting the opposing sides in alternating order, without any attempt to judge motives or to probe for hidden feelings; he proposes merely to set forth what has been alleged as fact by the participants and their friends, and to offer commentary on these allegations from a superior vantage point. The frequent repetition of the phrase *'they say'* illustrates this sense of perspective and non-involvement on the speaker's part; it also incidentally makes the recital less dramatic and emotionally exciting than the previous speeches. Allusions to his source of information become more marked as he gets to the thorniest part of the story – the introduction of Caponsacchi and his flight with Pompilia – but even before that he falls back on this method of reporting events from a sceptical and uncommitted position, with innumerable expressions like *'So say the Comparini'* (573); *'If, as is said'* (687); *'Guido says – that is, always, his friends say'* (905); *'at least so people tell you now'* (1425).[12]

12/See also 694, 698, 699, 769, 787, 797.

In the same vein, every change from husband's to wife's viewpoint and back again is introduced with a qualifying phrase to indicate its opposition to what has gone before: '*On the other hand "Not so!" Guido retorts*' (581); '*But then this is the wife's – Pompilia's tale*' (851); '*Accordingly one word on the other side*' (903); '*But then on the other side again*' (1043), and so throughout.[13] And as he denies one argument with the next, enjoying the sense of removed superiority to the petty passions of the actors in the drama, relishing the cut and thrust of the intellectual manœuvring, he notes the bewilderment of his audience and plays on it at will, inducing his hearers to acknowledge the rightness of one side, only to demolish their conviction with a stronger argument for the other side. All the time he insists that the case is quite clear, but that he is not yet prepared to tip his own hand in judgment: (505–7)

> *Now, here take breath and ask, – which bird o' the brace*
> *Decoyed the other into clapnet? Who*
> *Was fool, who knave? Neither and both, perchance.*

Or again: (629–33)

> *Which of the two here sinned most? A nice point!*
> *Which brownness is least black, – decide who can,*
> *Wager-by-battle-of-cheating! What do you say,*
> *Highness? Suppose, your Excellency, we leave*
> *The question at this stage, proceed to the next,*

and finally: (1580–4)

> *In truth you look as puzzled as ere I preached!*
> *How is that? There are difficulties perhaps*
> *On any supposition, and either side.*
> *Each party wants too much, claims sympathy*
> *For its object of compassion, more than just.*

At last he triumphantly concludes that he has settled all the questions he has raised: '*The long and the short is, truth seems what I show: – / Undoubtedly no pains ought to be spared / To give the mob an inkling of our lights*' (1618–20). In fact, of course, he has settled nothing, as his last lines imply, when the Cardinal and the Prince refuse to commit themselves to any position and leave him with the impression that all his blandishments have gone for nothing as far as his advancing himself by them is concerned. In truth, he has

13/See also 651, 699, 966, 1476.

tipped the scales somewhat to the husband's side simply by giving the Franceschini the last say, and by pointing out that the wife's partisans go to extremes in claiming sainthood for her (1593–5, almost a direct thrust at Other Half-Rome's argument):

> *No, they must have her purity itself,*
> *Quite angel, – and her parents angels too*
> *Of an aged sort, immaculate, word and deed*

and in their making Guido a monster: (1603–6)

> *Why, he's a mere man –*
> *Born, bred, and brought up in the usual way.*
> *His mother loves him, still his brothers stick*
> *To the good fellow of the boyish games. ...*

The facts revealed by this speaker's clever presentation are actually few in number and of little significance. He tends to agree more with Other Half-Rome in treating Violante tolerantly and accepting the role of Paolo as important in the marriage arrangements, adding the incident of the peruke-woman to give substance to the argument that the Abate actually engineered the alliance. The brief details of the police officer who died as a result of the pursuit, introduced chiefly for entertainment value, and of Guido's amazement when he learns that Pompilia lives even after the attack – this latter a piece of dramatic description that increases interest in the murderer – are among the few additional bits of information which he presents, along with the detailed account of Violante's arrangement for the purchase of Pompilia. One other new fact is brought in as having some bearing on Guido's reasons for the murder: that another court in Tuscany which had heard the same suit for divorce brought before the Roman court had found for him and dismissed his wife's counter-suit. This *'discrepancy of judgments,'* proving the law's inadequacy, drove the man mad, says Tertium Quid, and forced him to take revenge into his own hands – one more effective argument for Guido's side.

The opinions revealed by the speaker are carefully overlaid with that patina of impartiality afforded by the alternative presentation, so that except for a few instances, such as that mentioned above touching on Guido's motive for the murder, it is difficult to determine where Tertium Quid's real feelings lie. He does very little probing into the emotions of Pompilia and Caponsacchi, refusing them as strong a defence as he gives to Violante's and Guido's actions, which are objectively more blameworthy and therefore seem to call forth more interest on his part. He effectively indicates something of the ambiguities and complexities of the whole affair when he forces his hearers to compare their present easy circumstances of judgment to Guido's earlier desperate situation, to imagine how it must have been for him then: (1184–94)

> He has the first flash of the fact alone
> To judge from, act with, not the steady lights
> Of after-knowledge, – yours who stand at ease
> To try conclusions: he's in smother and smoke,
> You outside, with explosion at an end:
> The sulphur may be lightning or a squib –
> He'll know in a minute, but till then, he doubts.
> Back from what you know to what he knew not!
> Hear the priest's lofty "I am innocent,"
> The wife's as resolute "You are guilty!" Come!
> Are you not staggered? – pause, and you lose the move!

Even here, however, we are left with the strong suspicion that the emotional involvement in the husband's predicament springs less from genuine sympathy – the speaker has, after all, already taken sceptical note of the inexplicable delay in Guido's revenge – than from the irresistible attraction to introduce a climactic antithesis that will dramatically identify his listeners with the murderer. Hints of a leaning on his hearers' part toward the Franceschini, in spite of all evidence of their guilt, had best be exploited by the intelligent and ambitious manipulator of evidence, and this last subtle justification of their prejudice should not fail to have its effect.

What are we supposed to think, then, of the facts of the 'three-fold murder' story and the principals involved, as a result of the elaborate introduction we have received from the onlookers in these first three monologues? This examination from the point of view of "voice and address" seems to indicate that we can be confident that by now we have been given most of the significant facts of the case, that is, that we know in some detail just what took place in the days and months prior to the attack at the villa on the evening of January 2. We can be equally sure that we do not know WHY these incidents culminating in the murder occurred; at least, we know that for the bystanders the interpretations of the motives for the killing are a matter of personal opinion, highly divergent, influenced by many factors which have nothing to do with the case itself.

Our judgment of the speakers obviously influences our judgment of the principals involved. The vividness of the first speaker's personality and the obviousness of his bias, as well as his insistence on the accuracy of his facts and the superiority of his knowledge, force us to focus on his MANNER of telling the story and make his expressions of opinion more conspicuous than they would be if his personality were less stridently expressed. It is easy to see why such a speech should be placed first; since we have no other way of measuring the extent of the initial speaker's bias than by his own revelations, this bias must be made absolutely clear. With Other Half-Rome, who is much less colourful as a personality and whose personal reasons for prejudice are not as apparent, we are prepared to accept or at least recognize his strong leaning toward Pompilia because we have the advantage of the opposing viewpoint already presented. In other words, with the basic facts of the story given to us, we are more prepared to attend to the manner of their presentation and this manner need not be, indeed had better not be, for variety and interest, so obtrusive and insistent as that of the first speaker. By the time we come to the third speaker, we have heard both arguments in detail, so again it is the manner of telling that is made to dominate our attention; the manner here is so distinctive that we overlook repetitions of fact and concentrate on finding evidences of bias in the speaker, just as we found them in the other two. In point of fact, we do find the bias, this time not so transparently attributable to personal emotions, but all the more striking when it comes from an individual determined to be impeccably impartial. The bias toward Guido's side is subtle, and could even be missed or denied by a casual reader; however, the bias AGAINST both sides is clear, so that we are left with the feeling of a coldly negative and curiously unenlightening point of view.

How, if at all, does the question of the reader's sympathy enter here? It seems impossible for the reader to react with much sympathetic feeling for Half-Rome, the obsessively jealous husband, but it also seems quite possible to feel some degree of pity, however slight, for Guido, as a result of Half-Rome's argument for him; that is, we can suddenly see how the situation might have looked to the suspicious and tormented husband, scorned by family and friends for allowing his wife to leave him, without satisfactory recourse to law and desperate for revenge. This viewpoint might not be so effectively conveyed if it came from someone without Half-Rome's passionate intensity. We can never overlook the extent of his bias, but we feel the depth of the emotions agitating him personally, and this helps to make Guido a more human figure through identification with him. Arriving at a clear picture of the second speaker is more difficult. The impression given of a thoughtful, sensitive nature outweighs to some degree the obvious extremity of Other Half-Rome's adulation of Pompilia, and the tentative, probing quality of his discourse lends more, rather than less, strength to his argument, especially as he tries to work out a satisfactory explanation for the actions of the most ambiguous character of all, Caponsacchi. The third speaker's callousness, on the other hand, has the converse effect of increasing our sympathy for both sides, as we see how indifferent to human tragedy those in the seats of power can be, although the detectable leaning of the aristocrats toward Guido tends to repel us from his side.

In each case, the kind of language the speakers use contributes in large measure to our feelings toward them and our assessment of their veracity: the colloquial, undignified diction of the first contrasts unfavourably with the respectful, delicate language of the second; the consistent use of animal imagery by Half-Rome lends a disagreeable overtone to his narrative, while the flower and bird imagery of Other Half-Rome, often memorably beautiful, produces an aura of gentleness and innocence about his heroine. The obvious snobbery and calculated design of the third speaker make us trust his judgments even less than those of the first two; his mannered eloquence is aimed too much at producing an effect and not enough at presenting fact. On balance, then, as a result of the three monologues taken together, the weight of the reader's sympathetic response (apart from simply reasoned judgment) leans toward Pompilia's side and away from Guido's.

A secondary function of these three speeches is to supply an abundance of "local colour" and to set the scenes in rich detail for the principals about to appear. Henry James has spoken of the very "gold-dust" of Rome raised by the myriad details of place, time, custom, and character that are given in these early books.[14] With the presentation of minor actors like Luca Cini, Monna Baldi, Carlo Maratta, Fra Celestino, the maid Margherita, the peruke-woman,

14/"The Novel in 'The Ring and the Book,'" *Notes on Novelists with Some Other Notes* (1914), p. 400.

and the whole throng of bystanders who mill about the church of San Lorenzo and press about the hospital of Santa Anna, who lounge in the sun of the market-place to gossip, bargain, and argue, or who fill the card-rooms of the glittering salons of the nobility, there is a sense of the bustling, ceaseless activity of Rome of the *Seicento,* a sense of movement, life, and colour. Out of the ready comments on every speaker's lips, we piece together an historical and cultural background that is rich, convincing, and solid in texture. These comments naturally focus on the tortuous legal procedure now taking place, but they illuminate many other areas as well: the machinations of the Churchmen who claim Guido as one of their own, the claims of honour recognized by courts in crimes of violence, the marriage customs that allowed Pompilia to become the victim of a sordid bargain, the Molinist heresy so universally condemned and so eagerly discussed[15] – all the infinite variety of customs, beliefs, prejudices, and conventions that made up the social life of Rome in the last decade of the century.

But not only are we being exposed by these first three speeches to the very life and heartbeat of Rome, from the man in the street to the man in the palace, we are also being carried forward in time from the day after the murder to the day on which the actual trial proceedings begin with Count Guido Franceschini's testimony. And thus we are ready to listen with sharpened interest to the voices of the principal actors in the books to come.

15/In an important article, "Molinos: 'The Subject of the Day' in *The Ring and the Book*" (1952), William Coyle explores some thirty-five references to the heresy and shows how Browning makes each reference work as a means of dramatizing character as well as supplying historical background and ecclesiastical atmosphere, and, most importantly, notes how this one reference reinforces the theme of the imperfection of human judgment. The term "Molinist" becomes a calumnious epithet to be used indiscriminately against any deviation from accepted practices. Guido and Bottini use it most often; Tertium Quid, unwilling to commit himself on any controversial subject, not at all; only the Pope speaks of Molinism tolerantly.

Chapter III

Caponsacchi and Pompilia

I

COUNT GUIDO FRANCESCHINI is the first of the actors in the tragedy to appear on the stage. He makes his dramatic appearance to offer his own defence before the court which will shortly begin to weigh his fate. Because he makes another appearance later, it seems convenient to forego the detailed analysis of his first speech at this point and deal with both Guido's monologues later. However, the chronology of the court speech is most important. As it is being presented, the bodies of the Comparini are exposed for the third day to public view and word is still awaited of the death of the last victim, Pompilia. Under these circumstances, the Count's defence must be calculated to convince the judges of the overwhelming necessity he felt to commit the barbarous murders. The fact that he has a chance to present his case before the court hears the emotion-charged accusations of Caponsacchi is to his advantage, and he makes the most of the opportunity to create a sharp and favourable impression, mingling defence with attack in a brilliant rhetorical display.

He is followed in court by the Canon Giuseppe-Maria Caponsacchi who, some eight months before, had heeded the appeal of the Count's wife to help her flee her husband's tyranny at Arezzo. By his own admission a cleric who was living a worldly, religiously shallow life, devoted mainly to shaping sonnets and ladies' compliments, he still has a streak of idealism in him, and even before the flight had resolved to go to Rome and attempt to remedy the emptiness of his spiritual life. Overtaken in flight, he was sentenced by the ecclesiastical court to three years' relegation in a monastery some distance from Rome. Now he has been recalled before that same court to testify in the murder trial of Guido Franceschini. He is in a state of great emotional disturbance, compounded of feelings of grief for Pompilia and anger at the members of the tribunal. He is by turns reckless, bitter, and denunciatory in attacking Guido and the earlier decision of the judges, and quiet, respectful, and tender in defending the dying Pompilia.

He appears on the day after Guido. It is January 6, the fourth day after the attack, and Pompilia's death is expected momentarily. The scene is the same as the day before, the black-walled antechamber off the main courtroom, but the atmosphere is changed. Caponsacchi is no defendant and he knows it. He need not have come: *'For I might lock lips, / Laugh at your jurisdiction: what have you / To do with me in the matter?'*[1] he asks. From the first, he takes the role of accuser – *'now is grown judge himself,'* as the poet had said (I, 1067) – lashing out fiercely at the three judges before him whose short-sighted earlier decision has led to the tragedy. Where Guido had addressed the court from a sitting position, the better to play his role of injured victim, Caponsacchi stands, and the position emphasizes the commanding attitude he has assumed. He is the man of action; the gestures punctuating his speech mark the movements of a man indisposed to delay or impractical discussion. Twice he offers to demonstrate with his guard how he might have killed Guido: (1473–6)

> *I stood as near*
> *The throat of him, – with these two hands, my own, –*
> *As now I stand near yours, Sir, – one quick spring,*
> *One great good satisfying gripe, and lo!*

and: (1892–4)

> *I had him in arm's reach*
> *There, – as you stand, Sir, now you cease to sit, –*
> *I could have killed him ere he killed his wife, ...*

1/Lines 1623–5. All references in this section are to Book VI unless otherwise indicated.

Even his first words are accompanied by a dramatic gesture: '*I cannot see / My own hand held thus broad before my face / And know it again*' (3–5). When he wants to illustrate how he sought a solution to a pressing problem, he naturally uses a figure which denotes physical action, and he dramatizes it with an expressive motion: (939–41)

> *I have stood before, gone round a serious thing,*
> *Tasked my whole mind to touch and clasp it close,*
> *As I stretch forth my arm to touch this bar.*

His manner of addressing the court also is markedly different from Guido's. Whereas the latter showed deference and flattered ('*my sweet lords*'), the Canon castigates and shows contempt ('*You of the court!*'; '*Men, for the last time, what do you want with me?*'). Usually he calls the judges '*Sirs*' or simply '*Men,*' despite the fact that they sit as an ecclesiastical tribunal. He singles out one judge particularly for sarcastic abuse: '*You, Judge Tommati, who then tittered most*' (34), when the earlier case was heard, are now he says, in a quite different mood. The depth of the speaker's passion gradually elicits a correspondingly emotional response from his auditors. The judges at first are silent and sober in the face of his onslaught: '*Now no one laughs*' (9), he notes; '*And now you sit as grave, stare as aghast / As if I were a phantom*' (25–6). He plunges on, and they listen stunned into immobility: '*Well, Sirs, does no one move?*' (119). They are shame-faced when he sharpens the attack: (131–4)

> *You are all struck acquiescent now, it seems:*
> *It seems the oldest, gravest signor here,*
> *Even the redoubtable Tommati, sits*
> *Chop-fallen. ...*

Occasionally they make an attempt to pacify him: '*Yes,*' he responds once, remembering Pompilia, '*I shall go on now. Does she need or not / I keep calm?*' (214–16); later he assures them he can resume the narrative once more broken off in agitation: '*Sirs, I am quiet again*' (2069). Finally, one at least is moved to tears by the power of his words: '*Why, there's a Judge weeping!*' (1884).

Although he speaks for the express purpose of showing his audience the truth – he will, he tells them, '*For a moment, show Pompilia who was true! / Not for her sake, but yours*' (172–3) – his is not a rhetorical argument in the sense that Guido's preceding monologue is. He is too disturbed to marshal his thoughts in any logical progression; he hammers away at trivial points and passes over more significant ones, and repeatedly digresses from the narrative to vent his rage in long harangues against the negligent judges. He catches himself at this in dismay: (1955–8)

> *Why, Sirs, what's this? Why, this is sorry and strange! –*
> *Futility, divagation: this from me*
> *Bound to be rational, justify an act*
> *Of sober man!*

and again says ruefully: (1983–6)

> *While I was running on at such a rate,*
> *Friends should have plucked me by the sleeve: I went*
> *Too much o' the trivial outside of her face*
> *And the purity that shone there. ...*

Sometimes he appears to forget the presence of his auditors altogether as in the passages describing the flight with Pompilia, which are made up completely of quotations of her words and paraphrases of his answers, with little or no direct address to the court.

Pompilia as she lies dying is, in fact, the third person of his monologue. The thought of her desperate plight preys on his mind and lacerates him with remorse; even at the instant he speaks she may have breathed out her life. A half-dozen times in the course of his speech he breaks off to cry out in anguish at the realization of this fact. 'Pompilia is only dying while I speak!' (47) he exclaims at the outset; a few moments later (61–3) he cries out again:

> *Pompilia is bleeding out her life belike,*
> *Gasping away the latest breath of all,*
> *This minute, while I talk. ...*

Later, he asks how lenity to him can 'remit one death-bed pang to her,' Pompilia, 'that's fast dying while we talk' (125–7).[2] The persistent linking of her 'dying' with his 'talking' signals the anguished frustration of the man used to action here forced to stand idly by at the moment of crisis. The only time the thought of her suffering seems to cease briefly from burning 'his eyes and ears and brain and heart' is when he is describing Pompilia alive – at their first meeting and on the flight from Arezzo – and a measure of his agitation is the

2/See also 191–2, 1164.

fact that while reliving this memory he momentarily refuses to accept the truth of her death: (1593–9)

> *You tell me she is dying now, or dead;*
> *I cannot bring myself to quite believe*
> *This is a place you torture people in:*
> *What if this your intelligence were just*
> *A subtlety, an honest wile to work*
> *On a man at unawares? 'Twere worthy you.*
> *No, Sirs, I cannot have the lady dead!*

He will not take their word: 'Let me see for myself if it be so!' (1608) and again: 'Come, let me see her –' (1611). Then, under the weight of his emotion, he suddenly reveals the real reason why he answered the court summons: (1620–2)

> *... that is why*
> *– To get leave and go see her of your grace –*
> *I have told you this whole story over again.*

A moment later, seeming finally to accept the truth about her condition – it was 'Two days ago, when Guido, with the right, / Hacked her to pieces' (1632–3) – he confuses in his perturbation the time of the attack (four days before) with the time that he himself first heard of it. Only at the end of his speech can he say resignedly, 'Pompilia will be presently with God' (2074).

Not only his love for Pompilia – indicated, despite all his denials, by many lines like those mourning the extra half-hour he might have spent in her presence that last night – but the bitter knowledge that her death was unnecessary and all his sacrifice in vain account for the vehemence of his protest. The tone of his attack on the judges is impassioned, biting, contemptuous: (1783–6)

> *You blind guides who must needs lead eyes that see!*
> *Fools, alike ignorant of man and God!*
> *What was there here should have perplexed your wit*
> *For a wink of the owl-eyes of you?*

It is often steeped in scathing sarcasm, as when he reminds them how they claimed to deal with the Count Franceschini and now they tell him that Guido has again followed his wife to Rome: (37–43)

> *Three days ago, if I have seized your sense, –*
> *(I being disallowed to interfere,*

Meddle or make in a matter none of mine,
For you and law were guardians quite enough
O' the innocent, without a pert priest's help) –
And that he has butchered her accordingly,
As she foretold and as myself believed, ...

He is equally contemptuous of the worldly clergy who led him astray in his early years in the priesthood: his language is coarse and colloquial when he paraphrases them, as in the passage (373–85) on *'Brother Clout'* and *'Father Slouch'* who *'clump-clumped'* to Rome and *'flopped down'* before the Cardinal, *'two moony dolts'* who never once dreamed that their patron was more impressed by

> *"Heads that wag, eyes that twinkle, modified mirth*
> *"At the closet-lectures on the Latin tongue*
> *"A lady learns so much by, we know where. ..."*

But his harshest language is for Guido. He portrays the Count's behaviour at the inn in terms that stress his animal-like baseness and cunning: *'there / Scowled the old malice in the visage bad / And black o' the scamp'* (1437–8). The monster *'part howled, part hissed'* (1440); *'he shook, / Could only spit between the teeth'* (1551–2); taking his wife's name into his mouth, he *'Licked, and then let it go again, the beast, / Signed with his slaver'* (1493–4). He should not be allowed to die but made to *'slide out of life, / Pushed by the general horror and common hate'* (1911–12), the way a snake *'hatched on hill-top by mischance, / Despite his wriggling, slips, slides, slidders down'* (1924–5) to the outer place where there is no life. Here, at the edge of creation, let him meet Judas: (1938–40)

> *... Let them love their love*
> *That bites and claws like hate, or hate their hate*
> *That mops and mows and makes as it were love!*

Let them, he concludes in a veritable frenzy of rage, *'tear,'* *'fondle,'* *'grapple.'* Finally, he flings out: (1944–50)

> *Kiss him the kiss, Iscariot! Pay that back,*
> *That smatch o' the slaver blistering on your lip,*
> *By the better trick, the insult he spared Christ –*
> *Lure him the lure o' the letters, Aretine!*
> *Lick him o'er slimy-smooth with jelly-filth*
> *O' the verse-and-prose pollution in love's guise!*
> *The cockatrice is with the basilisk!*

The remarkable aspect of this outburst – apart from the level of passionate feeling unprecedented in the other monologues – is the presence of so many verbs of violent action. For Caponsacchi, the man of action who summed up the lesson of his experience by saying that man's destiny, whatever his calling, is to *act* – man must know *'How he is bound, better or worse, to act'* (159) – this Caponsacchi is overwhelmed by the realization that it was Guido and not himself who took the decisive action. There is self-loathing as well as hatred of the murderer, and perhaps a searing jealousy as well, in the furious attack.

The tone of passages describing Pompilia is in such sharp contrast that it is almost as though another man were speaking. Low-keyed, dignified, simple, these passages are laced with artistic imagery that relies on muted colour and indistinct outlines for its subdued effect. While Guido is fleetingly pictured as a black figure against a background of red, both colours signifying evil for Caponsacchi, Pompilia is repeatedly seen as pure white: she is *'The snow-white soul'* (195), approaching their appointed meeting as *'whiteness in the distance'* which *'waxed / Whiter and whiter'* until, he concludes, *'The white I saw shine through her was her soul's'* (1139–42). She lay at the inn, *'Wax-white, seraphic'* (1518), and he last sees her lying helpless there *'Dead-white and disarmed'* (1549). His other adjectives for her are equally generalized. He first saw her, *'A lady, young, tall, beautiful, strange and sad'* (399). She smiled *'the beautiful sad strange smile'* (412). He repeats this phrase (436), then speaks again of the *'sad strange wife'* (493) with the *'great, grave, griefful air'* (704) who looked out of a *'sad sweet heaven'* on him (1994). He particularly links the word *'Strange'* with her, quoting her use of it: his coming to her (758–61)

> *"... – were strange*
> *"But that my whole life is so strange: as strange*
> *"It is, my husband whom I have not wronged*
> *"Should hate and harm me. ..."*

He quotes her as adding, ' *"But there is something more,"* / *"And that the strangest"* ' (762–3) – her new reason for wanting to go on living is the ' *"one strange and wonderful thing more"* ' (791).

Even when he paraphrases the Augustinian's praise of her the words are the ones he has used over and over again: she is *'So sweet and true and pure and beautiful'* (2063). All the adjectives are notably simple and vague and the vocabulary surprisingly limited for one who could find such a wealth of distinctive epithets to describe

Guido.[3] It is as if Caponsacchi's image of Pompilia has become so etherealized that he cannot capture it in concrete terms. Hence the frequent use of the word *'dream'* to describe her disillusionment with life: it suggests the misty, other-wordly atmosphere he seems to feel surrounding her. She says that her parents told her she *'dreamed a dream'* in thinking that she was their child (784); *'the worst o' the dream'* to her is their forgetting her (819); since *'the way to end dreams is to break them,'* she will go to them (820). But, *'Just as in dreams,'* she cannot make them hear her (826). Now, she tells Caponsacchi, *'the dream gets to involve yourself'* (862). She knows instinctively the letters delivered to her are not his: ' *"Here too has been dream-work, delusion too"* ' (874). By the end of his speech, Caponsacchi comes to apply the term to himself: the quiet life of domestic comfort he might have lived is *'Mere delectation, meet for a minute's dream!'* (2097).

He uses none of the memorable flower- or bird-images of that other admirer of Pompilia, Other Half-Rome. Once he employs the familiar wolf–lamb figure in an indirect comparison: Pompilia tells him that Guido used to mistreat a lamb in the wood so that its cries would draw and thus trap the wolf, and she concludes that *'he practised thus with me'* (1364). Significantly, the one form under which Caponsacchi consistently sees her is the Madonna figure of Rafael's painting. This visual image, with its suggestion of unearthly beauty and goodness, seems the closest he can come to presenting the *'wonderful white soul'* he knew. He pictures his first sight of her at the theatre as like his first startling glimpse of the painting in the cathedral: (402–6)

> *I saw* facchini *bear a burden up,*
> *Base it on the high-altar, break away*
> *A board or two, and leave the thing inside*

3/Park Honan, in *Browning's Characters: A Study in Poetic Technique* (1961), finds that Caponsacchi's "vocabulary – with its high proportion of abstract nouns, many having to do with moral and religious concepts, with its adjectives frequently expressive of quality and often used in series, and with its paucity of concrete referents – reveals the morally intense, unworldly, idealistic man ..." (p. 236). This is demonstrably true of the passages dealing with Pompilia but other, more frequent and lengthy passages show another side of his nature (as in 667–700, 1433–1584). To call Caponsacchi "unworldly" and "idealistic" is to forget how full of "scorpions," "clowns," "gripes," and "dungheaps" his vocabulary is, and that he uses the most violent language of any speaker. Rather, it would seem more accurate to say that the Canon has two vocabularies, one "worldly" and one "spiritual," and the dual manner of expression reflects the division in his own mind.

> *Lofty and lone: and lo, when next I looked,*
> *There was the Rafael!*

The only way he can deal with the insinuation that Pompilia sent him the love letters is to revert to the painting: (668–76)

> *I told you there's a picture in our church.*
> *Well, if a low-browed verger sidled up*
> *Bringing me, like a blotch, on his prod's point,*
> *A transfixed scorpion, let the reptile writhe,*
> *And then said "See a thing that Rafael made —*
> *"This venom issued from Madonna's mouth!"*
> *I should reply, "Rather, the soul of you*
> *"Has issued from your body, like from like,*
> *"By way of the ordure-corner!"*

Even though he dismisses the accusation thus brusquely, it rankles and he returns to his metaphor: (679–82)

> *... the pest*
> *Was far too near the picture, anyhow:*
> *One does Madonna service, making clowns*
> *Remove their dung-heap from the sacristy.*

This preoccupation with the Rafael Madonna shows less the artist's appreciative eye for colour, line, or detail than a combination of the romantic's idealization of woman and the Churchman's reverence for virtue as represented by the Mother of God. When he first sees Pompilia standing at the window, she has the same sad air as the painting he knows of *'Our Lady of all the Sorrows'* (707). Once again he finds *'the first simile serves still'* to answer the criticism that Pompilia sent for him: suppose, he says (913–17), that

> *Pictured Madonna raised her painted hand,*
> *Fixed the face Rafael bent above the Babe,*
> *On my face as I flung me at her feet:*
> *Such miracle vouchsafed and manifest,*
> *Would that prove the first lying tale was true?*

He remembers how, on returning to her during a pause in their flight, he found her holding a peasant woman's baby in her arms — the Madonna image recurs, this time in real life rather than in art.

Only once he describes her features, admitting they are not those of the artist's flawless model: *'Her brow had not the right line,*

leaned too much, / Painters would say.' But, he insists, the brow was
bent thus with *'an invisible crown / Of martyr and saint'* (1989–92).
To emphasize further Pompilia's virtue he indirectly compares himself with the St. Thomas who saw Our Lady ascend into heaven – ' "I
too have seen a lady and hold a grace" ' (1105) – and with St. George
who rescued the maiden from the dragon.[4] Words like *'blessed,'*
'seraphic,' *'miracle,'* *'grace,'* *'faith,'* *'soul,'* *'heaven,'* and *'revelation'*
are interwoven into almost every sentence about her, constantly suggesting goodness and spirituality, in the manner of Other Half-
Rome, and suffusing her memory with an aura of sanctity.

It is difficult to reconcile the tender, reverential treatment of Pompilia with the coarse, even savage, diatribes against Guido, but the
differences in diction and tone apparently reflect the division in
Caponsacchi's own mind; he is drawn to the life of action in the
world of the flesh, but must live a life of contemplation in the world
of the spirit. The conflict is illustrated in his concluding lines: *'I mean
to do my duty,'* he says stoutly, and then (2081–4) adds, wistfully:

> *I do but play with an imagined life*
> *Of who, unfettered by a vow, unblessed*
> *By the higher call, – since you will have it so, –*
> *Leads it companioned by the woman there.*

His mode of address provides the best evidence of his troubled
state of mind. Neither a narrative like the first three monologues, nor
a defence like Guido's, his speech has elements of both but, despite
its powerful emotional impact, lacks clarity and coherence. The explanation for the confusion lies partly in the nature of its repetition –
he has told the whole story to the court before and counts on the
judges' remembering many of the details[5] – and partly in the fact
that he has so recently learned of the attack, scarcely two days ago,
and is still suffering the first shock of grief. His natural energy, exa-
cerbated by the months of enforced idleness in relegation, and his
powerful feelings toward Pompilia and Guido collide head on with

4/William C. DeVane, in "The Virgin and the Dragon" (1947), notes Browning's connection of the St. George legend with the Perseus-Andromeda myth
and shows how several speakers in *The Ring and the Book* use this myth, thus
giving us clues to their characters by their various treatments; for example,
Caponsacchi uses it ironically, showing his self-effacement.

5/He calls attention to this fact, pointing out that the judges have all his
testimony *'Noted down in the book there.'* He challenges them to *'turn and
see / If, by one jot or tittle'* he varies any in his presentation this time (1644–5).

his vow of detachment and his sense of obligation to do her justice before the law. His terrible effort to remain calm for her sake is moving testimony to the depth of the struggle within him: (215–20)

> I shall go on now. Does she need or not
> I keep calm? Calm I'll keep as monk that croons
> Transcribing battle, earthquake, famine, plague,
> From parchment to his cloister's chronicle.
> Not one word more from the point now!
>
> I begin.

But the practical result is that his discourse is only rarely a chronological narrative. He gives the details of his early priestly life clearly enough, and the account of Guido's machinations with the letters has obvious relish for plumbing the depths of the villainy, but at the most important part of his recital, the meeting and flight with Pompilia, factual details are lost or only incompletely remembered: 'It was at ... ah, but I forget the names!' (1208); 'This was – I know not where – there's a great hill / Close over' (1214–15). But every word, every gesture of Pompilia he recalls in minutest detail: how she looked, how she sounded as she asked him to read the Angelus, called him 'friend,' spoke the unknown name of Gaetano, her weariness when they stopped, her courage when they were overtaken by Guido. This was the last time he saw her; he goes on to paraphrase in sarcastic indignation the contradictory findings of the trial that followed, and ringingly asserts his innocence – 'I have done with being judged' (1859) – and his firm intention to live out his long life doing his duty as a priest. But his last words are an expression of desolation from the depths of his being: 'O great, just, good God! Miserable me!'

The uneven progression, broken sentences, abundance of exclamations make the whole discourse an eruption of personal feeling, lacking convincing logical or legal justification for his behaviour, but the weight of its emotion effectively characterizes Caponsacchi's intense temperament and presents him as a foil to the deliberate Guido of the previous speech. Beside this explosive excitement, Guido's self-justifying indignation pales to a kind of peevish complaint. The speech adds little to the narrative facts of the murder, since the Canon's involvement is so limited.[6] His knowledge of Pompilia ex-

6/The limited involvement of Caponsacchi – limited at least in scope and time, if not in emotional intensity – makes Henry James's famous assessment of

tends only to the few hours he spent with her; he knows nothing of her life with the Comparini or at Arezzo, of the birth of her child, or the circumstances of the attack. He contributes news of the fate of Conti and Guillichini, Guido's 'kinsfolk' to whom Pompilia had appealed for help and who would have come to court and 'told truth': the former was poisoned a month before and the latter condemned to the galleys. Not that this matters much: 'one mark more / On the Moor's skin, – what is black by blacker still?' (2034–5), he asks sardonically, making clear who is responsible for their disappearance. He is uncompromising in his denial that any letters passed between Pompilia and himself, and he gives a detailed account of the maid Margherita's role as willing instrument in Guido's plot to trap him with the letters.

Opinions revealed are limited to his attitude toward the two principals of the drama, and the simple 'black' and 'white' descriptions of them underscore the single-mindedness and intensity of his hatred for Guido – bitter, violent, and unrelenting – and of his love for Pompilia – sudden, strong, and pure. A significant fact about his feeling for her is its intuitive nature. He insists that he experienced an instantaneous conviction of her innocence, and he sees a similar reaction reflected in her attitude toward him. She knew immediately without a word from him that he could not have written the letters: (931–4)

> "As I
> "Recognized her, at potency of truth,
> "So she, by the crystalline soul, knew me,
> "Never mistook the signs. ..."

his role as a central one difficult to accept. In "The Novel in 'The Ring and the Book,'" James sees the poem's centre as "the embracing consciousness of Caponsacchi" (p. 395). Noting that he appears too late in the action to be a true "reflector," he claims that we "turn him on" before Arezzo, "place him there in the field, at once recipient and agent, vaguely conscious and with splendid brooding apprehension, awaiting the adventure of his life, awaiting his call ..." (p. 406). James here seems to be thinking less of Browning's poem than of the novel he himself can project from it, since nothing in the poem indicates that the Canon in his worldly life in orders ever had any significant contact with the Franceschini before his meeting with Pompilia. His passionate reaction to her fate and his sudden violent hatred of Guido also fail to bear out James's picture of him as the serene, detached observer at the end: "He *is* the soul of man at its finest – having passed through the smoky fires of life and emerging clear and high" (p. 397).

This instant apprehension of truth has for him the quality of a divine inspiration, above the possibility of, or need for, rational explanation: (1814–21)

> The spark of truth was struck from out our souls –
> Made all of me, descried in the first glance,
> Seem fair and honest and permissible love
> O' the good and true – as the first glance told me
> There was no duty patent in the world
> Like daring try be good and true myself,
> Leaving the shows of things to the Lord of Show
> And Prince o' the Power of the Air.

II

The next voice in the drama is that of Francesca Pompilia Comparini, adopted daughter of Pietro and Violante, and wife of Count Guido Franceschini. Married at thirteen, she had lived unhappily at the Count's family estate at Arezzo for over three years before making an unsuccessful attempt to flee some eight months past. After a short sentence in the house of the Convertites, she was released to the custody of her putative parents in a small villa on the outskirts of Rome. Here, just two weeks ago, her son had been born; then within the last few days she and her parents have been the victims of a savage attack by the Count and his four accomplices. Now, as she lingers for the fourth day on her deathbed, she tells her story. She is patient and resigned, not fully comprehending all that has happened, but anxious to set the true facts before the world in the best way she can for the sake of her child and the man who tried to save her, Canon Caponsacchi.

She speaks from a hospital bed in Santa Anna's on the evening of January 6, either at the same time as, or shortly after, the Canon's appearance before the court. Her audience is made up of nuns who staff the hospital – at one point she speaks of the difficulty of explaining all to 'Women as you are'[7] – along with Fra Celestino, her confessor: she refers to 'the Augustinian here' (1303). Apparently other visitors and curious spectators are allowed to approach her bedside, too – we have heard from Other Half-Rome about his visit and the presence of the artist Maratta and the superstitious Monna Baldi –

7/Line 720. All references in this section are to Book VII unless otherwise indicated.

but Pompilia makes no reference to anyone else, addressing her hearers simply as *'friends.'* Her contact with them is tenuous. At times she seems to be only vaguely aware of their identity and presence; *'Therefore I wish someone will please to say ...'*(72) is the way she words a request that her story be repeated when she is gone. She asks at one juncture, *'Say, if you are by to speak ...'*(74), indicating perhaps that she is unable to see them. Unlike other speakers, she notes little or no response from her audience; once she protests their assessment of Caponsacchi, suggested evidently by their silence, and she comments once on their patience in listening to the long recital. Despite her resolve to present the narrative in careful detail, her attention periodically wanders from the scene at hand to thoughts of her own mother, of Caponsacchi, and of God, and she addresses remarks directly to each of them in the form of a prayer. However, the great effort she exerts to hold the thread of her narrative shows how serious her purpose is and how well she realizes that only a little time is left to her.

The third person of her discourse at first seems to be her infant son Gaetano. She begins with a reference to him, returns to speak of him twice, and asks her listeners to remember what she says so that they can tell him when he is older. As she proceeds, however, it becomes clear that Caponsacchi's presence is even more vivid to her than that of the child she has hardly seen. She admits to the hope that her words may serve to clear the Canon's name: (930–5)

> *Then, I must lay my babe away with God,*
> *Nor think of him again, for gratitude.*
> *Yes, my last breath shall wholly spend itself*
> *In one attempt more to disperse the stain,*
> *The mist from other breath fond mouths have made,*
> *About a lustrous and pellucid soul ...*

so that when she is gone, others may invoke him who was to *'The weak a saviour and the vile a foe'* (939). She seems not to have heard about his court appearance, as she exclaims, *'Could he be here, how he would speak for me!'* (946). An unexpressed and perhaps only half-conscious motive for her speaking may be to bring him once more to her side. Later, she reminds herself that he cannot come: *'He is at Civita – do I once doubt / The world again is holding us apart?'* (1793–4). Passing over the three years of her marriage to begin her recital with the first sight of Caponsacchi at the theatre when *'he broke her dream,'* Pompilia compares him to the Star of Bethlehem, calls him a saint, and addresses her last thought to him in a paean of gratitude and devotion.

The tension that her words reveal springs from the desire to tell her story completely for Caponsacchi's sake, even while she shrinks from recalling the painful aspects of her life which led to his involvement. The difficulty is compounded by the need to explain what to her is essentially inexplicable; it is impossible for her to account for the depths of hatred and evil to which the events of the last few months have exposed her. She shows the extent of the conflict by the curious disparity in her discourse between explicitness in details surrounding the central issues of her story and vagueness about the issues themselves. Whole portions of her narrative are simply *'blank'* – she uses the word, for instance, to describe events after the marriage ceremony when Violante gave her to Guido: (574–7)

> *And so an end! Because a blank begins*
> *From when, at the word, she kissed me hard and hot,*
> *And took me back to where my father leaned*
> *Opposite Guido –*

and she repeats: *'All since is one blank'* (584), *'Blank, I say!'* (594). Even when Don Celestino bids her search her mind to forgive those who have offended her, she protests that she cannot remember; at the point of her marriage (599–602)

> *What was fast getting indistinct before,*
> *Vanished outright. By special grace perhaps,*
> *Between that first calm and this last, four years*
> *Vanish, ...*

The part of her life that is now blotted from her memory she also refers to as a *'dream,'* and the use of the word, to denote not an escape from unpleasant reality but a nightmarish confusion of deceit and disillusionment, immediately recalls Caponsacchi's use of it when quoting her on her life at Arezzo. She says of her son, for example, that she hopes he will regard her history as *'what someone dreamed,'* so that he can disbelieve it, because it has already dwindled for her to *'Sheer dreaming and impossibility'* (109–12). This *'terrific dream'* of hers is, thankfully, over and ended: *'It is the good of dreams – so soon they go!'* But their brevity is also *'the note of evil: for good lasts'* (585–95). And so she clings now to one or two truths only; *'the rest is death or dream'* (605).[8]

8/See also 213, 975, 1338.

As Pompilia cannot now clearly visualize past evil and suffering, so she could not see it when it first threatened; phrases like *'all blind! / As I myself was'* (655–6); *'I failed to apprehend its drift'* (702); *'Only, my dulness should not prove too much!'* (712) underscore her initial passivity and failure to grasp the fact of Guido's villainy. She describes her reaction to Violante's news that she is to be married with the same image of the helpless, uncomprehending lamb that Other Half-Rome had used: (386–8)

> *— Well, I no more saw sense in what she said*
> *Than a lamb does in people clipping wool;*
> *Only lay down and let myself be clipped.*

The impression of Pompilia as innocent pawn in a devious game is furthered by her use of other phrases, most notably, *'I was the chattel ... / I stood mute'* in conjunction with Pietro's cry: (520–5)

> *"She is not helpful to the sacrifice*
> *"At this stage, – do you want the victim by*
> *"While you discuss the value of her blood?"*

where the religious overtones in the image of the sacrificial lamb intensify the pathos.

The whole tone of the monologue can be summed up as one of wonderment, showing a gently surprised and puzzled effort to make sense out of the baffling things that have happened. Like *'dream,'* the word *'strange'* recurs – again in echo of Caponsacchi, but where he had applied it to the mysterious quality about her that drew him to her, Pompilia uses it to convey that sense of bewilderment and fore-boding with which she views the changes in her life. *'It got to grow so terrible and strange,'* she says of her marriage. *'These strange woes stole on tiptoe, as it were'* (118–19). She cannot explain the *'whole sad strange plot'* (706); the details of the journey are hard to recall: *'How strange it was –'* (1532).[9] Similarly, each new revela-tion is a *'surprise'*: the Comparini's declaration *'one surprising day'* that she is not their child; *'just such a surprise'* to learn what Guido is really like; and *'most surprise of all'* that the world should mis-understand Caponsacchi's role in her flight (139–62).

The cumulative effect of these repetitions is to emphasize the inexplicability of evil to a soul such as Pompilia's, which has never experienced any promptings but good. Yet, the over-all impression left by her discourse is of someone who is naturally exact, concerned

9/See also 429, 1031, 1713.

with details, scrupulous about imparting facts with thoroughness and accuracy. Her opening lines convey this idea so clearly that they underscore the significance of the *'blankness'* at the heart of her story. There is a quaint preciseness about her introduction, as she recites her full name, her exact age, her marriage date, and her child's name and age, in a conscious effort to keep the record straight, and concludes anxiously: *'All these few things / I know are true, – will you remember them?'* (35–6). Attention to exact numbers conspicuously marks these first 100 lines: she is *'just seventeen years and five months old,'* her child *'Exactly two weeks'* of age, she was married *'Four years ago,'* she has suffered *'twenty-two dagger-wounds, / Five deadly.'* They took her child away two days after he was born and he was to be kept for three weeks; the month she had to wait for his return wants *'two weeks this day.'* She has named him for one who has been made a saint for only twenty-five years – *'so, carefuller, perhaps, / To guard a namesake than those old saints grow,'* as, indeed, her own five patron saints have grown.

In the same vein, terms like *'just,' 'full,' 'exactly,'* qualify almost every statement; when she tells of the marble lion in San Lorenzo, she specifies parenthetically: *'(To the right, it is, of entry by the door)'* (25). Relating how the last four years have vanished, she reminds her listeners that these years were *'one quarter of my life, you know'* (602); concluding an account of a childhood fancy about some figures in a tapestry, she carefully draws the distinction between fact and imagination, lest any of the hearers be misled: *'You know the figures never were ourselves / Though we nicknamed them so'* (197–8). She corrects herself in a statement that the Comparini loved her as she loves her child: *'(– Nearly so, that is – quite so could not be –)'* (137). She is glad that her name is not a common one; it may help to keep the record straight in the future. All this punctilious concern with accuracy centres on the facts and events she knows and can grasp hold of; they do not elude her understanding the way evil and hate do. On these familiar points she is quite sure of herself and will preface a remark with a pointed reminder of its importance: *'Now, understand here, by no means mistake!'* (1260). Her obvious bent for neat and exact measurement of events causes her to indicate, when recalling others' words, that she is rendering them in the best way that she can: *'Something in this style he began with me'* (795), she says of the Archbishop's advice; she herself addressed Caponsacchi *'In some such sense as this, whatever the phrase'* (1417).

The sharp difference between her exact treatment of the familiar and her vagueness toward the *'strange'* aspects of her life is signalled by the uncertain, tentative way she sets forth those parts of her narrative which deal with the changes introduced into her life with Guido's appearance. At this point, she begins to rely heavily on two words – *'seem'* and *'somehow'* – which suggest that she can no longer trust appearances with her childhood faith. Violante arranged the marriage, ironically, only to do her child good: (334–7)

> *And I, whose parents seemed such and were none,*
> *Should in a husband have a husband now,*
> *Find nothing, this time, but was what it seemed,*
> *– All truth and no confusion any more.*

And so perhaps with her real mother; *'May not you,'* she asks, *'seeming as you harmed me most, / Have meant to do most good?'* (887–8). That she should somehow have her mother's rights, she admits, now *'seems absurd,'* but then *'So seems so much else, not explained but known!'* (1766–7).[10] Her frequent use of terms such as *'something'* and *'somehow'* to describe an event beyond her understanding expresses a similar element of doubt or cautiousness. All she knew of the strange arrangement with Guido was that *'Something had happened, low, mean, underhand'* (517), although Violante pretended that *'Matters were somehow getting right again'* (531). She felt that as Guido's wife she *'Was bound in some sort to help somehow there'* (658) to set matters right, but it seemed hopeless: *'Nothing about me but drew somehow down / His hate upon me'* (1725–6).[11]

She often quotes authority, keenly aware as she is of her own lack of experience, but even here a trace of scepticism creeps in about what *'they'* say; they were, after all, wrong about Caponsacchi: (168–70)

> *"That was love" – they say,*
> *When anything is answered that they ask:*
> *Or else "No wonder you love him" – they say.*

She is confident only about what *'God says'* (333) and perhaps what *'Don Celestino declares'* (371) or what her friend Tisbe has told her; all the others she refers to as the less trustworthy *'they,'* reporting what *'They said'* (861) or how *'they cry'* (871) dutifully, but without conviction. Within this framework, her use of derogatory animal

---

10/See also 98, 401, 454, 489, 659, 789, 1193, 1818.
11/See also 370, 420, 429, 667, 1439–40.

imagery to describe Guido seems quite natural, because that is how
other people have spoken of him to her. Friends ask her, figuratively
(124–7):

> "Why, you Pompilia in the cavern thus,
> "How comes that arm of yours about a wolf?
> "And the soft length, – lies in and out your feet
> "And laps you round the knee, – a snake it is!"

and Conti says (1315–17):

> "Guido has claws that scratch, shows feline teeth;
> "A formidabler foe than I dare fret:
> "Give me a dog to deal with, twice the size!"

Pompilia repeats the descriptions without commenting on their
appropriateness, merely recording what she has been told.

When using illustrations to make a narrative point clear, however,
Pompilia will not hesitate to draw directly on her own limited experiences. Because of her lack of formal education – she can neither
read nor write – her speech lacks literary allusions (except for a few
works she has *heard*: an *'old rhyme,'* the psalm of Don Celestino)
and she alone among the speakers does not refer to *'similes'* or identify other figures of speech or rhetorical usages as such. She uses
figurative language in an unself-conscious way, reaching back to the
few memorable incidents of an uneventful childhood in order to help
her hearers to see how a thing really was. The resulting figures are
not always clever or particularly apt, and some of the analogies
betray a discernible limp, as when she compares her instant recognition of Caponsacchi's innocence to her earlier recognition that the
maniac in the town square was not really the Pope he claimed to be.
Nevertheless, her images often have a blunt impact, just because of
their spontaneous quality: they are like the frank observations of a
clear-eyed child who sees reality in sharp outlines. When she recol-
lects that marriage to Guido had seemed at first like using a *'dirty
piece'* of coin to purchase a good end, or that he resembled in her
mind another *'scarecrow,'* the great, ugly doctor who once treated
her illness, the comparisons, while unflattering to Guido, do not seem
unkind on Pompilia's part, because they are so natural and un-
studied, so obviously the child's view. So, when she dismisses the
injuries committed against her as the *'yelp'* and *'bark'* of misunderstanding creatures into whose hovel she has mistakenly stepped, the

harsh image of the Franceschini is softened by the obvious objectivity and detachment of the metaphor's conclusion: (366-8)

> *The hovel is life: no matter what dogs bit*
> *Or cats scratched in the hovel I break from,*
> *All outside is lone field, moon and such peace. ...*

The comparison has an ingenuous quality which underlines the essential truth of the relationship it describes, without reflecting on the attitude of the speaker. In the same way, Pompilia's images of herself are acceptable as artless but truthful. When she likens herself to the virgin in the old rhyme pursued by the Paynims, she sees the similarity in the desperation of their imprisonment; when she compares herself to Mary with her Child, she is thinking of the similarity in their happiness. In both cases, the reader notes further overtones of virtue and spirituality linking the two, of which Pompilia is unaware, and this recognition increases the impact of the comparison without diminishing the impression of her naivety and simplicity.

One image she uses, however, differs from all the rest in the way it is introduced, elaborated upon, and repeated. Pompilia sees Caponsacchi as a *'star'* sent by God to guide her out of the darkness and misery of her life at Arezzo, and she uses this more sophisticated figure several times, specifically identifying the Canon with the Star of Bethlehem, and eventually broadening the image to include *'light'* as a symbol of all truth and goodness as shown forth through Caponsacchi.[12] At first, the sound of his name when she is on the point of despair is as if she had drowned, *'But woke afloat i' the wave with upturned eyes, / And found their first sight was a star!'* (1142-3). When he offers to help her, he is like a celestial guide: *'So did the star rise, soon to lead my step'* (1447). When he fails to come one night, *'darkness'* falls and does not break until the *'white star'* rises again (1460-70). Now he is the *'day-star'* that *'makes*

12/C. Willard Smith, in *Browning's Star-Imagery: The Study of a Detail in Poetic Design* (1941), traces in detail the use of the star-image throughout *The Ring and the Book*, finding thirty-two literal instances of its occurrence, with six dominating references appearing in Pompilia's book, and eight in the Pope's. He sees the star in general carrying symbolic meanings similar to those in Browning's earlier poems, of hope, aspiration, poetry, truth, and resolution, but he finds three meanings peculiar to this poem: (1) for Pompilia it signifies Caponsacchi, (2) for the Pope, truth, and (3) in the last book, Guido's "brilliant usurpature" (pp. 196-9).

night morn' (1785). The star-image thus represents for Pompilia not only a light piercing the present darkness, but a heaven-sent herald of the imminent passing of night and breaking of day. Caponsacchi is more than a guide and saviour; he is the reflection of God's own justice and truth on earth, showing her the promise of eternity. How can others fail to see this in him, she cries: (920–3)

> *That man, you misinterpret and misprise –*
> *The glory of his nature, I had thought,*
> *Shot itself out in white light, blazed the truth*
> *Through every atom of his act with me. ...*

This *'white light'* has another aspect, illuminating the darkest area of her life at Arezzo. On the morning of her decision to flee Guido's house, she recalls, after a night of *'darkness'* in which sleep seemed good because so near to death, she awoke to a strangely vivid daybreak: (1224–6)

> *Light in me, light without me, everywhere*
> *Change! A broad yellow sunbeam was let fall*
> *From heaven to earth. ...*

The light now signifies an awareness of the new life within her: (622–5)

> *That thrill of dawn's suffusion through my dark,*
> *Which I perceive was promise of my child,*
> *The light his unborn face sent long before, –*
> *God's way of breaking the good news to flesh.*

Finally, in her last words, Pompilia widens the significance of the *'light'* still further and makes the contrast with the earthly *'dark'* explicit: (1843–5)

> *Through such souls alone*
> *God stooping shows sufficient of His light*
> *For us i' the dark to rise by. And I rise.*

Caponsacchi's earthly love is the reflection of that divine love into which she now enters. The light–dark, good–evil antithesis here is a more complex and perceptive version of Caponsacchi's own white–black, love–hate dichotomy, and it serves to forge another link connecting her with him. Each is to the other a *'pure white soul'* illuminating the blackness of inexplicable evil that surrounds it.

Again like Caponsacchi's, Pompilia's mode of address is less narrative or dramatic than lyric, the artless expression of powerful feelings set forth in direct, simple language with little attention to rhetorical effects. Her style is largely unadorned, the star-image being the only figure extended or elaborated. Most of her sentences are simple and declarative, with few exclamations or apostrophes. The low-keyed, even expression contrasts, of course, with the explosiveness of Caponsacchi's utterance, but both speakers share a tone of helpless bewilderment in the face of the overwhelming force of evil. Many of Pompilia's passages are made up almost entirely of monosyllabic words (for example, 220–67); most of her words are common and simple and used repeatedly.[13] This simplicity of expression is in keeping with the precise, unimaginative, rather literal-minded characteristics which she has displayed. And yet for all her concern with order and exactness in factual details, Pompilia does not present a chronological or well-ordered summary of events; the ambivalence in her manner between careful delineation of minor points and blankness on more important issues is only one aspect of this inexpert and sometimes incoherent recounting of her story.[14] At the same time, the unimaginative and literal-minded quality of her

13/Park Honan, *Browning's Characters: A Study in Poetic Technique* (1961), points out that Pompilia has five favourite adjectives, all "among the more common in English: *good, poor, little, happy, kind*" and one noun and verb *love*, all of which seem to reveal her own image (pp. 216–17). Dealing with the criticism that some of the less frequent words in her vocabulary (*unperverse, perquisite, imposthume*, for example) are too complex or rare for her situation, he concludes that these may be ascribed either to her quoting of other people or to the fact that they are meant to suggest that Pompilia possesses "a wisdom that has not come directly from experience" and that she is no ordinary adolescent, but something "timeless and special and rare: part Virgin and saint" (pp. 240–2). (Browning himself claimed to have heard "abundant instances" of such elevated language from Italian peasant-girls. Richard Curle, ed. *Robert Browning and Julia Wedgwood*, p. 163.) It is difficult, of course, to say what words Pompilia uses that could not be found in the vocabulary of someone in her place and time; it can be said, however, that *every* speaker in the poem uses words unusual and difficult by our present-day standards, and that of them all, Pompilia uses by far the fewest. For this reason, I have taken the position that her diction is "common and simple."

14/The course of her narrative, for example, goes from the scene at the villa just prior to the attack (she breaks off with "the tap" at the door) back to the preparations for her marriage, and then ahead again to her pleas to the Archbishop. It is interrupted by addresses to her mother and Caponsacchi and then resumes again with the scene at the play, the letters, and the flight.

illustrations occasionally gives way to an impressionistic style of description, in situations where she gives up the attempt at rational explanation and simply tells of her emotional response to the incomprehensible. Such a situation is the secret marriage ceremony arranged for her; she remembers how oppressive and foreboding the atmosphere had seemed, how it suggested a moment of death to her impressionable mind: (425–33)

> ... I was hurried through a storm,
> Next dark eve of December's deadest day –
> How it rained! – through our street and the Lion's-mouth
> And the bit of Corso, – cloaked round, covered close,
> I was like something strange or contraband, –
> Into blank San Lorenzo, up the aisle,
> My mother keeping hold of me so tight,
> I fancied we were come to see a corpse
> Before the altar which she pulled me toward.

The familiar church had taken on a menacing air: the heavy church-doors seemed to 'lock out help,' as the tapers 'shivered,' while the priest made her say 'that and this,' Violante wept, and she herself stood 'silent and scared,' until they found their way 'on tiptoe' from the cold silent church (438–56).

In this same way, she feels, rather than knows, the threatening character of the marble lion-figure in San Lorenzo, 'With half his body rushing from the wall, / Eating the figure of a prostrate man'; it is 'An ominous sign' to one like her who feels that church to be her 'own particular place' (20–6). This acute susceptibility to impression, amounting almost to an instinctive apprehension of evil on Pompilia's part, belies her own description of 'blindness' and 'stupidity' and suggests a sensitivity and awareness beneath the child-like and submissive exterior. It also suggests a source for the vein of iron in her character so unexpectedly exhibited in the confrontation with Guido at the inn.

Even before this scene, Pompilia's discourse gives hints that, just as she is naturally exacting in small matters, so in more important matters she can be firm and forceful. If she cannot bear to remember the more painful aspects of her life and if she is helpless to explain the nature of, or the motives for, the evil that has been done her, still she can and does judge the morality of individual acts against her. Forgiving the sinner, she forthrightly condemns the sin. Violante meant no harm, but what she did was wrong: (270–1, 312)

Certainly she erred –
Did wrong, how shall I dare say otherwise? –

Wrong, wrong and always wrong! how plainly wrong!

She can forgive Guido, too, without ever understanding him, but she insists that, regardless of external circumstances, she was never his wife – only *'strange fate / Mockingly styled him husband'* (1713–14) – nor he Gaetano's father: (1762–4)

> *My babe nor was, nor is, nor yet shall be*
> *Count Guido Franceschini's child at all –*
> *Only his mother's, born of love not hate!*

Significantly, even in her carefully detailed introduction of herself giving all her *'many names,'* she calls herself Pompilia *'Comparini'* – not "Franceschini." She is firm in her insistence that the Archbishop's advice to return to Guido as a submissive wife was wrong and that she should not have followed it: *'But I did wrong, and he gave wrong advice / Though he were thrice Archbishop, – that, I know!'* (731–2).

This surprising element of firmness, more often concealed under the tone of uncertainty and perplexity, comes to the fore in the scene at the inn where Guido overtakes her in flight with Caponsacchi. The dramatic change in her demeanour at this critical moment, a change given varying interpretations by previous speakers, is explained by her conviction of the necessity for resisting evil wherever it is clearly revealed. The sight of her *'angel'* Caponsacchi helpless in the grip of the guards and Guido *'the serpent towering and triumphant'* – the only time she directly refers to him in such terms – drives her to snatch the sword from him and threaten him with it. The time for prayer and entreaty is over now, she knows: (1591–3, 1622–4)

> *I did for once see right, do right, give tongue*
> *The adequate protest: for a worm must turn*
> *If it would have its wrong observed by God.*

> *So, my first*
> *And last resistance was invincible.*
> *Prayers move God; threats, and nothing else, move men!*

She does not recall that here she was acting out a scene buried in her memory of the virgin in the *'old rhyme'* who, in flight from her pursuers, used the very lightning of the sky to confront them – *'And*

*lo, the fire she grasped at, fixed its flash, / Lay in her hand a calm
cold dreadful sword'* (1397–8); all she knows is that she was obeying
'the clear voice' which bade her rise: (1637–40)

> *I struck, bare,*
> *At foe from head to foot in magic mail,*
> *And off it withered, cobweb-armoury*
> *Against the lightning!*

The instinctive conviction of right which makes her strong in this
crisis has its roots in the same intuitive knowledge on which she
relies in judging Caponsacchi from the first. This knowledge has
nothing to do with reason; when comfits are flung in her lap at the
theatre, she understands immediately that they are not from him:
*'Ere I could reason out why, I felt sure, / Whoever flung them, his
was not the hand'* (982–3). That Margherita lies about him she is
certain, in the same way she knew as a child that the madman in the
square was not the Pope he claimed to be. She feels that Caponsacchi
shares this intuitive wisdom with her. *'Tell him,'* she cries to her
hearers, *'that if I seem without him now, / That's the world's insight! Oh, he understands!'* (1791–2). And, finally, *'Why explain?
/ What I see, oh, he sees and how much more!'* (1804–5).

Her faith in the rightness of the impulse that moves her in moments of crisis, that caused her to seek out Caponsacchi's aid and
flee Arezzo, leads her to apply two distinctive images to herself,
those of the homing bird and wild flower. Earlier speakers, notably
Other Half-Rome, had used similar figures to describe her gentleness
and beauty, but Pompilia uses them to convey the sense of natural-
ness she feels in her actions, to express her sensation that she experiences the same unreasoning, instinctive force of God's natural law
that the birds and plants know. Violante and her own mother were
wrong in *'transplanting'* her at her birth because (301–5)

> *God plants us where we grow.*
> *It is not that because a bud is born*
> *At a wild briar's end, full i' the wild beast's way,*
> *We ought to pluck and put it out of reach*
> *On the oak-tree top, – say "There the bud belongs!"*

But Violante moved first the *'wild-briar slip'* and then the *'wilding
flower-tree-branch'* after it had struck root and grown, and so began
all the evil. While she pines in the alien soil of Arezzo, she is like the
man in Fra Celestino's psalm who wishes for a dove's wings to fly

away and rest. But everything comes right again on that April morning when once more the impulse of nature stirs within her. She is as sure of her course as any creature of the air: '*I have my purpose and my motive too, / My march to Rome, like any bird or fly!*' (1245–6).

This one aspect of Pompilia's nature – her reliance on intuitive understanding, on following the dictates of her heart rather than reason or external authority – links her with Caponsacchi more strongly than any other correspondence between them. They are spiritually akin in their acceptance of the bond that draws them together as one of divine inspiration, beyond the possibility of rational explanation; they are one in their conviction that their actions are dictated by a law stronger and more binding than any on earth. This shared recognition of the demands of a higher law makes all the more striking the parallel conclusions which they reach independently: both reject thoughts of the marriage that might have been between them, Pompilia turning away trustingly from what Caponsacchi dismisses only reluctantly, and accept the authority of earthly law and institutions as a necessary alternative. Where he had made a weary resolution – '*I mean to do my duty and live long*' (VI, 2077) – Pompilia with her last breath urges him to spend '*God's instant men call years*' in holding fast to truth and '*Do out the duty!*' (1841–3). Thus, they both concede that their love was not meant for earth, that only in heaven can be found '*the real and true and sure.*'

The facts Pompilia reveals are few and serve mainly to corroborate Caponsacchi's testimony denying the writing of the letters and attributing them to the machinations of Guido and Margherita. Three times she mentions that she does not know how to write, regretting that she cannot leave her story in writing for her son, glad that she cannot read what vile pens have scribbled against the Canon, sad again that she was forced to rely on the wavering friar to write to her parents for her. She tells nothing of the attack, but sheds some light on the unhappy years at Arezzo and her desperate attempts to win freedom through the Archbishop and the Governor; the desperation is starkly expressed in the admission that she had briefly contemplated suicide before the flight (a point already hinted at by Other Half-Rome).

What happens when the strongly emotional Caponsacchi–Pompilia arguments come together and reinforce each other by their shared spontaneous, almost inspired quality is a counter-balancing of the impression produced by Guido's highly rhetorical presentation. They diminish the impact of his court defence by making it seem in retrospect overly controlled and contrived, relying too much on rationalizing and justifying by legal and traditional authority. In contrast, these two are uncalculated, almost lyrical expressions, bound together by an intricate pattern of cross-relationships and echoes: of words, like 'dream' and 'strange,' of motifs, like "light against dark" and "love against hate," and of beliefs, in intuitive apprehension and spiritual kinship. Thus they seem to present two sides of the same coin and constitute one argument – on a completely different level from Guido's rhetorical defence – powerful, moving, and unanswerable.

Chapter IV

Arcangeli, Bottini, the Pope

I

The next three monologues represent a reversion to the 'outside view,' this time giving not the reflection of popular opinion but the studied arguments of the two opposing lawyers and the final verdict of the Pope. The first speaker is Dominus Hyacinthus de Archangelis, Advocate of the Poor, appointed to present the written legal arguments for Guido Franceschini's defence. He is a domesticated, luxury-loving man whose two great interests in life are the enjoyment of home comforts, especially good food, and pride in his young son. A successful lawyer, he is somewhat jealous of the higher position which his opponent Bottini holds as Fisc but too complacent to let ambition interfere with the easy routine of his life. He applies himself to the task at hand with plodding thoroughness and little enthusiasm for Guido's cause, and has great difficulty in keeping his mind from straying from legal matters to thoughts of the pleasant pastime awaiting his work's conclusion. Two considerations prod him on, however: the awareness that this case presents a rare opportunity for professional advancement through a display of legal acumen before the ecclesiastical court – a promotion will not fail to pave the way for the son and heir to come after him – and the sheer delight he finds in employing his rhetorical skill in Latin. He fancies himself something of a poet and student of classical Latin form.

His opponent, Juris Doctor Johannes-Baptista Bottinius, is equally interested in impressing the court with a brilliant display of rhetoric, but his personality and presentation are totally different. A bachelor, he reveals a deep-seated distrust of women in general and of Pompilia in particular, although she is the ostensible subject of his '*defence.*' He is of a mean, suspicious nature, always interpreting events and motives in the worst possible light, and he presents his arguments in an oblique, insinuating fashion, contrasting with Arcangeli's assured manner. He is contemptuous of his good-natured opponent and perhaps somewhat envious of the Advocate's family pleasures as well. His presentation depends less on the careful mar-shalling of legal precedents than Arcangeli's, more on clever illu-stration and analogy to characterize Pompilia and her adversaries. Appointed to defend her interests, he can barely conceal his distaste for the task, and devotes his energies instead to exhibiting his skill with words and wide knowledge of classical literature.

Both monologues take place within a few weeks of the principals' pre-trial testimony and Pompilia's death. Arcangeli notes that it is '*Carnival-time*' – hence late in the month of January – as he sits in his study at noon of a blustery, rainy day and prepares his rough notes for the written argument to be submitted soon to the court for the trial proper. It is the eighth birthday of his son Giacinto, and thoughts of the jovial scenes to take place in the evening as relatives and friends gather to celebrate the happy occasion continually dis-tract the Advocate from his task. The boy Giacinto is, in effect, the third person of his monologue. In this son meet the two consuming interests of Arcangeli's life: domestic pleasure and the study of Latin rhetoric. Giacinto will emulate his father's skill with the classical language – he begins the study of Virgil this very day; symbolically, he will tonight actually play the part of the Don his father at the evening's entertainment. What is more, his birthday celebration will bring a special guest, the old grandsire who may yet be persuaded to alter his will in favour of this extraordinary grandson; then Giacinto will be well set even '*when poor papa / Latin and law are long since laid at rest.*'[1] Arcangeli speaks of the boy no less than

1/Book VIII, lines 1799–1800. All references in this section are to Books VIII (Arcangeli) and IX (Bottini) unless otherwise indicated. The Book number is included in the text wherever the discussion does not clearly indicate which of the two lawyers is speaking.

twenty-five times in the course of preparing Guido's defence, calling
him by eighteen different names, diminutives of endearment
('Cinone,' 'Cinoncello,' 'Cinarello,' and so on). Son and heir, the
child represents all the reasons for work and all the rewards of home-
life. There is sharp irony in the emphasis which Arcangeli places
on home and fatherhood as he prepares to defend Guido Franceschini, the wife-murderer and callously indifferent father. Quite unaware of its implications, the lawyer draws a parallel between his
own situation and that of Guido; to him the murder constitutes a
stroke of unlooked-for good luck which will help advance Giacinto's
future: (80–9)

> One might wait years
> And never find the chance which now finds me!
> The fact is, there's a blessing on the hearth,
> A special providence for fatherhood!
> Here's a man, and what's more, a noble, kills
> – Not sneakingly but almost with parade –
> Wife's father and wife's mother and wife's self
> That's mother's self of son and heir (like mine!)
> – And here stand I, the favoured advocate,
> Who pluck this flower. ...

No one else rates so much attention from the Advocate as his son;
he gives one passing thought to his client, languishing in a cold
prison cell, and several scornful thoughts to his arch-rival Bottini,
whose arguments he must prepare to answer – otherwise, all is
Giacinto.

Bottini, on the other hand, has no such pressing consciousness of
anyone else as he prepares his speech; his thoughts seldom move
beyond himself. He directs his argument at an imaginary audience
of fifty judges, a crowd of Roman citizens, and the Pope himself.
Alone in his study, some days after Arcangeli's monologue takes
place, he is reading aloud the findings of his month-long investiga-
tion of Pompilia's case, pretending that it is being presented in court
– where he can 'enliven speech with many a flower / Refuses obsti-
nate to blow in print' – and that 'This scurvy room' is turned into
an 'immense hall' where all can see and hear the Fisc in person (IX,
3–6). He speaks, then, directly to the judges ('O Court, O sun';
'How say you, good my lords?'), except for an occasional parenthetical remark to himself – '(– Did not he die? I'll see before I print)'
(118) – and opening and closing comments reflecting his personal

feelings. Unlike Arcangeli's speech, Bottini's is the finished product, in well-polished form and carefully timed to be delivered orally in the space of one hour. Occasionally, he allows himself the luxury of an address to Arcangeli, picturing his chagrined opponent in the audience, but here the polished language gives way to an undisguised snarl: *'Listen to me, thou Archangelic swine!'* (949). More often, he concentrates on anticipating objections from him: *'Does thy comment follow quick ... ?'* (952). If any third person exists for Bottini, it is this same Advocate, to whose feast he was not invited – *'(I heard of thy regale!)'* (987) – and whose inordinate love of food he continually jibes at, describing that *'rare pie / (Master Arcangeli has heard of such)'* (395–6) whose succulence makes fasting bearable, referring to him as his *'fat opponent'* (947), and recalling the doctor's advice to the latter to break his habit of indulgence. Finally, in an oblique defence, he accelerates the attack, hammering away at the same theme: (1401–6)

> *Yet let not some gross pamperer of the flesh*
> *And niggard in the spirit's nourishment,*
> *Whose feeding hath offuscated his wit*
> *Rather than law, – he never had, to lose –*
> *Let not such advocate object to me*
> *I leave my proper function of attack!*

The motive for both speakers is the same: apparently, to present the case for their clients; in reality, to advance themselves and their careers by an impressive rhetorical exhibition larded with no small portions of flattery for the judges. Both make this second motive explicit in their more honest moments. Arcangeli complains: (VIII, 1745–9)

> *It's hard: you have to plead before these priests*
> *And poke at them with Scripture, or you pass*
> *For heathen and, what's worse, for ignorant*
> *O' the quality o' the Court and what it likes*
> *By way of illustration of the law.*

Bottini in his last lines expresses envy of Isocrates, who as an ancient was free to say what he wished: (IX, 1576–9)

> *He put in just what rushed into his head:*
> *While I shall have to prune and pare and print.*
> *This comes of being born in modern times*
> *With priests for auditory. Still, it pays.*

Neither shows any concern at how the outcome of the case might affect his client's interests: Arcangeli seems not even to have consulted with Guido, and Bottini's remarks reveal a total ignorance of what Pompilia was really like. Hence, both freely employ specious reasoning and show no qualms about introducing irrelevant or even damaging material as long as it serves to exhibit their cleverness.

Arcangeli reveals little tension, except for that engendered by the conflict between his basic lack of interest in the case and his desire to shine in court for the boy's sake. He must make a continual effort to keep his mind on the text in preparation and time and again sternly corrects himself: *'Dispose, O Don, o' the day, first work then play!'* (18); *'If I one more time fly from point proposed!'* (423); *'Pen, truce to further gambols!* Poscimur!' (475). However, even if he can muster only scant interest in Guido's ultimate fate, his delight in publicly displaying his linguistic prowess rescues the assignment from boredom and lends a measure of excitement to the dry quoting of legal precedents. Today's task may be only to make rough notes – (1750–3)

> *To-morrow stick in this, and throw out that,*
> *And, having first ecclesiasticized,*
> *Regularize the whole, next emphasize,*
> *Then latinize, and lastly Cicero-ize,*

– but he cannot resist the temptation to try out the sound of different orotund Latin phrases. Whole passages (such as 1520–76 and 1633–1736) are made up of the Latin phrasing followed by the English equivalent, and Latinate terms are interspersed throughout the rest of the monologue.[2] Even his omnipresent references to food and eating, which play such a large role in characterizing him as luxury-loving and gluttonous, shrink in prominence when placed beside his revellings in classical phrase-making.[3] He speaks of the forth-

---

2/Charles W. Hodell, in "A Literary Mosaic" (1908), has collated the Latin expressions of Arcangeli in the poem against those in Browning's source document, and has found that 95% of the Latin, in 56 quotations, varying from two to 198 words long, "are taken directly from the source book" (p. 517). He notes, however, that the irony and humour are the poet's contributions. The glee with which Arcangeli experiments with the classical phrasing, along with the innumerable personal allusions to his son and his food, is obviously not to be found in the original document – an official court record – so that in spite of the heavy borrowing in this one area, Browning's advocate is an entirely different personality from the historical lawyer.

3/It is surprising to note that, despite the great number of food references in

coming feast and its delights of the palate some fourteen times, and
his attacks on Bottini number fifteen, but both of these pleasurable
topics yield to his obsession with Latin stylistics. Tantalizing as
is the thought of a satisfying meal, it cannot compete with the thrill
that comes from contemplating the newly coined epigram, the clever
witticism, or the dazzling riposte, or even, when creative opportunities are lacking, the catching of an authority in a grammatical error.

Well over one-half the speech is given over to experimenting with
such phraseology. For example, he gets as far as the first three words
of his argument ('*Count Guido married*') and then pauses to try out
some five different Latin versions of the idea, rejecting some as too
commonplace, others as having too much of a '*modern taint,*' before
recollecting that he is not to worry about the '*speech*' yet, but only
to make notes. Then he anticipates Bottini's charge and answers it
with relish; he will repeat '*charge with proper varied phrase,*' then
'*Cut away phrase by phrase from underfoot!*' – not the meaning, but
the expression of the idea matters. '*Bottini is a beast, one barbarous*'
when it comes to Latin, and the Advocate will show him so. '*That's
the way to write Latin, friend my Fisc!*' he cries, after one particularly good stroke (191–204). He gives up his plan to deny that Guido
carried a pistol, when he discovers that the Latin phrase for the
weapon provides all sorts of opportunities for cleverness; though the
concession '*make / Somewhat against us*' (211–12), he cannot resist:
(216–18)

> Better we lost the cause than lacked the gird
> At the Fisc's Latin, lost the Judge's laugh!
> It's Venturini that decides for style.

The judges are weary of facts and proofs by this time, so better to
leave dry logic and (259–62) look for

> ... the new, the unforeseen,
> The nice by-stroke, the fine and improvised
> Point that can titillate the brain o' the Bench
> Torpid with over-teaching long ago!

He even toys with the idea of claiming that Guido was not the

Arcangeli's monologue, they actually number less than those used by Bottini.
Possibly the fact that Arcangeli's are literal references for the most part and
most of Bottini's figurative helps to disguise their predominance in the latter.
This difference in usage obviously plays a role in characterizing the Advocate's
appetites as more natural and hearty and the Fisc's as unhealthy and perverted.

murderer at all – a fertile imagination can supply all sorts of ingenious explanations as to why the Count should innocently have happened on the scene at the fatal moment – but has to reluctantly
discard this touch at the recollection of Guido's open admission of
the killing. Mostly, he confines his cleverness to phrase-making
rather than reasoning; *'We'll garnish law with idiom, never fear!'*
(155), he says at one point, at once making a culinary reference
figurative and uniting it with the rhetorical theme as well.

He is gleeful to discover an error in one of his innumerable cited
precedents – an error in grammar: 'In monasterio! *He mismanages /
In with the ablative, the accusative!'* (963–4). At tonight's feast
Giacinto will enjoy some wine as reward for success in his classical
studies, with one important condition: (1770–2)

> *– Always provided that he conjugate*
> Bibo, *I drink, correctly – nor be found*
> *Make the* perfectum, bipsi, *as last year!*

He wonders if he himself dare make use of a *'neologism,'* is more at
ease quoting *'Ovid's phrase,'* or thanking *'Flaccus for the phrase'* he
makes bold to borrow; confidently, he sets out to coin *'Homeric
phrase'* and modestly concludes with a *'Horatian promise.'*

Arcangeli is, in fact, a frustrated poet. Not satisfied to turn a clever
phrase in Latin, he would like to be able to do it in verse as well, but
the law has allowed him no time to develop this talent: (148–51)

> *Such was the rule in Farinacci's time.*
> *Indeed I hitched it into verse and good.*
> *Unluckily, law quite absorbs a man,*
> *Or else I think I too had poetized.*

Elsewhere, the Cyriacus grammatical error reminds him what his
birthday present for Giacinto was to have been: (965–73)

> *(... I had hoped to have hitched the villain into verse*
> *For a gift, this very day, a complete list*
> *O' the prepositions each with proper case,*
> *Telling a story, long was in my head.*
> *"What prepositions take the accusative?*
> *Ad to or at – who saw the cat? – down to*
> *Ob, for, because of, keep her claws off!" Tush!*
> *Law in a man takes the whole liberty:*
> *The muse is fettered: just as Ovid found!)*

He finds some of his Latin models better for verse-making than for the present task: *'Virgil is little help to who writes prose. / He shall attack me Terence with the dawn, / Shall Cinuccino!'* (136–8). But he is fond of quoting a poetic line – *'Ah, fortunate (the poet's word reversed) / Inasmuch as we know our happiness!'* (358–9) – or tossing off a similar phrase of his own, as when he asks rhetorically of his audience: (537–9)

> *Shall man prove the insensible, the block,*
> *The blot o' the earth he crawls on to disgrace?*
> *(Come, that's both solid and poetic!)*

He even indulges himself in rhyme at times, as in this summary of his procedure: *'Regularize the whole, next emphasize, / Then latinize, and lastly Cicero-ize'* (1752–3), where the play on the verb form reflects his high spirits and the thwarted desire to *'hitch'* his words into verse.[4] A touch of this inclination to poetize appears in his last jubilant statement: (1738–42)

> *Landed and stranded lies my very speech,*
> *My miracle, my monster of defence –*
> *Leviathan into the nose whereof*
> *I have put fish-hook, pierced his jaw with thorn,*
> *And given him to my maidens for a play!*

The tone of Arcangeli's monologue is one of vast complacency, of hand-rubbing glee that he should be given this rare opportunity to display his skill before *'applausive Rome.'* He is pleased with himself, with his son, and even with God, and in no doubt that God is pleased with *him* (1782–4)

> *... – since, employing talent so, I yield*
> *The Lord His own again with usury, –*
> *A satisfaction, yea, to God Himself!*

He apparently feels not the slightest twinge of conscience in acclaiming himself as one *'vigilant for law, / Zealous for truth, a credit to his kind'* (1780–1); he has all along modestly attributed the stroke

4/Although he does not call him a "poet," Park Honan, in *Browning's Characters: A Study in Poetic Technique* (1961), notes Arcangeli's propensity for rhyme in the opening and closing lines of his monologue and in various couplings – *ermine-vermin, soar and pour, name and fame,* etc. – and concludes that "Although the device is not employed extensively in his portrait, it has the effect of emphasizing his obtuse and carefree nature ..." (p. 263).

of rare good luck of Guido's crime to the goodness of the Creator:
(75-80)

> Now, how good God is! How falls plumb to point
> This murder, gives me Guido to defend
> Now, of all days i' the year, just when the boy
> Verges on Virgil, reaches the right age
> For some such illustration from his sire,
> Stimulus to himself!

He calls himself a 'Solomon,' and 'Hortensius Redivivus,' and then
adds ingenuously, 'Pray God, I keep me humble' (93).

In spite of the Pharisaical note in so much self-praise, and the
complaint that because his audience is ecclesiastical he has to 'poke
at them with Scripture' (1746), Arcangeli is obviously familiar with
the Bible and able to quote from it with the ease of one who has committed much of it to memory. He may not be able to cite a passage
from St. Ambrose with accuracy, admitting '(I can't quite recollect
it)' (683), but he knows the words of Solomon by heart: '(The Holy
Spirit speaking by his mouth / In Proverbs, the sixth chapter near
the end)' (614-15). Many of his scriptural references are in asides
where he is speaking naturally and not for effect, as in the allusion
above to his drawing Leviathan and in this parenthetical passage:
(1464-71)

> (... – Ah, boy of my own bowels, Hyacinth,
> Wilt ever catch the knack, requite the pains
> Of poor papa, become proficient too
> I' the how and why and when, the time to laugh,
> The time to weep, the time, again, to pray,
> And all the times prescribed by Holy Writ?
> Well, well, we fathers can but care, but cast
> Our bread upon the waters!)[5]

This intimate acquaintance with Scripture, like the satisfaction in his
close relationship with God, makes all the more striking the dichotomy between Arcangeli's private and professional concerns: they
are on two different levels and never meet. The only time his complacent good feeling is disturbed when he thinks about the rival
who threatens his career: Bottini is the 'dog,' the 'fop,' the 'pale-
haired, red-eyed ferret,' the 'blazing ass.' Otherwise, everyone re-
ceives the blessing of his jovial nature, the 'hale grandsire,' the 'good

5/See also 554-7, 1202-7, 1417-22.

wife,' even the clever if worrisome cook Gigia who *'can jug a rabbit well enough'* though she may need help with the porcupine.

As indicated, legal arguments for the accused are all but submerged in the Advocate's warm glow of self-satisfaction and his glittering poetic phrases, but for the sake of Judge Tommati, who likes some legal justification in a defence, Arcangeli marshals an imposing and interminable array of precedents from ancient and modern Roman history, from the writings of the doctors of the Church, and from the Old and New Testaments, to show that Guido's act should not be considered a crime. No matter what charge Bottini may level, the Advocate will have an answer; *'Cite we an illustrative case in point'* becomes a monotonously familiar phrase. There is no end to the catalogue: Theodoric, Cassiodorus, Aristotle, Scaliger, Aelian, Solon, *'the Julian, Cornelian, Gracchus' Law,'* St. Jerome, Gregory, Solomon, Valerius, St. Bernard, Samson, St. Ambrose, Cyriacus, Leonardus, Aquinas, St. Paul, Castrensis, Butringarius, – *'Superabundant the examples be / To pick and choose from'* (569–70), Arcangeli notes, only too accurately.

On those rare occasions when he ventures into legal waters, his meagre arguments are generally couched in defensive terms – Guido having already presented his own positive arguments – and are aimed mainly at thwarting possible thrusts by the Fisc. A measure of Arcangeli's ingenuity and his disdain for the law can be gleaned from noting how he handles one such anticipated charge, that Guido hired base accomplices who turned on him in the end. Unable to deny the fact, he will smoothly turn aside the damning evidence by picturing the assassins as *'rustic souls'* with such an *'instinct of equity'* that they claimed their due pay even at the expense of their own lord's life; on the other hand, he will attribute the Count's failure to pay them to his complete sense of dedication to an affair of honour which should not be vulgarized: *'He spared them the pollution of the pay'* (1631). This ability to reverse direction in an argument will impress the court even if the argument itself is of doubtful worth, thinks Arcangeli, and in this opinion, at least, his opponent Bottini concurs.

In Bottini's case, the desire to impress the judges with his legal skill conflicts with his lack of interest in Pompilia and his dislike of women in general to produce a tension that seriously weakens his defence of her. Mainly to demonstrate his familiarity with figures of antiquity, he constantly forces comparisons of his dead client with characters who have nothing at all in common with her: Dido, Venus,

Helen, Lucretia and the like. The effect is so ludicrous as to nullify arguments for Pompilia's innocence while drawing attention to the most dubious aspects of her situation. His mode of address underlines this basic lack of sympathy even more sharply. He begins with the assumption that she was indeed guilty of indiscretion, deceit, and even infidelity to Guido, so that his whole defence of her actions must lie on one foundation: the concept that the end justifies the means and because of Guido's tyranny, anything she did to escape him, however unjust in itself, is excusable. In pursuing this argument, Bottini adopts a method of conceding as true all of Guido's darkest allegations, merely *'for the sake of argument,'* and ends by accepting them in fact. His "explanations" of Pompilia's alleged errors are so tortured and laboured as to make her actions seem both significant and blameworthy.

The most typical syntactical arrangement of his sentence is an introductory clause beginning with *'if,'* followed by a brief deprecatory phrase denying the truth of the *'if'* clause, the sentence then concluded by an elaborately detailed and over-extended *'defence'* of how the charge might be answered if it *were* true. The result is, of course, that the hypothetical nature of the charge is blurred and the audience is left only with the impression of a highly unconvincing justification offered for the misdemeanour. On Caponsacchi's reputed visits to Pompilia at the villa to *'brighten winter up,'* for example, Bottini will say: (1252–6)

> *If so they did – which nowise I believe –*
> *(How can I? – proof abounding that the priest,*
> *Once fairly at his relegation-place,*
> *Never once left it) still, admit he stole*
> *A midnight march. ...*

He offers none of the proof that abounds that Caponsacchi could not have been present, but develops at length a patently improbable version of how such visits might have been spent. Of Pompilia, he says: (298–302)

> *The lady, foes allege, put forth each charm*
> *And proper floweret of feminity*
> *To whosoever had a nose to smell*
> *Or breast to deck: what if the charge be true?*
> *The fault were graver had she looked with choice, ...*

where again he strengthens rather than refutes the charge, by prof-
fering such a glaringly inadequate defence of the action. This willingness to admit the demonstrably false is basic to the Fisc's mode of
address. Like the *'if'* construct, words like *'concede,' 'grant,' 'admit,'*
'put case,' or *'suppose'* (443–5, 473–4) introduce just such an in-
verted and damaging form of defence:

> *Grant the tale*
> *O' the husband, which is false, were proved and true*
> *To the letter – or the letters, I should say, ...*

> *Concede she wrote (which were preposterous)*
> *This and the other epistle, – what of it?*

Pompilia has denied writing any letters, but Bottini says: (808–24)

> *Admit the husband's calumny – allow*
> *That the wife, having penned the epistle fraught*
> *With horrors, charge on charge of crime she heaped*
> *O' the head of Pietro and Violante – ...*
> *Allow this calumny, I reiterate!*
> *Who is so dull as wonder at the pose*
> *Of our Pompilia in the circumstance?*[6]

In like manner, the word *'doubt'* recurs in the Fisc's speech, most
notably in the passage recounting Guido's furious reaction to the
news of his child's birth. The repetition of *'doubt'* here undercuts the
apparently indignant tone of the recital and contributes to the equi-
vocal effect of the whole passage: (1323–30)

> *So, father, take thy child, for thine that child.*
> *Oh nothing doubt! In wedlock born, law holds*
> *Baseness impossible: since "filius est*
> *"Quem nuptiae demonstrant," twits the text*
> *Whoever dares to doubt.*
>   *Yet doubt he dares!*
> *O faith, where art thou flown from out the world?*
> *Already on what an age of doubt we fall!*

He continues in this vein at length, purporting to answer doubts that
the child is Guido's by citing highly unlikely possibilities of *'some*
miracle' in this *'puzzling strait,'* like the *'strange favour, Maro mem-*
orized'; perhaps even *'Spontaneous generation'* marked the *'prodigy.'*

6/See also 261–72, 290–4, 653–6, 681–93.

He concludes the absurd argument with a heavy-handed attempt at irony: (1354–61)

> Let whoso doubts, steep horsehair certain weeks
> In water, there will be produced a snake;
> Spontaneous product of the horse, which horse
> Happens to be the representative –
> Now that I think on't – of Arezzo's self,
> The very city our conception blessed:
> Is not a prancing horse the City-arms?
> What sane eye fails to see coincidence?

This kind of presentation is intended not only to show the court how mockingly witty he can be, but also to show the world how well he knows women and their wiles: the Fisc is not one to be fooled.

Since Bottini's suspicious mind cannot accept the fact of Pompilia's innocence, he finds refuge in adopting a condescendingly amused attitude toward 'woman's weakness,' and asks the court to recognize that Pompilia acted only as women have always acted, with deceit and wiles to gain her own way. He makes this point in a tone that is smugly confidential and unctuous: (221–38)

> Know one, you know all
> Manners of maidenhood: mere maiden she.
> And since all lambs are like in more than fleece,
> Prepare to find that, lamb-like, she too frisks –
> O' the weaker sex, my lords, the weaker sex! ...
> And what is beauty's sure concomitant,
> Nay, intimate essential character,
> But melting wiles, deliciousest deceits,
> The whole redoubted armoury of love?
> Therefore of vernal pranks, dishevellings
> O' the hair of youth that dances April in,
> And easily-imagined Hebe-slips
> O'er sward which May makes over-smooth for foot –
> These shall we pry into? – or wiselier wink,
> Though numerous and dear they may have been?

The choice of words like 'wiles,' 'deceits,' 'pranks,' 'pry,' and 'wink' conveys the Fisc's leering attitude toward women, along with his conviction that beauty and deceit are inextricably bound together, and the sibilant sounds of the lines reinforce the impression of knowing slyness. Whenever he directly describes Pompilia's behaviour –

always ostensibly to defend it – this tone dominates and the language often becomes coarse and disagreeable. Why should Caponsacchi boast of his conquest with Pompilia, Bottini asks, when it is clear that *'The cup, he quaffs at, lay with olent breast / Open to gnat, midge, bee and moth as well?'* (313–14). And why should the husband complain, since his wife's charms are not diminished by the *'stranger's bite'* (324–6)

> *But rather like a lump of spice they lie,*
> *Morsel of myrrh, which scents the neighborhood*
> *Yet greets its lord no lighter by a grain.*

Similarly, in setting forth Pompilia's decision to flee Guido's cruelty, he pictures the conflict as one of brute strength – the husband is a hind who should treat the heifer with patience, *'for deem you she endures the whip, / Nor winces at the goad, nay, restive, kicks?* (255–6) – or treats it as a kind of coarse physical combat: (421–3)

> *Far better that the unconsummate blow,*
> *Adroitly baulked by her, should back again,*
> *Correctively admonish his own pate!*

The wife had to *'crush'* the crime and if she chose an indiscreet way to do it, the sullying of her pure whiteness is nothing serious: *'bruised, / She smarts a little, but her bones are saved / A fracture, and her skin will soon show sleek'* (1008–10).

As noted, many of the inappropriate analogies Bottini draws in presenting Pompilia can be explained in part as an attempt to demonstrate the breadth of his classical knowledge. Other unsympathetic speakers, notably Half-Rome and Guido, have compared her to Helen, and the situations of Venus and Dido might be granted at least a tenuous relationship in the Fisc's context, but the persistent recurrence of another kind of figure, that of the jewel or pearl lost in the mud, points up a more basic motive for Bottini's employing the unflattering comparison, his deep-seated distrust of woman's virtue. At least a half-dozen times he applies the lost jewel figure to Pompilia. At first, he simply praises her as a *'pearl,'* but notes that she was never a *'milk-white'* one, rather one suffused *'With here and there a tint and hint of flame, – / Desire'* (205–7). Then her bribing Caponsacchi with her love he justifies in these terms: (512–14)

> Shall she propose him lucre, dust o' the mine,
> Rubbish o' the rock, some diamond, muckworms prize,
> Some pearl secreted by a sickly fish?

This linking of the precious stone with discoloration, dust, rubbish, and the muckworm is carried out in the next passage, an attempt to extenuate Pompilia's deceit by citing the example of Ulysses' entering Troy in disguise; this hero, he points out (550–3)

> Entered Troy's hostile gate in beggar's garb –
> How if he first had boggled at this clout,
> Grown dainty o'er that clack-dish? Grime is grace
> To whoso gropes amid the dung for gold.

Here, the guttural sounds of the hard 'c's' and 'g's' and the explosive dentals echo the disgust Bottini cannot suppress at the notion that beauty is so often to be found *'amid the dung.'*

Gradually, the pearl image becomes subsumed for Bottini under the general symbol of whiteness signifying innocence. He claims he will show evidence of Pompilia's virtue *'Plain witness to the world how white she walks / I' the mire she wanders through ere Rome she reach'* (592–3). But whiteness cannot endure mud, he knows, and he must answer Arcangeli's anticipated jibe: ' *"But thither she picked way by devious path" / "Stands dirtied, no dubiety at all!"* ' (954–5). His opponent might further think to illustrate his point with the story of Hesione at Troy, forced to *'daub, disguise her dainty limbs with pitch'* to elude the monster, and taunt, ' *"The trick succeeds, but 'tis an ugly trick"* ' (977–9). To this accusation, the Fisc can only summon up a half-hearted reply that what the Advocate takes for pitch *'Is nothing worse, belike, than black and blue'* (1005), conceding once more that his client's innocence was indeed besmirched by her escapade. For his next illustration, he goes back to an old and discredited Hebrew writer whose many lies show forth just one true statement, a statement that shines *'(like jewel hid in muck)'* (1028); the phrase echoes again. Finally, speaking of Pompilia's return to her parents after flight and relegation, he uses the image of the gentle bird which other speakers have used, but with a difference; the white dove had been conspicuously besmirched and Guido should now be (1232–4)

> Proud that his dove which lay among the pots
> Hath mued those dingy feathers, – moulted now,
> Shows silver bosom clothed with yellow gold!

Another figure he uses for Pompilia is even more clearly debasing; right to the end, he claims, she played a deceitful part (1419–21)

> *And, wily as an eel that stirs the mud*
> *Thick overhead, so baffling spearman's thrust,*
> *She, while he stabbed her, simulated death. ...*

Here we have reference to the mud without mention of pearl or whiteness, but immediately before this the speaker indicates that he considers this last act of Pompilia *'one beauty more,'* the *'one crowning grace'* of her life (1414–15), and in this way once more connects beauty with evil and treachery. His concluding image for Pompilia calls up the first one, of the pearl. Her final falsehood – so the Fisc characterizes her deathbed statement – was, he suggests, expunged by the preceding confession. All that followed the confession, *'Subsequent talk, chatter and gossipry,'* which contradicts his own present statement of the facts, means nothing: (1497–1500)

> *The sacrament obliterates the sin:*
> *What is not, – was not, therefore, in a sense.*
> *Let Molinists distinguish, "Souls washed white*
> *"But red once, still show pinkish to the eye!"*

Once more, this time under guise of a jibe at heresy, the Fisc suggests that the pearl so snow-white and lustrous to other eyes shows discoloration to his jaundiced vision.

This obsessive image of the *'jewel hid in muck'* weaves its way around the more self-conscious imagery of the classical and legendary figures in such a way as to suggest that it represents a proclivity of Bottini rather than a deliberate attempt on his part to draw attention to a particular figure of speech. The classical images, on the other hand, are used so prominently and in so many inappropriate and over-ingenious parallels as to make clear that the speaker is bent on displaying his learned background at all costs. He speaks of Phryne, Lucretia, Hebe, Hymen, Venus, Cupid, Helen, Dido, Vulcan, Hesione, Jove, Hercules, Myrtillus, Amaryllis, Ulysses, Bacchus, Phoebus, and Icarus, all of whom have little or no connection with law in general and this case in particular. A key to their use is found in Bottini's earliest image, of himself as artist, painting for the delectation of his distinguished audience a new version of the Holy Family. It becomes clear, as he develops this *'conceit'* to almost 200 lines, that he is more concerned with emphasizing his own skill than with drawing out any significant relationship between the subject and the models. He will not put together 'bits of repro- duction' as the popular painter does; rather, he tells his lords, 'your artist turns abrupt from these' to brood on 'the inner spectrum,' to come to the 'soul o' the picture' (82–101). He compares himself to the master Ciro Ferri – 'engaged as I were Ciro's self, / To paint a parallel' (121–2); he will show every detail 'like as life' (139). At the start, he says he must claim 'the artist's ultimate appeal' (157); at the conclusion, he boasts: 'Point to point as I purposed have I drawn' (1565). The strained Holy Family 'conceit' has long since been dropped, but the artist image persists to the end.

This concept of himself as artist is reflected in the pompous, inflated style. Like the Homer and Virgil he quotes so often, he is daring an 'epic plunge,' and for his 'great theme' he invokes the Muse – '(Lend my weak voice thy trump, sonorous Fame!)' (186) – and apostrophizes to introduce his heroine: (196–8)

> What's here? Oh, turn aside nor dare the blaze
> Of such a crown, such constellation, say,
> As jewels here thy front, Humanity!

No classical form is too florid for his uses – Pompilia marries: 'For lo, advancing Hymen and his pomp!' (239). No Latinate polysyllabic word or phrase is too outrageous for him – his model shows 'Mar- moreal neck and bosom uberous' (53). But he can do more than list name and borrow style from classical literature; he can repeat the very words of antiquity's greatest writers. In the course of his speech, he quotes or paraphrases Tarquin, Virgil, Persius, Moschus, Homer, Archimedes, Nero, Tacitus, Horace, Thucydides, Sopho- cles, Ovid, and Isocrates. 'I, by the guidance of antiquity / (Our one infallible guide) now operate' (182–3), he claims. If few of the analogies he draws bear up under scrutiny, it is no matter: 'Any- thing, anything to let the wheels / Of argument run glibly to their goal!' (471–2). At one point, he is forced to give up in confusion an unworkable simile: (574–80)

> No damsel to convey in dish the head
> Of Holophernes, – style the Canon so –
> Or is it the Count? If I entangle me
> With my similitudes, – if wax wings melt,
> And earthward down I drop, not mine the fault:

> *Blame your beneficence, O Court, O sun,*
> *Whereof the beamy smile affects my flight!*

Even here, undismayed by the obvious unmanageability of his figure, he promptly turns it into flattery of the court, deftly incorporating a comparison of himself to the mythical Icarus.

This particular image also illustrates the difference between the two lawyers in their use of biblical allusions. The Fisc employs them much less frequently than Arcangeli; he refers only to Eve, to the Holy Family for his artist image, to Judith in the truncated figure above, and to Mary and Christ at the tomb in a most unlikely comparison. And he uses them with markedly less authority and interest. Sometimes he does violence to Scripture, as when in his zeal to paint Pompilia and the Comparini in the colours of the Holy Family, he relates how *'seeking safety in the wilderness,'* they *'Were all surprised by Herod, while outstretched / In sleep beneath a palm-tree by a spring'* (127–9). At another point, he feels the need to enhance a description of the *'flower of wifehood'* with a reference to Solomon, but cannot call on one readily, as Arcangeli could, and has to remind himself: *'(Confer a passage in the Canticles)'* (289). In one of his strangest illustrations, he cites the example of the Magdalen's mistaking Christ for the gardener at the tomb as an explanation of how Pompilia chose Caponsacchi to be her guardian in flight; he pointlessly quotes Mary – ' *"Sir"*, *said she, and so following,* '– and then, either forgetting what she did say, or suddenly aware of the irrelevancy of the example, adds, *'Why more words?'* (941) and abruptly changes the subject. The impression left is of a speaker who feels the need occasionally to introduce a biblical reference to keep his ecclesiastical auditors from becoming restless amid the welter of pagan allusions, but who is himself far more at home in the world of myth and god.

The facts revealed by the two lawyers are negligible for the most part, although Arcangeli admits that Baldeschi, one of Guido's accomplices, confessed on the third day of torture and disclosed that all four assassins had resolved to murder the Count after the attack to assure collecting their fee. A minor revelation reflecting on Arcangeli's professional character is that he has bought, at half their value, Violante's pearls which Pietro was forced to pawn and will use them to bribe his own wife on behalf of son Giacinto; the Comparini's murder has already proved of some benefit to the Advocate of the Poor.

Both speakers deal more in opinion than in facts. Arcangeli shows not only a lack of interest in his client, but a kind of contempt for Guido, especially his breaking down under torture and confessing; *'Men are no longer men!'* (420) exclaims the comfort-loving gourmand reprovingly. His one most sympathetic trait, love for his son, is shown ultimately to be another aspect of his self-love; Giacinto represents for him a projection of his own personality, as symbolically the boy is going to act the part of his father at the night's entertainment: *'Done up to imitate papa's black robe, ... And call himself the Advocate o' the Poor'* (1763–6). Bottini's most obvious opinion is belief in Pompilia's guilt; it runs like a dark thread through his whole *'defence'* of her. The two lawyers meet on common ground in basing their arguments on the concept that "the end justifies the means" and their assumption that truth and the objective facts of the case are less important than the opportunity to display their respective professional skills. In their different ways, they both use classical allusions, specious arguments and outright lies, strained analogies and grandiose rhetorical flourishes, and consider themselves creative artists in their chosen medium of words.

The contrasting styles of the two monologues, however, produce an interesting difference in result. Of the two, the defender of Guido the murderer plays the more sympathetic role: his jovial good nature and pride and pleasure in domestic life are more attractive, in spite of his egotism, than the suspicious, leering nature and insinuating manner of Pompilia's advocate. Nevertheless, the ultimate effect of both monologues taken together is of increased sympathy for Pompilia, condemned to be misunderstood and basely attacked even in death by the ignorant and biased, and a correspondent weakening of sympathy for Guido, whose unnatural lack of family feeling is sharply underscored by his advocate's domestic happiness. With every word about the joys of fatherhood and *'home-sanctitudes'* Arcangeli unwittingly cuts away at the case for the man who wrecked two homes and wantonly destroyed the most sacred of relationships, and the attack is all the more effective because the speaker is unaware of the irony in his words. Bottini's defiling touch, on the other hand, conveyed by the persistent linking of beauty with mud and dirt, is too obsessive to stain the memory of Pompilia at all; it simply brands him as blind to goodness, incapable of appreciating or even recognizing innocence when he sees it, and suggests by indirection something of the distorted mentality of Guido, who killed innocence.

II

The final legal judgment to be rendered is that of the man who, as Antonio Pignatelli, served *'the many years / I' the school, i' the cloister, in the diocese / Domestic, legate-rule in foreign lands'*[7] and is now completing the seventh year of his reign as Pope Innocent XII. Eighty-six years old, he struggles now with one of the most difficult decisions of his long ecclesiastical career. A man of prudence and probity – *'simple, sagacious, mild yet resolute,'* the poet had called him in Book I – in the course of his current deliberation he shows himself to be also a man of deep humility and strong religious sense. He is acutely aware of his declining years, his human fallibility, and the seriousness of the decision that awaits him. Firm in his moral certitude of Guido's guilt, he has yet to contend with doubts and uncertainties as to his own role in pronouncing judgment against the murderer. The study of his predecessors' differences of opinion on earlier papal decisions is not encouraging, and a survey of the current state of Christianity leaves him disturbed and disillusioned.

He muses alone in his sparsely furnished study in the Vatican, overlooking the wet, deserted Roman streets at twilight of a grey winter day. It is February 21, a month after Arcangeli's speech and a few weeks after Bottini's; when he takes up the handbell to call his servant, the message will go out that the prisoner is to die at sunset of the following day, February 22. The Pope has been studying the trial records of the opposing lawyers' views and now turns to his daily custom of reading from a history of the papacy in an effort to glean some inspiration from the example of his predecessors; today, however, he finds only confusion and contradiction in the eight-hundred year old history of Formosus, and he is forced to rely on his own judgment and conscience to find the right way. Just as he read aloud, now he lets his thoughts flow forth *'Likewise aloud, for respite and relief'* (I, 1259); in point of fact, then, his words form a soliloquy, with no one but himself to act as audience. He does address in his imagination a whole series of individuals as he summons up the principals in the murder case to stand before the bar of judgment in his mind; once he addresses Pompilia directly in a kind of prayer, and again he directs a prayer to God for help. Nevertheless, the Pope is actually carrying on a dialogue only with himself. The men and women he calls before him are shadowy figures and dim outlines who

7/Lines 385–7. All references in this section are to Book X unless otherwise indicated.

appear briefly and withdraw without affecting the course of his deliberations. This dialogue gives the feeling of a divided mind behind the apparently resolute exterior of Innocent XII. He even calls himself by name at times, as though his earlier self were a separate entity: '*Wherefore, Antonio Pignatelli, thou / My ancient self, who wast no Pope so long*' (383–4). Only once, briefly, is the soliloquy interrupted: at the end, the servant who answers the handbell enters to receive the handwritten message and the terse order, '*Carry this forthwith to the Governor!*' (2135).

The sense in this monologue of the presence of another person is created by the aged prelate's intense awareness of his obligations to his Creator and last Judge. Antonio Pignatelli's whole life has been lived in the service of God, and the knowledge that he makes the present decision in His name, acting as His '*Vice-gerent*,' shapes every thought and emotion: (163–9)

> *In God's name! Once more on this earth of God's,*
> *While twilight lasts and time wherein to work,*
> *I take His staff with my uncertain hand,*
> *And stay my six and fourscore years, my due*
> *Labour and sorrow, on His judgment-seat,*
> *And forthwith think, speak, act, in place of Him –*
> *The Pope for Christ.*

This awesome responsibility presses heavily on him. He holds a man's life in his hands, he reminds himself: (194–202)

> *And I am bound, the solitary judge,*
> *To weigh the worth, decide upon the plea,*
> *And either hold a hand out, or withdraw*
> *A foot and let the wretch drift to the fall.*
> *Ay, and while thus I dally, dare perchance*
> *Put fancies for a comfort 'twixt this calm*
> *And yonder passion that I have to bear, –*
> *As if reprieve were possible for both*
> *Prisoner and Pope, – how easy were reprieve!*

But he pushes aside the temptation to shrink from the decision; there can be no reprieve, because he is God's vicar, by God's own choice: (1333–47)

> *It is I who have been appointed here*
> *To represent Thee, in my turn, on earth, ...*

> *Choice of the world, choice of the thing I am,*
> *Both emanate alike from Thy dread play*
> *Of operation outside this our sphere*
> *Where things are classed and counted small or great, –*
> *Incomprehensibly the choice is Thine!*
> *I therefore bow my head and take Thy place.*

Innocent XII is by no means unaware of public opinion in Rome. Again and again he adverts to the intense concern abroad for Guido's fate, the mounting tide of public sentiment favouring the prisoner's release: (289–91)

> *But wheresoe'er Rome gathers in the grey,*
> *Two names now snap and flash from mouth to mouth –*
> *(Sparks, flint and steel strike) Guido and the Pope.*

He knows how the Count's friends agitate for his release and mur-mur against the aged prelate who has turned a deaf ear to bribes, how they whisper about his declining powers – '*Nay, if the popular notion class me right,*' he admits, '*One of well-nigh decayed intelli-gence*' (1246–7). He even knows about the Swedish numerologist who, given the facts of the Count's powerful allies and the old man's failing strength, predicts the Pope's death first. He devotes a lengthy passage at the end of his monologue to a summary of these views, to the reasons advanced on all sides for Guido's acquittal – the prosper-ity of the Church, the integrity of the family – and to a consideration of the thinly veiled threats against his own person if he fails to heed them. He is sharply aware, too, of history's verdict on him, a verdict he sees rendered by the Greek dramatist Euripides, who judges those who enjoy faith in '*the blaze of noon*' against those like himself who followed virtue's path at '*midnight*'; such a one would admonish him: (1763–5)

> *"You have the sunrise now, joins truth to truth,*
> *"Shoots life and substance into death and void;*
> *"Themselves compose the whole we made before. ..."*

He hears all these voices and for them has only one answer: (2099–101)

> *... but a voice other than yours*
> *Quickens my spirit. "Quis pro Domino?*
> *"Who is upon the Lord's side?"*

All other voices are drowned out by the awesome demand: (338–42)

> But say the Swede were right, and I forthwith
> Acknowledge a prompt summons and lie dead:
> Why, then I stand already in God's face
> And hear "Since by its fruit a tree is judged,
> "Show me thy fruit, the latest act of thine! ..."

Innocent XII's imminent appearance before the bar of final judgment weighs more heavily than any other consideration. His only
motive for condemning Guido Franceschini to death is the moral
obligation, imposed by his station and office, to ensure justice. The
tension revealed in the growing indecisiveness and doubt which
threaten to shake his initial resolve is due less to uncertainty about
Guido's guilt, or still less to fear of public opinion, than to the crush-
ing awareness of man's innate limitations and his proven unworthi-
ness. There is no encouragement to be gained from a study of papal
history; in the face of so many conflicting opinions on Formosus,
first maligned and then revered, he can only ask despairingly, 'Which
of my predecessors spoke for God?' (152). But neither does he have
any sense of divine guidance to direct his own wavering hand:
(1243–5)

> I find the truth, dispart the shine from shade,
> As a mere man may, with no special touch
> O' the lynx-gift in each ordinary orb. ...

He realizes only too keenly how the Church's chosen few of his own
day have betrayed their teaching, and this betrayal is to him far more
frightening than that the pagans should not accept the truth: (1440–
50)

> But this does overwhelm me with surprise,
> Touch me to terror, – not that faith, the pearl,
> Should be let lie by fishers wanting food, –
> Nor, seen and handled by a certain few
> Critical and contemptuous, straight consigned
> To shore and shingle for the pebble it proves, –
> But that, when haply found and known and named
> By the residue made rich for evermore,
> These, – that these favoured ones, should in a trice
> Turn, and with double zest go dredge for whelks,
> Mud-worms that make the savoury soup!

Added to this disturbing thought is the rankling remembrance that he himself judged wrongly in selecting as guardian of his flock one who cast out Pompilia in her hour of need: (987–92)

> Archbishop, who art under [me], i' the Church,
> As I am under God, – thou, chosen by both
> To do the shepherd's office, feed the sheep –
> How of this lamb that panted at thy foot
> While the wolf pressed on her within crook's reach?
> Wast thou the hireling that did turn and flee?

This combination of awed humility and deep disillusionment colours the Pope's thoughts and accounts for the tone of weariness, the mood of doubt, and the ruminative mode of address. In point of fact, the ultimate decision is already made – he states explicitly almost from the first his conviction that Guido must die – 'to-day / Is Guido's last' (336–7) – and his final words solemnly repeat this conviction: 'Enough, for I may die this very night: / And how should I dare die, this man let live?' (2133–4). But the continued questioning, the tortuous re-examination of every aspect of the case which he has already studied, pondered, and decided upon, is inevitable in his present melancholy mood, when an aching sense of human frailty conflicts headlong with the obligation to condemn a fellow man. The desire to go over the whole case, step by step, still one more time, is partly a result of this present mood; it is also partly a manifestation of the habitual philosophical bent of his mind, which sees the present particular reality in terms of universal truth and believes in the ultimate capability of man's reason to arrive at a just evaluation of human conduct: (228–32)

> All's a clear rede and no more riddle now.
> Truth, nowhere, lies yet everywhere in these –
> Not absolutely in a portion, yet
> Evolvible from the whole: evolved at last
> Painfully, held tenaciously by me.

Hence the distinction he makes in his speech between himself as Innocent XII, philosopher, judge, Vicar of Christ on earth, and as Antonio Pignatelli, fallible and fearful human creature. It is the philosopher who asserts he has at last evolved the truth that Guido Franceschini is guilty and must die; it is the uncertain man who, immediately afterward, comforts himself thus: (260–4)

So and not otherwise, in after-time,
If some acuter wit, fresh probing, sound
This multifarious mass of words and deeds
Deeper, and reach through guilt to innocence,
I shall face Guido's ghost nor blench a jot.

If time shall prove him wrong, he can only assert that he acted according to his best lights, reached as far as his limitations would permit.

The sombre, weary tone is conveyed largely through the recurrent use of words suggesting darkness, finality, and the passing of time. The Pope speaks of the need for a decision *'While twilight lasts and time wherein to work'* (164), in a phrase echoing the biblical warning to act before *'the night cometh when no man can work,'* and he refers to the lateness of the day in a figurative as well as a literal sense: (212–15)

I have worn through this sombre wintry day,
With winter in my soul beyond the world's,
Over these dismalest of documents
Which drew night down on me ere eve befell. ...

The dispiriting greyness and cold outside creep upon him and he cries out impatiently: (283–5)

O pale departure, dim disgrace of day!
Winter's in wane, his vengeful worst art thou,
To dash the boldness of advancing March!

He notes the *'grey'* streets on this *'dull eve'* and the wording echoes in the phrase about himself – *'this grey ultimate decrepitude'* (389) – where the fading light of day is linked with the waning hours of his own life. He speaks often of his advanced age: he needs God's staff to stay his *'six and fourscore years'* (166); he imagines others contrasting Guido's relative youth with one *'twice eight years beyond the seven-times-ten'* (319), or calculating the accomplices' combined ages against his own – ' *"all four lives together make"* / *"Just his own length of days"* ' (2080–1). He always addresses himself as *'old'*: *'mere old man'* (393), *'poor old Pope'* (1007).

In a similar vein, he continually refers to the *'end'* that is near: man, he says, must always be aware of the accident linked to the *'smoking flax'* (the symbolic reminder to the newly crowned Pope of

his mortality) which 'Hurries the natural end and quenches him!'
(331). Again, he remarks, 'I am near the end; but still not at the end;
/ All to the very end is trial in life' (1303–4), with a tinge of regret
that all is not over yet. Later, he connects his approaching death with
the passage of historical time, with a touch of bitterness: (1903–7)

> Do not we end, the century and I?
> The impatient antimasque treads close on kibe
> O' the very masque's self it will mock, – on me,
> Last lingering personage, the impatient mime
> Pushes already, – will I block the way?

In this stage image, he sees himself the superannuated Churchman,
trying to live by the law of Christ, but soon to be followed by those
who reject such law as meaningless. Extending the simile, he concludes with a refusal to be hurried off the world's stage before his
task is 'ended': (1955–60)

> Still, I stand here, not off the stage though close
> On the exit: and my last act, as my first,
> I owe the scene, and Him who armed me thus
> With Paul's sword as with Peter's key. I smite
> With my whole strength once more, ere end my part,
> Ending, so far as man may, this offence.

He recalls how Guido's friends have reminded him of the closeness
of death, of (2059–63)

> " ... How one hears
> "The howl begin, scarce the three little taps
> "O' the silver mallet silent on thy brow, –
> " 'His last act was to sacrifice a Count
> " 'And thereby screen a scandal of the Church!' "

There is irony in the Count's supporters' issuing this bold warning,
for it is just this awareness of impending death that stiffens Innocent's resolve against freeing Guido. He has never needed the howls
of the mob to remind him of his mortality; the repeated allusions to
'age' and 'the end' show how the shadow of death falls across every
conscious moment.

As the monologue proceeds, the references to greyness, age, and
finality gradually fuse into one dominant image of night, the darkness of which comes to represent for him the receding tide of faith

and the growing spirit of doubt and scepticism he feels engulfing the world. He first acknowledges a *'quite new quick cold thrill'* that *'cloud-like'* creeps on him out of the skies he scans nightly (1253) and a voice that derides him for missing the signs he points out to others, for failing to face *'the doubt / I' the sphere above,'* that *'darkness to be felt'* (1283–4), in his preoccupation with lifting the light for others. His answer is that his *'poor spark'* had its source in the sun, and he acts according to this light: *'I reach into the dark / Feel what I cannot see, and still faith stands'* (1373–4). When the terrifying possibility of the total obliteration of faith in an indifferent age threatens to overwhelm him, he clings to one thought: (1635–43)

> *I must outlive a thing ere know it dead:*
> *When I outlive the faith there is a sun,*
> *When I lie, ashes to the very soul, –*
> *Someone, not I, must wail above the heap,*
> *"He died in dark whence never morn arose."*
> *While I see day succeed the deepest night –*
> *How can I speak but as I know? – my speech*
> *Must be, throughout the darkness, "It will end:*
> *"The light that did burn, will burn!"*

With increasing frequency from this point, the word *'light,'* representing the antithesis of doubt and despair, appears.[8] His conclusion to the passage above, declaring a final victory for faith, *'No, – I have light nor fear the dark at all'* (1660), is unmistakably related to the last lines of Pompilia's monologue, in which she resolved the opposition between the forces of good and evil in the same trusting manner: *'God stooping shows sufficient of His light / For us i' the dark to rise by. And I rise.'*

When he thinks back to the way in which the bards and philosophers of antiquity faced the problem of religious belief, the Pope

8/C. Willard Smith, *Browning's Star-Imagery: The Study of a Detail in Poetic Design* (1941), pp. 205–18, develops the significance of the Pope's light imagery at great length. He sees the star integrated with the basic figure of light, but here limited to "the function of association with other images of light that, through their cumulative effect, produce the grand image of 'white light' thoroughly appropriate to his principal theme, universal truth and justice" (p. 208). Among these "other images" he includes the "optic glass" and the "ancient river of light." For a further discussion of this basic image, see Barton R. Friedman, "To Tell the Sun from the Druid Fire: Imagery of Good and Evil in *The Ring and the Book*" (1966).

again turns to the image of darkness. The great Euripides could evolve only *'fragmentary truths where light / Lay fitful in a tenebrific time'* (1761–2) and men of the present day *'Who miss the plain way in the blaze of noon'* (1785) can hardly criticize their predecessor *'For not descrying sunshine at midnight'* (1782). But how might Euripides blame these Christians who *'have got too familiar with the light'* (1794), who might have to lose that light to realize its worth. The Pope muses on the doubtful future: (1852–7)

> *What if it be the mission of that age*
> *My death will usher into life, to shake*
> *This torpor of assurance from our creed,*
> *Re-introduce the doubt discarded, bring*
> *That formidable danger back, we drove*
> *Long ago to the distance and the dark?*

His last words, spoken after he has written the order for Guido's execution, repeat the dark–light image, this time applying it hopefully to the prisoner's last hours: (2119–28)

> *I stood at Naples once, a night so dark*
> *I could have scarce conjectured there was earth*
> *Anywhere, sky or sea or world at all:*
> *But the night's black was burst through by a blaze – ...*
> *So may the truth be flashed out by one blow,*
> *And Guido see, one instant, and be saved.*

One other revealing image Pope Innocent uses even more frequently than the dark–light figure is that of life as garden, men as plants. Instead of employing the common metaphor of the Pontiff as fisherman or shepherd, he prefers to see himself as a gardener, tilling the soil of the Church and nurturing the seeds entrusted to him in the form of souls. The seed-plant-garden image becomes so preponderant that it suggests a natural attitude of the speaker, rather than a studied figure of speech – a particular way of viewing the world, which reveals his basic simplicity and humility and leavens the otherwise abstract philosophizing of his speech with the concrete and earth-bound. The figurative expressions in this group are rarely involved or ingenious. Often they are brief, obvious comparisons. To deny his own irresoluteness, for example, the speaker will point to a nearby hill – *'Irresolute? Not I, more than the mound / With the pine-trees on it yonder!'* (236–7) – finding a kinship between his own firmness and the sturdy trees. In a somewhat more elaborate metaphor, he compares his intentions to seeds of a tree: (272–80)

> For I am ware it is the seed of act,
> God holds appraising in His hollow palm,
> Not act grown great thence on the world below,
> Leafage and branchage, vulgar eyes admire.
> Therefore I stand on my integrity,
> Nor fear at all: and if I hesitate,
> It is because I need to breathe awhile,
> Rest, as the human right allows, review
> Intent the little seeds of act, my tree. ...

Carrying this idea a step further in the passage on his own final judgment, he sees man as the tree whose worth is judged by its fruits: (340–5)

> Why, then I stand already in God's face
> And hear "Since by its fruit a tree is judged,
> "Show me thy fruit, the latest act of thine!
> "For in the last is summed the first and all, –
> "What thy life last put heart and soul into,
> "There shall I taste thy product."

In paraphrasing Guido's friends, he uses the tree-branch metaphor to represent the earthly lives of the Count and himself: (318–23)

> Again, there is another man, weighed now
> By twice eight years beyond the seven-times-ten,
> Appointed overweight to break our branch.
> And this man's loaded branch lifts, more than snow,
> All the world's cark and care, though a bird's nest
> Were a superfluous burthen. ...

He sees Guido's sin as blasting man's natural growth: (736–40)

> Greed craves its act may work both far and near,
> Crush the tree, branch and trunk and root, beside.
> Whichever twig or leaf arrests a streak
> Of possible sunshine else would coin itself,
> And drop down one more gold piece in the path. ...

Such a twig or leaf, violence says, must be cut down or ripped from earth.

The blighted tree with its barren branch is a deeply disturbing sign of nature frustrated and outraged. Innocent shudders at the 'mass of men' daily sinking into the mire of sin and tells himself that they are 'grafted, barren twigs, / Into the living stock of Christ: may bear / One day, till when they lie death-like, not dead' (1897–9). Even Guido's supporters might well use such an argument on behalf of reprieve; they might hold out the promise of reform, urging the Pontiff to spare 'this barren stock' and to 'dig about and dung and dress / Till he repent and bring forth fruit even yet!' (1968–70). Here the subtle appeal is to the Pope's conception of himself as gardener responsible for the healthy growth of his afflicted plants. He consistently views the world as a kind of garden enclosure for man: (361–7)

> But when man walks the garden of this world
> For his own solace, and, unchecked by law,
> Speaks or keeps silence as himself sees fit,
> Without the least incumbency to lie,
> – Why, can he tell you what a rose is like,
> Or how t. e birds fly, and not slip to false
> Though t .th serve better?

There is a slight suggestion in these lines that for Innocent the pressing consciousness of human weakness is connected in his mind with man's original fall in the garden of Eden: the 'swerve' toward falsehood is so ingrained in man that he hardly needs a conscious motive for speaking a lie. At another point, he says: (1838–44)

> "We fools dance thro' the cornfield of this life,
> "Pluck ears to left and right and swallow raw,
> "– Nay, tread, at pleasure, a sheaf underfoot,
> "To get the better at some poppy-flower, –
> "Well aware we shall have so much less wheat
> "In the eventual harvest: you meantime
> "Waste not a spike, – the richlier will you reap!"

Focusing on his own role as husbandman and nurturer, the Pope's thoughts turn inevitably back to how soon his task is ended and how small the return he will make to God: can this be all he will take with him, he asks anxiously, 'to show as stewardship's fruit, / The best yield of the latest time' (1533–4)? More hopefully, he hails the dead Pompilia as the one bright flower of his tenure as tiller of otherwise barren ground: (1031–47)

> *Seven years a gardener of the untoward ground,*
> *I till, – this earth, my sweat and blood manure*
> *All the long day that barrenly grows dusk:*
> *At least one blossom makes me proud at eve*
> *Born 'mid the briers of my enclosure! Still*
> *(Oh, here as elsewhere, nothingness of man!)*
> *Those be the plants, imbedded yonder South*
> *To mellow in the morning, those made fat*
> *By the master's eye, that yield such timid leaf,*
> *Uncertain bud, as product of his pains!*
> *While – see how this mere chance-sown cleft-nursed seed*
> *That sprang up by the wayside 'neath the foot*
> *Of the enemy, this breaks all into blaze,*
> *Spreads itself, one wide glory of desire*
> *To incorporate the whole great sun it loves*
> *From the inch-height whence it looks and longs! My flower,*
> *My rose, I gather for the breast of God, ...*

This one passage gathers up all the major motifs of the Pope's soliloquy: his role of gardener (papal responsibility) in the growing dusk of a long day (his age and approaching death), rejoicing at the blaze of the one flower which longs for the sun (Pompilia's recognition of truth) when all hope is dimmed by the *'nothingness of man'* (discouragement at human frailties) and the sense of his own inadequacy (his one blossom, the rose he gathers for God, is, after all, not one he chose and imbedded in the warm sunlight, but a mere *'chance-sown cleft-nursed seed'*). The single new idea introduced here into the soliloquy, of Pompilia as rose, immediately recalls the dominant flower imagery of her earliest defender, Other Half-Rome, who saw her as an abandoned blossom growing into beauty amid alien surroundings. The Pope's figure gains significance from its association with these earlier memorable comparisons as well as from his own strongly developed cluster of images having to do with seeds and nurtured plants, and it prepares the way for another link with Other Half-Rome: the view of Pompilia as saint. Her first defender had called her that, always associating her name with religious terms – miracle, soul, angels, and the like. Now the Pope hails her as *'Armed and crowned'* (1011) in heaven like Michael; without sword or shield, she earned her crown and now her soul, *'earth's flower / She holds up to the softened gaze of God!'* (1018–19).[9]

9/Smith, *Star-Imagery*, notes the imagistic echo of Other Half-Rome in the

These two ideas, of Pompilia's flower-like quality and her angelic innocence, merge in the Pope's monologue to produce another concept, of Pompilia as part of nature, unself-consciously following instinctive promptings within her in the same way as birds of the air and plants of the soil. A sensitive, intuitive responsiveness had been the dominant impression left by her own monologue (as she likened her flight to that of the birds before winter) and Innocent once more reinforces an idea already presented by making it a part of his pervasive garden metaphor: (1072–81)

> ... But, brave,
> Thou at first prompting of what I call God,
> And fools call Nature, didst hear, comprehend,
> Accept the obligation laid on thee,
> Mother elect, to save the unborn child,
> As brute and bird do, reptile and the fly,
> Ay and, I nothing doubt, even tree, shrub, plant
> And flower o' the field, all in a common pact
> To worthily defend the trust of trusts,
> Life from the Ever Living. ...

What happens as a result of this emphasizing of man's role as an essential part of nature, fruitful only when he fulfils the role assigned by God and blighted and barren when he distorts this role, is a kind of "humanizing" of the speaker, and further a significant development of the idea, first set forth in the Caponsacchi-Pompilia monologues, that intuitive knowledge is ultimately superior to that of the rational intellect. Pope Innocent XII may be wise and philosophical, but he is not infallible, and his abstract, theological speculations can never lead him to unswerving truth in the tangled threads of human conduct. He can only approach this kind of truth when he speaks as Antonio Pignatelli, fallible and uncertain, but with an understanding of human motives that springs from a deep-rooted love of his fellow-

Pope's lines, 'Promptings from heaven and hell, as if the stars / Fought in their courses,' which recall the earlier speaker's description of Pompilia's and Caponsacchi's meeting: it 'Blazed as when star and star must needs go close / Till each hurts each' (III, 1058–9), and he states: "Browning has evidently intended to recall the sentimental opinions of The Other Half-Rome, and to review them in the light of the Pope's conception of truth" (p. 207). Actually, this echo is only one of a whole series in the Pope's monologue, the most notable of which are the flower, bird, and saint parallels to characterize Pompilia.

creatures and from the desire to protect and nourish those given to his care. Something of the vigour and depth of his sympathy shows in the terminology he spontaneously uses in speaking of men: terms of the natural processes of nurture and growth, solid images of plants and soil, seeds, branches, trees, and gardens. The Pope must express lofty thoughts in lofty language, he must view the world from a higher plane than other men, but at the same time, the man Pignatelli knows his roots go deep in the same soil as Guido Franceschini's and the *'mass of men'* daily sinking in the mire. And he knows, too, that it has not been the philosophers but the simplest souls, like Pompilia, who have been *'obedient to the end.'* Popes have been wrong – witness their judgments on Formosus – and the unlearned or unreasoning right – witness the intuitive and impulsive acts of Pompilia and Caponsacchi – and the difference is that these last two knew *'love without a limit'* in yielding to the promptings of the heart.

With this concept in mind, Innocent feels that he *'dares'* to decide this case because his motives are *'pure,'* springing from some instinct of good: (1248–52)

> ... *Through hard labour and good will,*
> *And habitude that gives a blind man sight*
> *At the practised finger-ends of him, I do*
> *Discern, and dare decree in consequence,*
> *Whatever prove the peril of mistake.*

The reference to the blind man's *'practised finger-ends'* suggests, besides the skill of experience, a kind of inborn sensitivity or *feel* for the truth, not an exercise of intellectual powers. Never does he imply that the intellect is not to be trusted; only that it is not *enough*. Unaided reason here below can see partial truth, he concludes, but only when it is supplemented by love and self-sacrifice can it see truth in its eternal aspect: (1367–72)

> *What lacks, then, of perfection fit for God*
> *But just the instance which this tale supplies*
> *Of love without a limit? So is strength,*
> *So is intelligence; let love be so,*
> *Unlimited in its self-sacrifice,*
> *Then is the tale true and God shows complete.*

It was love and self-sacrifice that guided Caponsacchi *'straight'*; the Pope returns to the metaphor of the blind man to represent the

Canon's acting by the impulse of the heart, not the direction of the head: (1559–65)

> How does he lay about him in the midst,
> Strike any foe, right wrong at any risk,
> All blindness, bravery and obedience! – blind?
> Ay, as a man would be inside the sun,
> Delirious with the plenitude of light
> Should interfuse him to the finger-ends –
> Let him rush straight, and how shall he go wrong?

Here he identifies the priest's vision of the light with his own – 'Yet my poor spark had for its source, the sun' (1285), he had said earlier – and establishes his emotional and spiritual kinship with the priest, just as he had done with Pompilia by the use of plant imagery.

The long, troubled progress of the monologue, before this final victory for the emotion of love over the demands of reason, is embodied not only in the sombre tone and diction but in the distinctively speculative mode of address. The Pope's manner of speaking is neither narrative nor dramatic nor logically expository. His soliloquy falls into three sections: the first, a review of instances of papal fallibility, second, a judgment on each of the principals in the murder trial, and last, an assessment of the state of Christianity in his own day. Thus, the dominant mood of the first and last sections is one of uncertainty and discouragement, and only in the central passage is the Pope's resolution clearly manifested.

In this central section lies the basis for his decision on Guido's guilt and Pompilia's innocence. Putting aside the trial documents as well as the papal history as useless, he proceeds to call up before the judgment bar of his mind's eye each of the actors in the Franceschini drama and to pass sentence on them individually. He uses phrases which indicate that he can 'see' these figures before him as he speaks, as in: 'I sit and see / Another poor weak trembling human wretch' (170–1). On Guido's formative years, he says: 'I see him furnished forth for his career' (400); then, 'I see a trial fair and fit / For one else too unfairly fenced about' (427–8). After Guido come the Franceschini family and the hired assassins; picturing them all as a huddled mass in the dark of a cave, he says, 'I detect each shape' (875), with special note of the youngest brother Girolamo: 'For there's a new distinctive touch, I see' (906). As this group passes from view, he is conscious of still other dim shapes: 'Nay, more i' the background yet? Unnoticed forms ... ?' (965). These are the Governor and the Archbishop who spurned Pompilia's pleas for help. He calls on her next to appear as she was on earth: (1009–11)

> *Let me look at thee in the flesh as erst,*
> *Let me enjoy the old clean linen garb,*
> *Not the new splendid vesture!*

Caponsacchi, too, he pictures in his imagination, as a kind of athlete-warrior in the act of a *'Great undisguised leap over post and pale / Right into the mid-cirque, free fighting-place'* (1142–3) to save the helpless Pompilia. The Comparini appear next and he admonishes them to *'hide'* until a *'gracious eye'* may find them (1216–17), since neither is all good or all bad. When the last of the figures has faded from view, he sums up the process thus: *'So do I see, pronounce on all and some / Grouped for my judgment now'* (1239–40). No question remains in his mind about their respective guilt and innocence (this whole passage, like the rest of the monologue, reveals no new facts at all, but is composed entirely of opinions); the Franceschini and henchmen he pronounces wholly wrong, the Comparini partly so, and Caponsacchi and Pompilia wholly innocent. In a following passage, he adds severe judgments on the hypocritical Churchmen and the Convertites of Rome who turned on Pompilia for money, and he commends the noble Greeks who followed the path of virtue without the light of faith.

This peculiar procedure of passing summary judgment on a visible but silent parade of witnesses is what gives the Pope such an air of wisdom and lofty detachment in this passage. The effect is enhanced by the frequent interpolation of exclamations and reminders to himself to observe all; *'I remark'* (532), *'(note the point!)'* (599), *' – see!'* (658), *'I note how'* (802), he will comment, demonstrating a painstaking determination to let nothing of importance escape his vigilant eye. Perhaps the most significant effect of the *'I see'* mode of discourse, however, is the evidence of how penetrating is the Pope's insight into human motives. Here he has abandoned the inadequate trappings of law and logic to look directly into the hearts of men; he "sees" all in a flash of light, as it were, without benefit of argumentation or reflection.

This exhibition of firmness in judgment sets off by contrast the passages preceding and following, where the Pope's resolution falters as the awareness of his own human fallibility becomes more acute and the consequent mood of weariness and uncertainty dominates. In these passages, every statement of resolve to condemn Guido is followed by a new expression of doubt. The assertion, *'So do I see, pronounce on all'* and *'profess no doubt / While I pronounce'* (1239–41), is followed almost immediately by the fearful admission of a *'quite new quick cold thrill'* of doubt (1253), and so throughout, in an irregular fluctuation of emotion that forms a counterpart pattern to the alternating dark–light imagery.

The over-all effect of the Pope's monologue is, consequently, not one of serenity or detachment as has so often been suggested by critics, but rather one of passionate involvement and soul-searing struggle. That a man, prompted by no other motive than desire to see justice and God's will done, should find passing sentence on his fellow-creature such a tortuous and uncertain procedure throws into bold relief the inadequacy of human reason to analyse truth in the affairs of men. Though his selflessness and human sympathy eventually guide him to the right decision, Pope Innocent xii, far from being an omniscient and dispassionate judge, is simply one more in the circle of questioning and limited observers of human conduct.[10] His conclusions, although imparted in language more philosophical and exalted than that of any other speaker, make him one of a group, composed of Other Half-Rome, Pompilia, and Caponsacchi, who approach truth through an emotional, intuitive response to good, and they similarly set him apart from the cold, casuistical, and distorted rationality of Tertium Quid, the two lawyers, and Guido Franceschini.

10/Although the Pope has generally been held to be Browning's "spokesman" in the poem, it is clear from the plan of *The Ring and the Book* that his view of truth is not to be taken as synonymous with the poet's as expressed in Book 1. Since both come to virtually the same conclusions regarding the guilt and innocence of the actors in the drama, Browning apparently intended to show the main difference as lying in their *method* of arriving at these conclusions; hence, the wavering, troubled progress of Innocent's speech, the stress on its painful evolving of truth in contrast to the poet's excited, instant apprehension of it. Hence also Browning's explicit insistence on the Pope's fallibility – he has no special *'lynx-gift in each ordinary orb'*; and the history of Formosus merely proves how often his predecessors in the papacy have been wrong. That Browning was opposed to the whole idea of Papal Infallibility (declared a doctrine of the Roman Catholic Church in 1870 and much discussed in the preceding decade when he was working on *The Ring and the Book*) is clear from his scornful references to it in letters. (He speaks, for example, of "the Spiritual Head" in Rome excogitating dogmas "to all eternity ... poor old 'infallibility.'" *Letters of Robert Browning Collected by Thomas J. Wise*, ed. Thurman L. Hood (1933)). The Pope is wise, but uncertain; to Browning, clearly only the poet can claim infallibility in judging the affairs of men.

Chapter V

The Two Guidos

I

As NOTED IN chapter III, the first appearance of Guido Franceschini comes after the three speeches by the representatives of public opinion in Rome. The second comes much later, after Caponsacchi, Pompilia, and the lawyers have all voiced their views and the Pope has rendered his final judgment. However, because Guido is the only actor in the drama to speak twice, an examination of the two speeches consecutively is both convenient and helpful in shedding light on important aspects of Browning's dramatic method.

Count Guido Franceschini is a Tuscan nobleman of ancient lineage, son of Countess Beatrice and brother of the Abate Paolo and Canon Girolamo. He has received *three or four* minor orders in the Church himself but, despairing of advancement after thirty fruitless years, has contracted marriage to the youthful Pompilia, adopted daughter of the Comparini, and he now in his first appearance stands on trial for his life, accused of the brutal murder of his wife and her parents. He has been subjected to the torture of the Vigil and comes to address the judges in his own behalf while still suffering the after-effects, but this defence is a brilliantly conceived and presented appeal for sympathy and clemency. His speech reveals a combination of deference and boldness, of apparent candour and wily evasiveness, of passionate feeling and cold intellectuality, as he frankly admits his guilt and proceeds to explain what he thinks are the extenuating circumstances which should spare his life and restore his liberty.

The time of the speech is apparently January 5, the same day as Tertium Quid's monologue,[1] and the place a small antechamber off the courtroom – the same place, the speaker notes, in which he testified only eight months before in the trial of his wife and Canon Caponsacchi for their flight from his home in Arezzo. The audience is composed of the same three judges who heard the earlier case and who are now engaged in taking evidence to be used in the trial proper which begins in a few days. No nuance of the effect his words produce on the three men is lost on the speaker, as he addresses them from a seated position, necessitated, he says, by the effects of his rigorous treatment. *'And never once does he detach his eye / From those ranged there to slay him or to save,'* as the poet had said (I, 975–6). He calls them by their titles or uses some other form of respect, sometimes singling out one, sometimes another, usually addressing all three at once. He uses the form *'Sir'* (or *'Sirs'*) fourteen times in all, *'my lords'* (or *'my sweet lords'*) seventeen times, and various other epithets (*'you of the court,' 'my masters'*) at least a half-dozen times. These frequent vocatives are so spaced throughout the more than 2000-line speech that at no time is the audience's attention allowed to flag; contact is constantly maintained by the attention-controlling forms of address. The entire monologue is a direct address, devoid of digressions, asides, or personal reflective passages. Occasional oblique references to the out-of-court activity of individual judges are not in the nature of digressions, but rather a device for capturing their interest and flattering their vanity, as in:

> *So, my lord opposite has composed, we know,*
> *A marvel of a book, sustains the point*
> *That Francis boasts the primacy 'mid saints;*
> *Yet not inaptly hath his argument*

1/Guido makes no mention of the previous speeches and at one point says that four days have passed *'Since this adventure'* (1683). He seems to imply at times that Pompilia is already dead (109, 936) but his one clearly literal statement on the subject establishes that she is still living at the moment he speaks: *'But my wife is still alive, / Has breath enough to tell her story yet'* (1687–8). All references in this section of the chapter are to Book v unless otherwise indicated.

Obtained response from yon my other lord
In thesis published with the world's applause
– Rather 'tis Dominic such post befits: ... (147–53)

These personal allusions and the regular recurrence of the second
person grammatical forms "you" and "yours," in close conjunction
with the dominant first person references, point up the fact that this
speech does not constitute a narrative at all, but is rather intended as
a personal appeal by the accused to those in authority. Guido does
not, for instance, speak of the force of the law as an impersonal
agent; he says, *'You came on me that night, / Your officers of justice,*
– caught the crime' (1670–1). That the judges respond with close
attention to the directness of the appeal can be seen in their reactions
as the Count notes them: *'Now, – I see my lords / Shift in their seat'*
(1374–5), he says, after scoring with a telling point. Commenting on
the *'few days'* since the murder, he acknowledges their correction:
'Do you tell me, four?' (1683). Alert to every opportunity for keeping the interplay between his audience and himself alive, he asks if
Caponsacchi has been sent for and is told the Canon is not at hand
yet, having had so far to come. In other remarks, he anticipates a
response or imputes agreement for the benefit of his argument: *'The*
wife, you allow so far I have not wronged' (1869); claiming that the
court found the Canon and Pompilia guilty after their flight, he over-
rules an objection – *'Not guilty? Why then did you punish them?'*
(1898) – and then proceeds as though the tribunal had agreed with
his judgment: *'You righted me, I think? / Well then, – what if I, at*
this last of all, / Demonstrate you ... ?' (1943–5). This procedure
effectively diminishes the distance between judges and accused,
raises the Count to a level of equality with his questioners, and
establishes a subtle bond of sympathy between them.

So involved is Count Guido in his delicate task of persuading his
audience, so totally committed to the desperate cause of pleading his
life and freedom, that in his speech no effective third person presence
can be detected. He is aware that Pompilia still lives – he mentions
with some bitterness how she is even now still clinging to life[2] – but
her condition is a source of annoyance rather than concern to him,
since she must die in a short time anyway and her weak testimony
can easily be overshadowed by his expert argumentation. Even his
ostensible rival Caponsacchi is of little interest to him; he refers to
him with surprising infrequency and then in comparatively mild

2/See n. 1 above.

language (1049–56, 1978–82). He directs sharper words at Pompilia's behaviour in their life together at Arezzo: he should have cut off a joint of her finger, he says, when he first discovered her attentions had begun to stray. He adds almost as an afterthought, perhaps metaphorically, that he believed some of his stabs were in Caponsacchi's heart or he might not have been so lavish with them: '*less had served*' (1693). But, on the whole, neither of the principal antagonists in his drama affects his thinking as he speaks; they are merely peripheral figures now in the deadly duel with the judges in which he is locked.

By the last part of his speech his new-born son Gaetano seems to have taken a dominant role in his consciousness, but a curious inconsistency develops in his attitude toward the child. He wavers between expressions of a father's love for his '*first-born child*' (1519) and a denial that the boy is his own. He describes the torment of doubt and rage that engulfed him on hearing the news of the child's birth, and then talks of the tortuous thought that his son will be bred by those most hateful to the Franceschini. And he finally pictures himself, in some hopeful brighter day, telling the whole story of the murder and trial to his son, who will honour him for the role he played. The contradictory nature of the references to Gaetano suggest that for Guido the boy constitutes an argument to be wielded for the defence rather than any strong influence in his own right, and that at this crucial moment no one enters Guido's consciousness meaningfully except the judges to whom he is speaking.

He makes his motive for speaking quite clear. He has not come to deny the murder, only to explain it. The frank admission of his crime makes an arresting introduction to his defence: (109–15)

> *I killed Pompilia Franceschini, Sirs,*
> *Killed too the Comparini, husband, wife,*
> *Who called themselves, by a notorious lie,*
> *Her father and her mother to ruin me.*
> *There's the irregular deed: you want no more*
> *Than right interpretation of the same,*
> *And truth so far – am I to understand?*

He is anxious to live. The desire to die that overwhelmed him after the shame of the earlier trial has given way to a new hope now that the killing has restored his honour: '*I find the instinct bids me save my life*' (1742). When he fears he may have been too daring in his illustration of the injury done him, he inserts a deprecatory parenthetical remark – '(*save* / *The ears o' the Court! I try to save my head*)' – as an excuse (758–9). '*I want my head* / *To save my neck*' (7–8), he admits at the outset, and again, '*I need that life*' (2011). The explicit admission of his motive for speaking helps to strengthen the appearance of disarming candour and co-operative friendliness already established by his intimate address to the court.

A further element in his motivation, not so frankly expressed, is the intent to play upon the sympathy of his hearers and to sway their judgment by appeals to emotion rather than to reason or justice. This element accounts for a certain wariness in answering some questions, notably those concerned with the authenticity of the love letters alleged to have passed between Pompilia and Caponsacchi, a wariness which may escape the judges but which is apparent to the reader who has heard all the previous speakers emphasize the "true" facts about the disputed letters. Guido acknowledges that it is a commonly held suspicion that he himself penned the notes and, although never admitting that he did, he allows the possibility merely for the sake of argument: '*Mine and not hers the letter, – conceded, lords! / Impute to me that practice! – take as proved ...* ' (852–3), but even then, he asks, who could blame him? Later, however, when describing the encounter at the inn, he states the finding of the letters as a fact: '*We searched the chamber where they passed the night, / Found what confirmed the worst was feared before*' (1133–4), the '*Love-laden*' missives.

Another passage where apparent frankness appears more like evasiveness on closer scrutiny is that where Guido describes his journey to Rome on the fateful errand. All is haste, confusion, obscured by clouds of passion: (1567–81)

> *And out we flung and on we ran or reeled*
> *Romeward. I have no memory of our way,*
> *Only that, when at intervals the cloud*
> *Of horror about me opened to let in life,*
> *I listened to some song in the ear, some snatch*
> *Of a legend, relic of religion, ...*
> *Then the cloud re-encompassed me, and so*
> *I found myself, as on the wings of winds,*
> *Arrived: I was at Rome on Christmas Eve.*

In the actual moment of the killing, he was '*rapt away by the impulse*,' '*mad*,' '*blind*' (1662–8); only after it was done was he himself again, restored to health and sanity: (1707–12)

> *I am myself and whole now: I prove cured*
> *By the eyes that see, the ears that hear again,*
> *The limbs that have relearned their youthful play,*
> *The healthy taste of food and feel of clothes*
> *And taking to our common life once more,*
> *All that now urges my defence from death.*

This rendering of his state of mind in the moment of the murder as confused and cloudy not only eliminates the need to set forth any details of the savage attack, and denies the allegation of malice aforethought, but also serves to emphasize the abnormality of his situation prior to the murder and the beneficial results that followed the deed: the cleansing and purging of the sore of dishonour, the restoring of health, order, and justice to a disordered society. So strong is his insistence on the advantages flowing from his act of violence that he claims finally, in contradiction to the anxiety he has been professing, to be indifferent to the outcome of the trial: *'The trial is no concern of mine; with me / The main of the care is over'* (1699–1700). He then proceeds to the next bold stroke of his defence, the assertion that in committing this act of retribution he was only accomplishing what the court had intended in its original decree: (1987–9)

> *Will you not thank, praise, bid me to your breasts*
> *For having done the thing you thought to do,*
> *And thoroughly trampled out sin's life at last?*

He has only, he continues, *'Blackened again, made legible once more / Your own decree, not permanently writ,'* and he concludes ringingly: *'Absolve, then, me, law's mere executant! / Protect your own defender, – save me, Sirs!'* (1997–2004).

The tension which in other speeches resulted from the relationship of the speaker to the third person of the monologue here is rather generated by the conflict in Guido between the necessity to win over the judges through an appeal to their sense of pity and their vanity and, on the other hand, the urge to assail them bitterly for their cowardly earlier decision which solved nothing and only aggravated the situation. At times this bitterness cuts through the veneer of frank good nature in those *'Incisive, nigh satiric'* phrases that bite *'Rough-raw, yet somehow claiming privilege,'* as the poet had described them (I, 965–6). *'Read it, lords,'* he cries, as he cites the bland sentence handed down earlier against Pompilia by a court once noted for the fierceness of its penalties. *'You mete out punishment such and such,'* for minor misdemeanours, he concludes sardonically, *'yet so / Punish the adultery of wife and priest!'* (1226–37). Indirectly, he accuses them of succumbing to the popular cry, of making *'common cause / With the cleric section'* in favouring Caponsacchi over himself, and warns them that posterity may *'blast'* them (1853–61). Daring as these verbal assaults are, they serve to relieve the burning sense of injury that consumes him and at the same time put the judges on the defensive. He can then provide an escape for them by establishing the position that his action was merely an attempt to help them right their original wrong, so that now they need only acknowledge his innocence to vindicate themselves. His argument that he is the *'law's mere executant'* thus serves as a two-edged sword, at once implicating the court while justifying himself.

The tension makes the tone by turns conciliatory and bitter, defensive and accusing. This combination of conflicting attitudes is carefully controlled by Guido's rhetorical skill so that passionate feeling never becomes unrestrained ranting; the attack stops just short of invective, is always counteracted immediately by the respectful salutations, the deprecatory remarks – *'(save / The ears o' the Court! I try to save my head)'* – or by flattering personal allusions to the judges. For the most part the Count deftly balances the easy familiarity of the aristocrat addressing his equals against the deference of the prisoner before the bar. For example, of the bargain between himself and the Comparini he says smoothly: (484–8)

> *They straight grew bilious, wished their money back,*
> *Repented them, no doubt: why, so did I,*
> *So did your Lordship, if town-talk be true,*
> *Of paying a full farm's worth for that piece*
> *By Pietro of Cortona –*

making the analogy between his case and that of the judge pointed but inoffensive, with its implication that the latter can be counted on to understand the accused's situation and sympathize with it, just as he, Count Guido, knows and sympathizes with the judge's chagrin at being caught in a bad bargain.

This meticulously maintained balance of expression marks the whole speech as an exercise in persuasion rather than a forthright explanation or revelation of a state of mind. It is significant that Guido describes his *'irregular deed'* with an expression of the rhetorician: *'I have heightened phrase to make your soft speech serve'*

(1990), meaning that his radical action was only the implementation of their too-cautious decree. Rhetorical argument is his basic mode of address. He declares from the beginning that his own eloquence is all that remains to him as a weapon and he will use it with all the skill at his command, as in this reference to the long list of injuries he might enumerate: (77–82)

> But I curtail the catalogue
> Through policy, – a rhetorician's trick, –
> Because I would reserve some choicer points
> O' the practice, more exactly parallel
> (Having an eye to climax) with what gift,
> Eventual grace the Court may have in store. ...

He thus deliberately draws his hearers' attention to his knowledge of the art of effective speech, in a show of confidence and candour. The implication is that he will not flatter himself that he can delude such a knowing and experienced audience, but will lay all his cards on the table immediately, so to speak. The modest comparison of his own testimony to the forthcoming speech of Caponsacchi – the priest's will be *'florid prose / As smooth as mine is rough'* (1694–5) – is not meant to deceive the court.

The entire speech follows the classical oration in outline. Lines 1–120 form an exordium, with the establishment of the speaker's background and situation, the arousal of interest and sympathy, and the introduction of the proposition. The narration follows (121–1738), with the detailed delineation of events leading up to the murder and arguments explaining these events. Some of the devices Guido uses for presenting these arguments include illustration by concrete visualized experience, analogy, syllogism, rhetorical question, and *reductio ad absurdum*. The refutation follows (1739–1939) and includes *argumentum ad hominem* and the device of begging the question. Finally comes the peroration (1940–2058) in which all the arguments are summed up in a logical appeal to precedence and authority, culminating in a powerful emotional plea for life and liberty.

The oratorical effect of the speech, resulting not only from its general structure but from the contact early established and assiduously maintained between speaker and audience by the frequent vocatives and personal allusions, is further enhanced by the regular recurrence of certain key words and themes which act as another device for controlling the audience's response. The location and frequency of these references set them apart from similar recurring words in earlier speeches which might be taken as indicating unconscious self-revelation or an innate habit of mind (as with Half-Rome's *'angler'* and Tertium Quid's *'mob'*); in Guido's monologue they are always coupled with a direct address to the court or a remark or gesture intended to draw attention to them. These repeated ideas fall into two main themes on which the entire defence rests: one is a bid for the court's sympathy, the other, a claim of privilege. The first of these themes takes the form of references, primarily, to the physical torture which Guido has undergone and, secondarily, to his mental sufferings, his poverty, and his material disappointments. The claim of privilege consists in allusions to the nobility of the Franceschini family, its honourable history, and its ecclesiastical connections. A measure of Guido's rhetorical brilliance is the way he eventually manœuvres his defence to the point where both of these arguments merge in one incisive attack on the court which has exceeded its prerogatives in applying torture to a noble.

The first 120 lines are solely concerned with these two appeals, weaving them smoothly together: the apologies for his condition after coming so soon from the vigil, the assertions that his family's suffering constitutes far worse pain, the assurance that such torment was hardly necessary for one so anxious to tell the truth. From this point on, allusions to his *'nobility'* and *'rank'* abound, usually with relation to his father's position and the illustrious history of the family line, summed up as *'all that hangs to Franceschinihood'* (437). He speaks of his *'good name'* (31), the *'poor old noble House'* (39), the *'great line'* (140); he points with scorn to the court physician – *'My father's lacquey's son we sent to school'* (299) – and the *'father's chaplain's nephew, Chamberlain'* (309) who ignores him now. He likens himself to the Franceschini who fell in battle against the Paynims. Whenever he refers to himself it is by family name or title: *'Count Guido Franceschini had hit the mark / Far better'* (456–7); *'I am Guido Franceschini, am I not?'* (1790). He even quotes Abate Paolo as referring to him by title: ' *"Count Guido and brother of mine"* ' (399); ' *"Count you are counted"* ' (406).[3]

At the same time that he plays on this theme, with its calculated attempt to impress and perhaps intimidate the judges, he misses no opportunity to return to his original emphasis on the physical torment inflicted by the court authorities prior to his court appearance. After the initial extended commentary on the inappropriateness of

3/See also 188, 225, 350–5, 419, 439, 515–16.

the use of the *'Vigil-torment,'* he reverts at least ten times in the course of his defence to the effects of the torture-irons, noting that he is unable to stand, that his arm and shoulder pain him, that he will be permanently disabled. All the while he ostentatiously minimizes his bitterness at the use of such methods on such a one as he: *' 'Tis my wrist you merely dislocate'* (65); *'Humbly I helped the Church till here I stand, – / Or would stand but for the omoplat, you see!'* (247–8); *'I shall sleep now, / Spite of my shoulder'* (1679–80).[4] Most effectively, he climaxes his emotional plea with the picture of the son one day stooping to kiss his father's hand and starting to see the traces of the torture-iron still there. *' "That was an accident," '* the vindicated Count will be able to say generously, *' "Hardly misfortune, and no fault at all" '* (2055–8). Here he smoothly juxtaposes veiled criticism of the law's inquisitorial methods against the engaging picture of familial affection and restored honour, concluding the whole on a note of confidence and magnanimity.

By constantly stressing the physical pain he has suffered, Count Guido makes all the more impressive the description of his mental anguish. He repeats the idea, for instance, that the court's torture was almost a relief from the terrible torment that Pompilia and the Comparini have caused him: (23–30)

> *This getting tortured merely in the flesh,*
> *Amounts to almost an agreeable change*
> *In my case, me fastidious, plied too much*
> *With opposite treatment, used (forgive the joke)*
> *To the rasp-tooth toying with this brain of mine,*
> *And, in and out my heart, the play o' the probe.*
> *Four years have I been operated on*
> *I' the soul, do you see. ...*

Later, subtly making the assumption that the court already regrets its harsh treatment, he exclaims: *'Apologize for the pincers, palliate screws? / Ply me with such toy-trifles, I entreat!'* (1275–6), implying that their practised methods are as nothing compared to what he has been suffering. And he underscores this idea by repeating that only the *'irregular'* but honourable killing of his tormentors restored him to his present peace of mind, just as a lance must be wielded boldly to draw out the poison.

The word *'poison,'* recalling Half-Rome's frequent use of it, is second in prominence only to the word *'torture'* in the Count's

4/See also 16–17, 75, 118–20, 845, 924–5, 1166–7.

vocabulary of sympathy-evoking terms. He uses it, just as his earlier defender had done, in both a literal and a figurative sense, always connecting it with the Comparini's mistreatment of him. He describes himself on the morning after Pompilia's flight: '*Well, this way I was shaken wide awake, / Doctored and drenched, somewhat unpoisoned so'* (1037–8), having to fight off the effects of her drug potion. '*Poison-torture*' (1042) he calls the feeling with which he began the pursuit. In a metaphorical usage, he vividly describes how continued injuries turned the wine of his cup of life bitter and poisonous; Half-Rome's use of the term '*drop*' to suggest slow torture – '*on Guido's wound / Ever in due succession, drop by drop, / Came slow distilment*' (II, 1267–9) – is called irresistibly to mind by these words: (879–81)

> Yes, this next cup of bitterness, my lords,
> Had to begin go filling, drop by drop,
> Its measure up of full disgust for me,

by which Guido pictures the discovery of Pompilia's deceit. This torture goes on, he continues passionately: (903–7)

> Till one day, what is it knocks at my clenched teeth
> But the cup full, curse-collected all for me?
> And I must needs drink, drink this gallant's praise,
> That minion's prayer, the other fop's reproach,
> And come at the dregs to – Caponsacchi!

He describes his bleak return home after the final humiliation of the inn encounter, how he '*ate the coarse bread, drank the wine / Weak once, now acrid with the toad's-head-squeeze*' (1388–9), his wife's bestowment – echoing Half-Rome's characterization of Pompilia as a poisonous serpent or toad. Guido himself caps his tale by calling Pompilia a '*reptile*': (1958–65)

> There was the reptile, that feigned death at first,
> Renewing its detested spire and spire
> Around me, rising to such heights of hate
> That, so far from mere purpose now to crush
> And coil itself on the remains of me,
> Body and mind, and there flesh fang content,
> Its aim is now to evoke life from death,
> Make me anew, ...

Violante, too, is a poisonous snake; when the door of the villa opened that fateful night, the sight of her drove him mad: '*I had stumbled, first thing, on the serpent's head / Coiled with a leer*' (1659–60). Now, after the murder, he can sleep again, his soul '*safe from the serpents*' (1678).[5]

The combined impact of the torture and poison references in Guido's speech is thus strengthened for the reader by recollections of the earlier speaker's use of them to arouse sympathy for the tormented husband; for the audience in the court-chamber, which has not heard Half-Rome's speech, the impact comes largely from the stress which Guido puts on the dubious legality of applying the Vigil-torture to one of his rank. By uniting these two ideas in one passage, the injustice of the court's punishment and the aggravation of the stained family honour caused by this court's mistreatment, he achieves an effect of deep pathos, as in the passage where he figuratively depicts the gradual unfolding of the details of Pompilia's flight: (1030–4)

> Bit by bit thus made-up mosaic-wise,
> Flat lay my fortune, – tessellated floor,
> Imperishable tracery devils should foot
> And frolic it on, around my broken gods,
> Over my desecrated hearth.

He strikes a similar note in a final moving appeal for the restoration of his son to him: (2029–34)

> Let me lift up his youth and innocence
> To purify my palace, room by room
> Purged of the memories, lend from his bright brow
> Light to the old proud paladin my sire
> Shrunk now for shame into the darkest shade
> O' the tapestry, showed him once and shrouds him now!

Frequent religious and biblical allusions also contribute to the aura of respectability and virtue. In the course of the monologue Guido mentions St. Peter, Lazarus, St. Francis, St. Dominic, St. Paul, Lucifer, Rachel and Leah, Solomon, the Holy Infant, Christ, the Trinity, and the Cross. He makes innumerable references to God, usually calling upon Him to witness the justice of his act or attributing it to divine inspiration: '*I did / God's bidding and man's duty*'

5/Other terms he applies to Pompilia and the Comparini for a similar effect are '*toad,*' '*cockatrice,*' '*worm,*' '*vermin,*' and '*asp.*' See 636, 657, 1485, 1537–41, 1666–8.

(1702–03); the triple killing was 'God's decree, / In which I, bowing bruised head, acquiesce' (1417–18), he asserts. He uses invocations and prayers liberally: 'I' the name of the indivisible Trinity!' (121); 'I pray God that I think aright!' (1637).[6] He quotes Scripture to his purpose, using the biblical injunction that a woman shall leave father and mother and cleave to her husband as an argument against Pompilia's flight, assuring the judges that they 'have chosen the happier part with Paul / And neither marry nor burn' (723–4), comparing his anticipated restoration by the law to that of Lazarus raised from the dead, and sarcastically likening Caponsacchi to the provident shepherd who leaves the flock to follow the stray lamb. Clerical figures likewise fill his illustrations and analogies: the priest, the monk, the deacon, the bishop, the cardinal. Even his boasts of Franceschini heritage are linked to the Church; he reminds his hearers of his last patron, a cardinal, of the ancestor who became a pope, of another who fell in the Crusades, of his descent from the Guido once Homager to the Empire, and of his family's present poverty which stems from generations of generous giving to the Church. He implies a comparison of himself with St. Peter who 'took the efficacious way' (969): better had he treated his wife from the first with the impulsiveness that caused Peter to cut off Malchus' ear.

Only one element in the speech militates seriously against the sustained tone of injured righteousness. The figure which Guido uses at one point to describe Pompilia – the hawk – strikes a false note by its obvious unsuitability. He says that his wife was 'no pigeon' but 'a hawk, / I bought at a hawk's price and carried home / To do hawk's service' (701–5); he bought her as he would any falcon, to 'hoodwink, starve and properly train' and, if necessary, to 'twist her neck!' (709–10). He cannot be blamed, he insists, for not treating her as gently as his finch. The juxtaposing of the gentle finch with the fierce hawk underscores the incongruity of linking the helpless girl-wife to the untamed bird of prey. She who has been compared by other speakers to the finch, the dove, and the martin – even the vitriolic Half-Rome saw her only as a harmless insect – cannot now be accepted as fierce and predatory. Even the invidious serpent image of Guido's, with its suggestion of stealth and poison, does not have the striking inaptness of the hawk figure. Guido himself later, in complete contradiction, speaks of Pompilia as 'the tender thing / Who once was good and pure, was once my lamb / And lay in my bosom' (1638–40). At another point, he links her with a song-bird,

6/See also 1464, 1542, 1586, 2009, 2045, 2051.

and the description, despite a context similar to that of the hawk image, strikes the mind as more apposite: (604–6)

> With a wife I look to find all wifeliness,
> As when I buy, timber and twig, a tree –
> I buy the song o' the nightingale inside.

Although some of his crudest language is directed at Pompilia's person – 'that thief, poisoner and adulteress' (1975) he calls her, for example – such epithets are in the nature of direct attack in the heat of emotion, whereas the hawk comparison, not calculated to arouse pity or admiration for himself, seems to reveal him in a role directly opposed to the one he has been assuming. It implies his position as master and lord, the callously tormenting, not the tormented: (748–51)

> Put case that I mishandle, flurry and fright
> My hawk through clumsiness in sportsmanship,
> Twitch out five pens where plucking one would serve –
> What, shall she bite and claw to mend the case?

The streak of brutality that flashes out in these lines is a new note; emphasis on a husband's proprietary rights over his wife is not unexpected – such an attitude appears matter-of-fact and natural, for example, in the "bought nightingale" metaphor above – but the insistence on his right to exercise deliberate cruelty is. In spatial terms, the hawk image is not the most important in Count Guido's speech (he does not revert to it as he does to the serpent figure, for instance) but it stands out so conspicuously just because its obvious discordance calls attention to itself, so that it seems to take on the quality of a sudden, illuminating revelation of an otherwise hidden side of the speaker's personality.[7]

Despite his apparent candour, Guido reveals few new facts. He admits to deliberately misleading Pietro and Violante about the extent of his wealth, but passes this off as 'A flourish round the figures of a sum / For fashion's sake, that deceives nobody' (498–9). He does nothing to clear up the controverted question of the love

---

7/Park Honan, Browning's Characters: A Study in Poetic Technique (1961), arrives at this same conclusion by a somewhat different route. He analyses in detail the hawk passage to show how Guido's "negative rhetoric," a series of technical elements such as alliteration, syntax, phonetics, rhythm, and diction, makes it a "false image," since "We are led to feel that 'hawk' and 'Pompilia' have no natural or self-evident relationship with one another" (p. 302 n.).

letters, evading the question of their forgery, but he claims to have himself found some letters at the inn. He elaborates on the reasons for the delay in executing his murder plan, attributing it to a religious impulse, born of the sound of bells on Christmas Eve.

The significant opinions he reveals, besides those concerning his own justification, deal mainly with his conception of the relationship between Pompilia and himself. As the lines of the hawk image, quoted above, indicate, in their brief married life he regarded her without affection or interest and was more disturbed that the flight involved an invasion of his proprietary rights than that it meant the end of their life together. Other than to make this point, explicitly and repeatedly, that Pompilia's escape from him required an act of revenge to expunge the stain on the Franceschini honour, he shows surprisingly little personal feeling toward her, the Comparini, or even Caponsacchi. His rage toward the latter he frankly ascribes to injured pride in the face of neighbours' scorn and not to jealousy or fear. His final summation reveals a serene confidence, real or assumed, in his ultimate vindication, strengthening an already impressive defence. The emphatic conclusion serves to increase further the interest in the two monologues to follow, those of the two people most intimately involved in his story, Caponsacchi and Pompilia.

II

Since Guido is the only speaker in *The Ring and the Book* to have more than one monologue, his second speech might be expected to reveal a hitherto concealed side of his personality. The poet indicates this change in Book I where he speaks of the second appearance as that of *'the same man, another voice'* (I, 1285). The titles of the two monologues also point up the difference: the first is *'Count Guido Franceschini,'* because title and family name are significant elements in the defence; the second is simply *'Guido,'* because for the condemned man neither position nor connections matter any more. The second Guido has many of the same characteristics as the earlier one – he is bold, defiant, wily, persuasive, desperate – but his voice is rougher, sharper, his words less calculated. This time he foregoes the elaborate justification for his deed and instead makes an outright appeal for release on the grounds that he has only done what was heretofore accepted by a hypocritical society which now wants to make him a scapegoat. He flatly rejects his visitors' pleas for repentance. He reveals himself as having feigned Christian belief for his own ends and fiercely accuses his listeners of leading him astray and then betraying him.

His speech follows within hours of Pope Innocent's rejection of the last appeal. It is early in the morning of February 22, dawn has not yet broken, and the prisoner has just been awakened in his cell in the New Prison with the news that he must die at sunset. Two Churchmen come to stay with him on this last day; they are sent by the Pope to hear his confession, absolve him, and reconcile him to his fate. One is the Cardinal Acciaiuoli, the patron and family friend Guido had spoken of before the court, the other Abate Panciatichi, a friend of Guido's youth. Despite their mission, however, both have little or nothing to say in the hours they crouch on a bench opposite the condemned man and listen awestruck as he pours forth a steady stream of vituperation and bitterness – until the sounds of the approaching Brotherhood of Death are heard on the stair outside.

At no point in his long harangue is Guido unaware of his visitors' presence, in spite of their silence and his preoccupation with his wrongs; he addresses them by name or title with extraordinary frequency, the Cardinal some twenty-one times, the Abate fifteen, and both of them together as 'Sirs' or 'Friends' another twenty times. The frequency of these vocatives far exceeds even his habit in his other speech in which he had sought the court's attention so determinedly, and gives a clue to the extent of his desperation. It suggests that perhaps a faint light of hope still flickers in him that he can exert his old rhetorical skill to win a reprieve yet. His acute awareness of their horrified reaction to his outbursts indicates that he still measures the effects of his words, possibly even finds a certain satisfaction in shocking his visitors. 'Don't fidget, Cardinal!'[8] he exclaims, or 'Contort your brows! You know I speak the truth' (695), and 'Grind your teeth, Cardinal: Abate, writhe!' (943). Apparently their silence is due to their shock at the torrent of words which Guido pours out on them; 'Be tacit as your bench, then!' he orders them, 'Use your ears, / I use my tongue' (137–8). But even when he stops for a time, apparently exhausted, they say nothing, perhaps praying silently. Guido admonishes them: 'Come, I am tired of silence! Pause enough! / You have prayed: I have gone inside my soul' (2290–1). At least twice they try to put the crucifix to his lips but he rebuffs them fiercely: 'Cardinal, take away your crucifix! / Abate, leave my lips alone, – they bite!' (2221–2); 'take / Your crucifix away, I tell you twice!' (2288–9).

8/Line 553. All references in this section of the chapter are to Book xi unless otherwise indicated.

Guido's attitude toward these two visitors is confused and contradictory. He often inserts a cajoling plea in the midst of his
denunciations of them, swinging wildly from despair to hope, from
insult to flattery, for brief fitful periods. Always in the background
as he speaks is the shadow of the mannaia, the dread engine which
faces him at day's end, and the awareness of it is so acute that the
machine becomes for him a kind of third person, an inescapable
presence not to be conjured away by argument, threat, or bribe. He
never strays far from it in his discourse. He has seen it – once many
years ago on an evening walk in an out-of-the-way part of Rome –
and he hates it, and he will make his hearers see it, too. The man-
mutilating engine was painted red and stood on a twelve-foot square
of scaffold, railed about; it had a *'half-moon'* iron plate fitted into
its other half to complete a *'neck's embrace'* (228–9). Guido then
describes the hideous details of the execution procedure with a kind
of horrified fascination: the sound of the cleaving blade, the sight of
the pitcher and the *'unnamed utensil'* standing by to keep the blood
from leaving its mark on the stand. He recalls how the lovely crescent
moon of that May evening – *'no half-moon of red plank'* (251) –
appeared between the bars of the engine, and how he shuddered to
see it framed by that machine he *'Understood, hated, hurried from
before, / To have it out of sight'* (255–6) and cleanse his soul.

Time and again after this he returns to the dread subject of *'the
red thing.'* His knowledge of anatomy makes him feel that the sage
who declares there is *'not much pain i' the process'* (297) of beheading is wrong. It would be better to die by the *'cold pale lightning of
a knife'* in fencing than by the *'Brute force'* of the engine (313–16).
He castigates the Pope for seeing *'hell yawn / One inch from the red
plank's end'* (338–9) and remaining silent. And what if he should
repent, he cries, *'Will that assist the engine half-way back / Into its
hiding-house?'* (450–1). Everything serves to remind him of the
engine. When he is citing the example of the Refendary who has an
argument that will *'cut the spinal cord'* of Molinism, the anatomical
phrase recalls the grisly fate awaiting him, and with an exclamation
of disgust he hastily abandons the figure. He abruptly pulls himself
back to his discourse from a digression by remembering that *'each
minute's talk'* pushes *'this Mannaia-machine'* an *'inch the nearer'*
him (847–8).[9]

By the last part of his speech, Guido declares that death will be a
relief, that he is ready, like an ancient Roman, to fall on his own
sword, but this air of resignation is contradicted by the ever-present

9/See also 707–13, 782–4, 1750–3, 2266–7.

references to the passage of time. He is keenly conscious of how few hours are left to him and his repeated reminders of this fact serve to focus the reader's attention on the dramatic passage of time within the monologue. Thus, the setting of early morning hours of darkness is presented first, as Guido complains of being awakened *'ere break of day'* to find he must die *'at sunset'* (24–5), and he demands to know why he should have to die *'twelve hours hence'* (32). He mentions the *'twelve hours'* interval five times after this first allusion to it, as for instance when, describing his first acquaintance with the mannaia, he concludes, *'Twelve hours hence, I may know more, not hate worse'* (258). Again, he says, *'If I pass / Twelve hours repenting, will that fact hold fast / The thirteenth at the horrid dozen's end?'* (445–7). Later he accuses his visitors of being so stony-hearted that if he were to *'Rave / Another twelve hours, every word were waste!'* (2229–30).[10]

All these remarks but one come in the first part of the discourse (within the first 500 lines) and indicate time to pass *before* the execution hour; the exception is the last quoted reference which comes near the end of the speech and indicates that he has been talking continuously throughout the course of the twelve hours and the execution hour is now at hand. Interim passages between the early remarks and the last have also alluded to the time element, in terms of minutes and hours passing; Guido remembers *'this Mannaia-machine, each minute's talk / Helps push an inch the nearer'* him (847–8); he breaks off a thought to ask, *'What hour is fleeting now?'* (920); he blames himself for preaching *'while the hour-glass runs and runs!'* (1520). The reader is in this way being asked to accept the fact that Guido's monologue has begun with the early hours of dawn and continued into the afternoon, to conclude with the sounds of the approaching executioners at the cell door sometime near sunset. Even while recognizing that Guido's is a long speech (by far the longest of the monologues at over 2400 lines), that it is marked by at least one lengthy pause (*'Come, I am tired of silence! Pause enough!'*) and perhaps more, and that the arrival of the executioners may precede the actual execution by some time[11] – even taking all these points into account,

10/See also 123, 354.

11/The Pope has given orders that the nobleman Franceschini is to be put to death, not at the usual place near the prison *'where die the common sort,'* but at the more distant People's Square, frequented by his peers (x, 2107–14). The Venetian visitor indicates that the procession's route was a lengthy one (xII, 138–46).

it is still clear that the rendering of the speech could not, realistically speaking, encompass several hours' time. Dramatically speaking, however, the telescoping of time is not only acceptable but vastly effective in building up to the shocking change in Guido's demeanour at the climactic moment. It has something of the powerful effect of the final scene of Marlowe's *Dr. Faustus*, where the last irretrievable moments of life slip from the lost soul's grasp with incredible swiftness, and even prayer is powerless to hold off doom.

The tone of Guido's discourse is the most striking departure from his earlier monologue. At the outset, it reflects the same attitude that he had displayed toward the court: he flatters the Abate with references to the latter's ancient family seat, linking himself with that noble heritage: '*My blood / Comes from as far a source*' (15–16). However, the tone soon changes to one of undisguised contempt for those in league against him, the Pope, the clergy, and particularly the two men sent on their pious mission to him. He abruptly stops their attempts to reason with him and begins to vent his outrage in an almost uncontrollable outpouring of words: '*Let me talk, / Or leave me, at your pleasure! talk I must: / What is your visit but my lure to talk?*' (130–2). He passionately asserts his right to live and paints a shudderingly vivid picture of the death that awaits him because of the old Pope's obduracy. He lashes out at the hypocrisy of those who call themselves believers in Christ. Suddenly he catches himself, and in a swift change of pace, claims that his attack is not directed at his two hearers at all, but is a mere '*expedient to save life*' (852). Now he begins in a quieter vein to explain how his pride in the marriage bargain turned to smouldering resentment when he saw how impervious Pompilia was to his mistreatment of her. He rises to a new pitch of indignation: '*What you call my wife / I call a nullity in female shape, / Vapid disgust, soon to be pungent plague*' (1112–14), and concludes with another savage attack on his visitors: (1500–3)

> You, – whose stupidity and insolence
> I must defer to, soothe at every turn, –
> Whose swine-like snuffling greed and grunting lust
> I had to wink at or help gratify, –

where the "s" sounds of the words echo his snarling ferocity and the "d" and "t" sounds his snapping bitterness. He has to pull himself up short again at the recollection of how time is fleeing while he raves; he resumes in a new tenor, a rueful surveyal of how close his well-laid plan came to success but for *'the luck that lies beyond a man'* (1567). Now he is coolly realistic as he assesses the life he would have led had he been freed, seeing it as *'sad and sapless'* (1822). Stoically, he accepts the inevitability of death, claiming an affinity for the ancient pagans and wishing he might have married a Circe or a Borgia fit for him. Another outburst then breaks the reflective mood, and he alternately bribes and threatens the Cardinal, baits him on his dead mistress, and mercilessly reminds the Abate of the disease eating away his life. Finally, he boasts defiantly: *'I lived and died a man, and take man's chance, / Honest and bold: right will be done to such'* (2412–13). But with the sounds at the door, the bravado suddenly cracks and the terrified prisoner denies all he has said before: *'All was folly – I laughed and mocked!'* and incoherently pleads for life: *'Don't open! Hold me from them! ... Pompilia, will you let them murder me?'* (2419–27).

The highly erratic tone of the speech is reflected in the mode of address. Exclamatory and interrogative sentences predominate and, like the alogical development of thought, reveal the intense agitation of mind. Just as certain words and phrases lead inevitably back by association to the thought of the dread mannaia, with the memory of the mannaia leading in turn to thoughts of the fleeing time, so both of these ideas are connected in the speaker's mind with the pressing need to talk, to express himself. He does not want to waste time – *'And, fool-like, what is it I wander from? / What did I say of your sharp iron tooth?'* (178–9) – but he cannot hold back the flood of words: *'Talk I must,'* he admits at the start, and a short time later breaks off to exclaim: *' – how I speak! / Lucidity of soul unlocks the lips: / I never had the words at will before'* (158–60). He is aware of a strange new articulateness, *'this voluble rhetoric'* which has come to the fore *'of a sudden'* (170–4). At one point he acknowledges, *'Yes, friends, / I go too fast: the orator's at fault'* (1292–3), indicating that his listeners are having difficulty keeping up with the rush of words.

These phrases about "words" and "talk," and others like them, point to a significant similarity to his first speech; both show a concern with rhetoric. In the speech before the court, he was the orator delivering his most persuasive arguments in a deliberate and controlled presentation. In his speech to the Cardinal and Abate, he is neither deliberate nor controlled, and the apparent candour of the earlier appearance has given way to the devastatingly real candour of despair. Nevertheless, certain elements of the second speech suggest that the Guido of the prison cell is not completely unmasked until the last fifteen lines of his monologue, that throughout the other 2400 lines he is playing a role, not entirely for his audience, but also for himself. The allusions to "rhetoric," to "talk," and to "words" that stud his sentences and the way in which he plays with particular images and figures of speech point to this conclusion. For example, in addition to lines like those quoted above, where he comments on his new-found skill with language, he repeatedly refers to the practice of embellishing his thoughts with rhetorical flourishes. He excuses his excesses of language at one point thus: 'I blame you, tear my hair and tell my woe – / All's but a flourish, figure of rhetoric!' (850–1). When he describes Pompilia being led to the altar for the marriage ceremony, he likens her to the heifer led to sacrifice, noting that 'the old simile comes pat' (978). In comparing himself in one of several instances to the wolf in sheep's clothing, he exclaims: '(How that staunch image serves at every turn!)' (1179). Picturing himself metamorphosed after death, he enjoys playing upon the idea with words: 'Do I ring the changes right? / Deformed, transformed, reformed, informed, conformed!' (2062–3). At the conclusion of his extended wolf analogy, sensing his hearers' revulsion, he admits that all is imagination: (2318–22)

> Don't mistake my trope!
> A Cardinal so qualmish? Eminence,
> My fight is figurative, blows i' the air,
> Brain-war with powers and principalities,
> Spirit-bravado, no real fisticuffs!

He calls himself 'orator' and 'preacher,' and in the last few horror-stricken moments, he abjures all that he has said before as 'words' only:

> Sirs, have I spoken one word all this while
> Out of the world of words I had to say?
> Not one word! All was folly – I laughed and mocked!
> Sirs, my first true word, all truth and no lie,
> Is – save me notwithstanding! (2417–21, emphasis mine)

His discourse is marked by a naturally figurative turn of expression: three times, for instance, he uses the phrase 'to wave wand' to signify the conjuring up of a paradoxical situation. Other figures of speech abound. The most prominent is the wolf image to represent Guido himself. Because almost every previous speaker has used it to describe him, most notably the Pope in the preceding monologue, it seems neither unexpected nor unnatural to find it in Guido's own mouth, but the weight he gives to it is surprising. A common critical assumption is that in this image Guido the murderer unconsciously reveals that darker side of his nature he had kept so carefully hidden earlier. There are signs, however, that he uses the wolf figure here quite consciously, that he finds some satisfaction in the likeness, and that he returns to it again and again deliberately in order to savour its cleverness and its shock value. He uses it extensively five times, each time with different elaborations, so that the suggestion is that as he had earlier wanted his listeners to think of him as having a sheep's nature,[12] he now wants to be thought of as wolf-like – ferocious, savage, bold. A noteworthy point, however, is that in four out of five of the uses of the figure to describe himself, the wolf characteristics that emerge are not fierceness or boldness, but rather craftiness and a skulking meanness. In each of the four images, he admits his wolf nature has been masked in sheep's clothing: first, by claiming he is now casting off the mask – *'There, let my sheepskin-garb, a curse on 't, go'* (443); second, by accusing the ecclesiastics of teaching him hypocrisy – *'But you as good as bade me wear sheep's wool / Over wolf's skin'* (824–5); third, by criticizing the Comparini for not placating the wolf they found when they reached for the sheep in the marriage bargain – *'these, forsooth, / Tried whisker-plucking, and so found what trap / The whisker kept perdue, two rows of teeth'* (1188–90); and fourth, by conjecturing about whether the wolf at bay should try to escape through trick or give up the fight – *'Shall he try bleating?'* or *'die fighting quietly?'* (2308–11). In each instance, the wolf is seen as furtive, treacherous, cowardly, although these qualities are obviously not those that Guido wants to claim for himself.

Only in the fifth use of the image is there a touch of the fiercely audacious: (2056–60)

> *Let me turn wolf, be whole, and sate, for once, –*
> *Wallow in what is now a wolfishness*
> *Coerced too much by the humanity*
> *That's half of me as well! Grow out of man,*
> *Glut the wolf-nature, –*

12/In his first speech, for example, he had said: (v, 1094–8)
> *Say I stand*
> *Convicted of the having been afraid,*
> *Proved a poltroon, no lion but a lamb, –*
> *Does that deprive me of my right of lamb*
> *And give my fleece and flesh to the first wolf?*

but this is a grandiose vision of what he would like to be, not a description of himself as he is, and serves only to emphasize by contrast the real weakness and baseness of his past behaviour. He later admits the exaggeration of the lines, calling them *'Spirit-bravado'* (2322). The fact is that Guido aspires to a kind of magnificence in evil; he would like to see himself in the role of heedless challenger to conventional morality. But the truth about his behaviour pierces through the figurative language almost, it seems, in spite of himself. Except for this revealing side of the animal imagery, Guido's characterization might indeed have projected a grandness of unadulterated malevolence that would have outweighed the pitiful impression of his abject end. As it is, the wolf image he wants to project becomes a false image: he is not the wolf he tries to be, able to end *'fighting quietly,'* but a sheep who must go to his death *'bleating.'* His own language betrays the truth he had tried to hide even from himself.

Another image which illuminates a facet of his personality only hinted at before is the figure of the horse which he applies several times to Pompilia. Like the hawk comparison of his other monologue, it reflects more about the speaker than the object described. It is notably inapt to portray the sensitive dignity of Pompilia, but Guido seems unaware of its incongruity. He says, for example, of the way she bore herself in church at the marriage ceremony: *'So have I brought my horse, by word and blow, / To stand stock-still and front the fire he dreads'* (1045–6). She submitted to his maltreatment *'As if one killed the horse one could not ride!'* (1364). He rails at her failure to at least feign some affection for him: (1397–1403)

> *Just as we bid a horse, with cluck of tongue,*
> *Stretch his legs arch-wise, crouch his saddled back*
> *To foot-reach of the stirrup – all for love,*
> *And some for memory of the smart of switch*
> *On the inside of the foreleg – what care we?*
> *Yet where's the bond obliges horse to man*
> *Like that which binds fast wife to husband?*

Although none of these comparisons is intended to be an exact analogy, their spontaneous quality and their frequent recurrence suggest that Guido naturally thinks of himself as a demanding taskmaster and of Pompilia as a creature made for obedience and submissive service. Even when he is calling up the memory of his licentious youth, he falls into the metaphor of the dashing cavalier horseman: (96–112)

> *As forth we fared, pricked on to breathe our steeds*
> *And take equestrian sport over the green*
> *Under the blue, across the crop, – what care?*
> *If we went prancing up hill and down dale,*
> *In and out of the level and the straight,*
> *By the bit of pleasant byeway, where was harm?*
> *Still Sol salutes me and the morning laughs:*
> *I see my grandsire's hoof-prints, – point the spot*
> *Where he drew rein, slipped saddle, and stabbed knave*
> *For daring throw gibe – much less, stone – from pale:*
> *Then back, and on, and up with the cavalcade.*
> *Just so wend we, now canter, now converse,*
> *Till, 'mid the jauncing pride and jaunty port,*
> *Something of a sudden jerks at somebody –*
> *A dagger is out, a flashing cut and thrust,*
> *Because I play some prank my grandsire played,*
> *And here I sprawl. ...*

The lines seem to waver between figurative and literal expression. The elaboration of the image and the excited tone arouse a suspicion that they may contain an element of wishful thinking, that the Count would prefer to see himself still the privileged nobleman commandingly astride his finely trained horse as he boldly overcomes every obstacle in his path. But the reality mocks him. Just as he was never really the lordly and dashing cavalier, so Pompilia was not the high-spirited creature curbed and trained to respond to her master's slightest pressure of command; he has insisted all along that it was her imperviousness to his cruelty, that peculiar withdrawn quality by which she put herself out of his reach, that so infuriated him. Hence, where the hawk image struck a false note in his first speech by reflecting his true attitude, this master–horse image proves revealing, not of the actual relationship between him and Pompilia, but of the way he wishes to view it.[13]

Other images he uses for her are less incongruous. He calls her a stream *'Fit to reflect the daisies on its bank'* (2055), and a *'faint fine*

13/In the first speech, significantly, he had pictured himself as a pathetic, plodding beast of burden: (v, 133–7)

> *I protruded nose*
> *To halter, bent my back of docile beast,*
> *And now am whealed, one wide wound all of me,*
> *For being found at the eleventh hour o' the day*
> *Padding the mill-track, not neck-deep in grass. ...*

gauze' needleworked 'with its lily and rose' (2130–1); although he intends these phrases to describe her pallid and weak personality, he succeeds instead in conveying a sense of the transparent purity of her nature. He also has a wealth of contemptuous expressions to depict the Comparini: they are 'insects,' 'scorpions,' 'a pander-pair,' 'tiger-cats,' and together with Pompilia 'a three-headed beast.' But since these phrases are not made part of a well-developed or consistent image, they seem indiscriminate name-calling and lack the impact of the "serpent-poison" figures of the first speech.

Like the references to his family name and heritage which were so prominent in the first monologue and are so rare in the second, Guido's allusions to his father and his child show a marked difference. He passes over the former with a slurring remark – 'I know how to suppress rebellion there, / Being not quite the fool my father was' (1877–8) – and dismisses the supposed consolations of his own fatherhood as meaningless: 'Therefore no sort of use for son have I' (1902). This time when he tells an anecdote about his illustrious ancestor, it is to sneer at the empty symbolism of the furze on the family coat of arms. His attitude toward religion reveals an even more conspicuous change. He denies the existence of Christianity:

> I say, if ever was such faith at all
> Born in the world, by your community
> Suffered to live its little tick of time,
> 'Tis dead of age, now, ludicrously dead;
> Honour its ashes, if you be discreet,
> In epitaph only! (558–63)

His frank avowal of amorality, the profession of his creed that pleasure is the sole good in the world, is the one outstanding fact revealed by this speech. He adds nothing new to the narrative; most of what he discloses for the first time has to do with his opinions, such as the admission that the indifference he earlier professed toward Pompilia was a disguise for a consuming hatred: 'I grow one gorge / To loathingly reject Pompilia's pale / Poison my hasty hunger took for food' (2404–6). He never mentions the 'cloud of passion,' the raging shame that he once claimed drove him to desperation, he omits all mention of the child Gaetano's role in his decision to kill; instead he describes the plot in terms of an artistic creation spoiled by a twist of fate. Revealingly, he calls himself an 'artist' and 'painter,' his plan a 'masterpiece,' the 'spoiled work' of 'Artistry's haunting curse, the Incomplete' (1561).

Although the two monologues of Guido Franceschini are obviously not intended to be read side by side, certain advantages derive from such an examination as this, and illuminate some of Browning's dramatic methods. First of all, it can be seen more clearly how the impressive effect of the first monologue depends primarily on its position in the series, coming after the "outside" view (which is slightly weighted toward Guido's side) and before the versions of Caponsacchi and Pompilia (which substantiate each other and detract materially from the credibility of Guido's defence). Secondly, we see more clearly to what extent the aura of trustworthiness in the first speech depended on the Count's artfully manipulated tone and his carefully selected allusions. Furthermore, it becomes evident that at least some of the impact of this first monologue comes from the repetition of ideas presented in previous speeches, particularly Half-Rome's. The echoes of terms like "poison" and "serpent," designed to arouse sympathy, have been noted, and there are many others.[14] No claim can be made that the reader will remember, as he listens to Guido, exactly where or when he has heard these ideas before, but the fact that he *has* heard them reinforces their present expression through the subtle suggestion that what the speaker is saying represents widely held public opinion.

Of the conclusions emerging from this juxtaposing of the two speeches, the most significant is the light shed on the nature of the first by the second. Many clues in the first monologue point to the appeal in the courtroom as an elaborately fashioned rhetorical performance, of course, but there is no way for the reader to know, during the course of it, the full extent of Guido's play-acting: what had seemed mere exaggeration in the exploiting of family and religion is seen only in retrospect as blatant lying. The position of the second speech is of paramount importance for several reasons. It follows the Pope's reasoned and impartial judgment, when the last appeal has failed; it is the eleventh book of the eleventh hour, as one commentary has put it.[15] It comes after Pompilia's death, and Guido's indignant references to her deathbed words of forgiveness for him —

14/For example, Guido calls Pompilia and Caponsacchi 'Helen and Paris' (v, 1264), refers to the Comparini and himself as 'anglers' and 'fish' respectively (1400–3), abuses Violante as the 'mock-mother' (1651), and the passage on his unjust treatment at the hands of the authorities repeats the word 'law' ten times in the space of fifteen lines (1749–63) just as in Half-Rome's concluding passage.

15/Charlotte Porter and Helen A. Clarke, in their introduction to The Ring and the Book, The Complete Works of Robert Browning (1898), VI, xiii.

he mentions twice that they have been reported to him – gives a new insight into the depths of his brutality, just as his indignant quoting of her words while she was still alive increased sympathy for him. It is noteworthy in this regard that the second Guido never uses long direct quotations from Pompilia as all the other speakers do; this serves to make her very spirit absent from the monologue and gives a terrible poignancy to his last anguished utterance of her name.

Most striking revelation of all in a comparison of the two monologues is the way in which Browning has made the Guido of the second reflect the first in so many characteristic touches of speech habits and rhetorical expressions and especially of tone. This last element is a remarkable link between the two speeches. That unique blend of deference and boldness, barely concealing a corrosive bitterness, is still recognizable – under totally different circumstances of audience, setting, occasion, motive – in the half-snarl, half-whine of the condemned prisoner. An intricate web of cross-references, verbal echoes, and recurring motifs, woven around Guido's concept of himself as rhetorician, links the two so that we actually do recognize '*the same man*' although he speaks with '*another voice.*'

Chapter VI

The Book and the Ring

THE LAST BOOK of the poem is a summary of events following Guido's death by the same speaker as in Book I: the nineteenth-century English poet who discovered the source materials for the Franceschini murder story and who has introduced the 'voices' of the seventeenth-century actors in the intervening ten monologues. It is, in fact, a kind of continuation of the earlier speech, in which the poet repeats his basic assumptions about his high office and reinforces them with further proof of the unreliability of human testimony without the artistic intermediary to interpret it. The speaker's earlier excitement is somewhat subdued; he is less intense in his expression, although still deeply stirred by the events of his story and convinced of their significance. He speaks much less, Book XII being little more than half as long as Book I and most of it being direct quotation of other speakers. After commenting on Guido's end, he notes that his source-book contains the only four additional extant written reports on the execution and subsequent events, and he quotes at length from each report in turn, interspersing ironic comments on the veracity of the writers – a Venetian visitor to Rome and the two opposing lawyers, Arcangeli and Bottini (the

latter's letter containing an excerpt from the sermon of Fra Celestino). Then, drawing attention to the printed note at the end of his
old yellow book, he reads the Pope's decree restoring Pompilia's
good name. He notes the fact of the Pope's death a year after the
trial, and reveals that his own search has failed to uncover any trace
of Pompilia's son Gaetano – has failed to find any other reference
to the entire story, in fact, than a record entered in the Arezzo
annals by Guido's sister, lauding the name of Franceschini. Finally,
he concludes with an exhortation to the 'British Public' to accept
the lesson demonstrated by his poem, 'That Art remains the one way
possible / Of speaking truth.'[1]

The circumstances of this speech are apparently the same as those
of the poet's first monologue, as indicated by the allusions to his
concluding the story – 'And so an end of all i' the story' (779). The
only concrete localizing effect comes from the references to the old
yellow book: (225–8)

> To this Cencini's care I owe the Book,
> The yellow thing I take and toss once more, –
> How will it be, my four-years'-intimate,
> When thou and I part company anon?

The exuberant gesture and the allusion to the long, affectionate
association of the poet with his raw materials recall similar expressions in Book I which helped to establish the monologue's setting.
Audience references, too, are the same as in I: the poet addresses
himself to some interested, receptive members of his public who
have been involved in his artistic process; 'you have seen his act,'
the poet says of Guido's murder, 'By my power – may-be, judged it
by your own' (9–10), and he continues to imply the closeness of the
speaker–audience relationship throughout, speaking of Arcangeli
as 'him I made you mark' (212), hinting that the listeners are too
familiar with his procedure to need further explanations: 'you know
where, / Whence came the other stuff, went, you know how, / To
make the Ring' (236–8). That the listeners represent the poet's
general reading public is made explicit in the last direct address,
with this time a slight change in wording – from 'ye who like me not'
– to suggest the poet's hopes for greater receptivity to this more
significant work: (835–40)

1/Lines 843–4. All references in this chapter are to Book XII unless otherwise
indicated.

> *So, British Public, who may like me yet,*
> *(Marry and amen!) learn one lesson hence*
> *Of many which whatever lives should teach:*
> *This lesson, that our human speech is naught,*
> *Our human testimony false, our fame*
> *And human estimation words and wind.*

This last passage, like earlier ones, embodies a kind of tension between the need to justify his ambitious undertaking in the face of past failure and a confident assertiveness about the significance of his task. Because he is an artist, he maintains, he can tell a truth, *'write a book shall mean beyond the facts, / Suffice the eye and save the soul beside'* (866–7). This impressive claim is only a more explicit restatement of what he had said in the opening book, when he compared himself to Elisha who with God's help restored life to the dead. The poet considers himself sharing the Creator's power in a lesser degree, able to restore life where it once was; just as he had said earlier

> *That, although nothing which had never life*
> *Shall get life from him, be, not having been,*
> *Yet, something dead may get to live again,*

in defence of the artistic act (1, 727–9), now he claims to have accomplished this himself, the rescue of dead men from the tomb. The earlier exhilaration of anticipation has given way to a quiet satisfaction: (830–4)

> *So did this old woe fade from memory:*
> *Till after, in the fulness of the days,*
> *I needs must find an amber yet unquenched,*
> *And, breathing, blow the spark to flame. It lives,*
> *If precious be the soul of man to man.*

Even in the abbreviated space of the poet's second monologue, all the characteristic speech habits of Book 1 are repeated: the topical allusions and puns – noting that the year of the Pope's death marked the birth of Voltaire, he comments, *'Terrible Pope, too, of a kind'* (778); the colloquialisms – *'Eh! What ails the man?'* (405), he asks of Bottini's choleric letter; the mocking references to his own poetic reputation – *'There, would you disbelieve the annalist, / Go rather by the babble of a bard?'* (808–9); the explanation of foreign terms to the English audience – *'For Guido had so nearly nicked ... / At Tarocs, – or succeeded, – in our phrase'* (222–4); the constant references to the old yellow book; the address to the British Public; and the prayer to his 'lyric Love.'

It becomes clear that we are to see this speech as a continuation of the first, but there are other indications that we are also to notice the modification of tone that takes place in the final quiet lines. The dominant ring metaphor of the first book, for example, is used only briefly – once, in a reference to the letters as material that made 'the Ring that's all but round and done' (238) and once, in the concluding lines, where it is offered as a graceful tribute to his 'lyric Love.' The ring now stands completed, pure and golden, its alloy removed with the completion of the ten monologues, and it is no longer needed to symbolize the poetic process; the title of Book XII, 'The Book and the Ring,' reversing that of Book I, shows that the ring has taken a subordinate position. Another figure takes its place in XII: the image of the poet's life-giving breath blowing on seemingly dead ashes and producing a vital spark.

At first, the poet refers to the actors in the drama as 'shooting stars,' or 'streaks' that flash across the sky momentarily and then disappear: Guido is the 'Wormwood Star' whose 'act, over and ended, falls and fades' (13) until nothing is left in the darkness; to the Venetian letter-writer he says, 'You've sputtered into sparks,' and then asks of Arcangeli, 'What streak comes next?' (210). Later, he reverts to Guido's role: 'So / Did the Star Wormwood in a blazing fall / Frighten awhile the waters and lie lost' (827–9). The emphasis is on the transitory nature of their brilliance, destined in brief time to fade out of memory into eternal darkness – except that it was seen and saved by the poet. 'In the fulness of the days,' he found 'an ember yet unquenched' in the pages of the old book, 'And, breathing,' found he could 'blow the spark to flame.' The tone of this imagery is more subdued, more retrospective than the earlier excited, insistent description of his ring-craft. It is almost as though the poet's energy had gone into the exhausting task of breathing life into the half-extinguished ashes and all that he feels now is a sense of quiet satisfaction, in contemplating the enduring flame which he has restored. The "unquenched ember" image calls to mind lines from his first speech: (I, 735–8)

> Man's breath were vain to light a virgin wick, –
> Half-burned-out, all but quite-quenched wicks o' the lamp
> Stationed for temple-service on this earth,
> These indeed let him breathe on and relume!

The diminution of the speaker's dynamism in Book XII is due in large measure to the limited number of personal references, since approximately two-thirds of his speech (which at 874 lines is the shortest by far of all the monologues) is made up of direct quotations of the four documents. For the most part, then, the mode of address resembles the first part of Book I, with heavy emphasis on the written character of the source materials. Introducing Arcangeli's words, the poet notes parenthetically that they are all *'in this paper that I touch'* (220) and points out to his auditors that the sand that dried the ink is still not rubbed away. Bottini's letter is introduced the same way, with attention called to its appearance: *'(The print is sorrowfully dyked and dammed, / But shows where fain the unbridled force would flow ...)'* (399–400). So with the Pope's decree clearing Pompilia's name: *'The Instrument / Is plain before me, print that ends my Book'* (752–3).

In the earlier monologue, the emphasis on the printed character of the source-book served to establish the "inertness" of the written facts and to bring out by contrast the vitality of the poet-created *'voices'*; here obviously the purpose is somewhat different. The poet quotes directly from the documents rather than paraphrasing them as he had done with the trial records, and since three are private letters (the fourth an outspoken sermon), they represent the frank views of the quoted individuals and are akin in effect to the dramatic monologues. The manner in which the poet indicates the speaker's audience and the time and circumstances for each (with Bottini accomplishing this task for the friar's sermon) further underscores their dramatic quality. The emphasis on their printed nature, then, seems to be directed toward an end similar to that achieved by the first monologue's references to the old yellow book (*'Here it is, this I toss and take again'*) which concretized the existence of the source materials and provided a substantial link between the poet's present situation and the dead past. In Book XII, the poet reminds his audience that these views he now presents are found here *'in this paper'* that he *touches*, that they represent, not the creations of his imagination, but the actual, tangible record of historical fact. For the same purpose, he quotes directly from the Pope's decree clearing Pompilia – ' "In restitution of the perfect fame" / "Of dead Pompilia ... " ' (757–8) – and even from the insignificant entry in the Arezzo annals praising the Franceschini; in the latter case, he feels it necessary to explain the quoting: *'I like and shall translate the eloquence / Of nearly the worst Latin ever writ'* (798–9). It is all here, he seems to be repeating, all part of the verifiable historical record.

It might be asked, why then the dramatic monologue form for the epistles? All the letters' information might have been disclosed by the poet's paraphrase – factual details such as the Pope's death and Gaetano's disappearance are, after all, given in the poet's own words – with due acknowledgment of the source. The answer must be that the writers' own words reveal something further which would be lost or distorted in paraphrase or summary; it is not fact alone they reveal but, once more, a point of view. Serving a larger purpose than merely to tie all the loose ends of the story together, they reinforce and expand the basic concept underlying the poem's structure by demonstrating, finally and forcefully, human inability to see truth whole. Two of the writers, Arcangeli and Bottini, have spoken in previous monologues, Fra Celestino has been quoted by other speakers, and only the unnamed visitor from Venice is new to the scene. Their words form a kind of postscript, or post-mortem, to the events of the drama, reflecting the city's reaction in the aftermath of the trial which has held its attention for weeks. The point made unmistakably clear by their self-expressed views, following one upon another in the first hours and days after the execution, is that for all the controversy and excitement that enveloped the trial of Count Guido Franceschini, its dramatic consummation leaves the hearts and minds of men untouched.

The first writer is the aristocratic visitor from Venice who is informing a friend at home of the news of the day: gossip about the Carnival gaiety, the Pope's health, the Fenelon case, and finally the beheading of the Roman count who murdered his wife. An outsider who has not been involved in the controversy, he considers himself a superior reporter, and he endeavours to render a lively narrative, full of scornful references to the 'mob' (a half-dozen such allusions in 150 lines), while he maintains the pose of a judiciously detached observer: (169–73)

> "We hardly noticed how the peasants died,
> "They dangled somehow soon to right and left,
> "And we remained all ears and eyes, could give
> "Ourselves to Guido undividedly,
> "As he harangued the multitude beneath."

His attitude is strongly reminiscent of the self-consciously uncommitted position of that other outsider, Tertium Quid. The reminder serves notice that 'men of quality' find nothing in the fate of their fellow nobleman Count Guido Franceschini but a momentary titillation and a source of gossip.

Arcangeli's letter follows in two parts: the first half is an obsequious official report to Guido's friend Cencini on the failure of their efforts to secure the prisoner's reprieve, full of pious wishes for the departed and exaggerated apologies; the second half is the true voice of Arcangeli as he slips in a personal note to his friend, complete with plans to snare a new, more remunerative case. Writing only hours after Guido's execution, he wastes no tears for his client's end. The familiar classical phrasing mingles with paternal boasts: ' "hoc malim," *raps me out / The rogue: you notice the subjunctive?'* (338–9). Jibes at his court opponent are coupled with unflagging attention to furthering his own professional prospects: *'Success with which shall plaster aught of pate / That's broken in me by Bottini's flail'* (364–5). All these sharply underline the callous indifference and acquisitive egotism of the executed man's defender. Guido alive or Guido dead, it is all the same; Arcangeli's interests never move beyond the narrow sphere of his own pleasures.

Next comes Bottini, and his long letter, repeatedly echoing the ideas and phrasing of his earlier monologue, indirectly highlights the essential insignificance of Pompilia's life and death to her advocate. The erstwhile defender of her name is now engaged in trying to wrest her estate from her heir on the grounds that she was, after all, guilty. Again, all is tediously familiar: the spiteful attacks on his opponent – *'Not that the burly boaster did one jot / O' the little was to do'* (435–6); the vicious diatribe against Fra Celestino – *'this virulent and rabid monk'* (664); the obsessive linking of dirt and beauty – the friar will find his *'Noah's-dove'* Pompilia turned into *'quite the other sooty scout, / The raven'* (727–9).

Bottini's ugly and distorted viewpoint sets off by sharp contrast the sermon of Fra Celestino which it encloses. This excerpt from the sermon which was delivered the day after the execution is the first direct word of the Augustinian priest who defended Pompilia on her deathbed, but it too awakens echoes, in this case of Pope Innocent XII. The tone, of troubled faith and wearied wisdom, is the same, and so is the basic image of light in conflict with dark. Like the Pope, Celestino goes back to the *'twilight day'* of the pagan Romans to show how, as they mistook the *'morning star'* of Christian faith for a false superstitious belief, so present-day Romans misinterpret goodness because it is obscured by *'vapoury films, enwoven circumstance'* of darkness. The darkness is only thickened by the machinery of law intended to disperse it and were it not for *'the true instinct of an old good man / Who happens to hate darkness and love light'*.

(593–4), the earthly mists enfolding Pompilia's name would never have been pierced.

This direct reference to the Pope is reinforced by other echoes. The dove figure for Pompilia, recalling for the reader Innocent's recognition of her gentleness and oneness with nature, is the very allusion which enrages Bottini, bringing on his *'raven'* comparison. Celestino uses the image to emphasize the sheer chance involved in Pompilia's final vindication, as he asks: (472–86)

> *"Because Pompilia's purity prevails,*
> *"Conclude you, all truth triumphs in the end?*
> *"So might those old inhabitants of the ark,*
> *"Witnessing haply their dove's safe return,*
> *"Pronounce there was no danger, all the while*
> *"O' the deluge, to the creature's counterparts,*
> *"Aught that beat wing i' the world, was white or soft, –*
> *"And that the lark, the thrush, the culver too,*
> *"Might equally have traversed air, found earth,*
> *"And brought back olive-branch in unharmed bill.*
> *"Methinks I hear the Patriarch's warning-voice –*
> *" 'Though this one breast, by miracle, return,*
> *" 'No wave rolls by, in all the waste, but bears*
> *" 'Within it some dead dove-like thing as dear,*
> *" 'Beauty made blank and harmlessness destroyed!' "*

The heavy concentration of explosive *p*'s, *b*'s, *d*'s, *t*'s and *k*'s in these lines – hardly a word here that does not have at least one of these sounds – gives a sharp edge to the general feeling of dispiritedness they convey; the old priest reveals a sense of disillusionment amounting almost to bitterness in the realization of how empty is man's justice on earth. The friar's viewpoint is similar to the Pope's, it is wide, deep, sympathetic, sensitive to the evidences of man's limitations. But he lacks an element of hope that caused Innocent to pray for Guido's soul to be saved and for a new light to dawn among the modern Romans. Celestino's conclusion is more profoundly pessimistic (600–3): the story of Guido and Pompilia is merely

> *"... one proof more that 'God is true*
> *" 'And every man a liar' – that who trusts*
> *"To human testimony for a fact*
> *"Gets this sole fact – himself is proved a fool. ..."*

In this way, through the invoking and repetition of previously employed motifs of human prejudices, blindnesses, and distortions, all four writers are made to strengthen and enhance one of the poet's major themes: the untrustworthiness of human speech.[2] His other basic theme, so prominent in Book I – the power of the creative process to open man's eyes to truth – is also expanded here, mainly by the direct statement in the poet's concluding lines. Repeating the friar's text that *'God is true / And every man a liar'* in different words (838–40)

> *This lesson, that our human speech is naught,*
> *Our human testimony false, our fame*
> *And human estimation words and wind*

he answers the question *'Why take the artistic way to prove so much?'* with an explicit restatement of the concept he had expressed in the ring metaphor of Book I: (842–4)

> *Because, it is the glory and good of Art,*
> *That Art remains the one way possible*
> *Of speaking truth, to mouths like mine at least.*

A man's attempt to speak truth to another man is doomed to failure because his words take on the appearance of falsehood as soon as they are uttered, expressing as they do a particular, human, limited viewpoint: (858–61)

> *But Art, – wherein man nowise speaks to men,*
> *Only to mankind, – Art may tell a truth*
> *Obliquely, do the thing shall breed the thought,*
> *Nor wrong the thought, missing the mediate word.*

The creative process, then, does not involve a presentation of truth directly to man, but a gradual revelation, indirectly, by the poet-agent working through the medium of other human voices. In the

2/C. Willard Smith, in *Browning's Star-Imagery: The Study of a Detail in Poetic Design* (1941), notes the echoes in Book XII: "The Venetian's letter recalls the matter of *Half-Rome, The Other Half-Rome*, and *Tertium Quid*; the lawyers' letters recall the themes of Books VIII and IX; and the sermon recalls the idealism of the Pope" (p. 219). I feel that the Venetian letter more specifically recalls Tertium Quid in its conspicuous references to "rank" and the "mob" and its attitude of indifference – Half-Rome and Other Half-Rome were at least strongly committed to one side. It seems to me also less "idealism" than disillusionment that the friar and the Pope share as an attitude. Smith also finds innumerable links between the star images used in Book XII and those used by previous speakers.

process, through his special gifts of insight and *'outsight'* and extraordinary will-power, the poet gives to the final revelation a spiritual and eternal value: this poem will *'Suffice the eye and save the soul beside'* (867).

Fra Celestino has usually been called Browning's "mouthpiece" in expressing his solemn views on the futility of human speech,[3] but this interpretation overlooks the fine distinction Browning makes between the friar's pessimistic conclusion (of *'every man a liar'* and *'truth reserved for heaven not earth'*) and his own hopeful, even exalted, view of the poet as instrument of an earthly epiphany of eternal truth. At the same time, there is evidence that Browning intends to show Fra Celestino – a man, like all others, with only one facet of the truth – groping blindly toward some sort of vision of a human achievement that would transcend the mundane and transitory. In his sermon, he hesitatingly reaches out, first toward the role of human love in reaching this goal, and finally toward the role of human art. Claiming contentment at having renounced the rewards of earthly fame, he still must admit to some haunting doubts that his was the only or the best choice of life: (625–34)

> "For many a doubt will fain perturb my choice –
> "Many a dream of life spent otherwise –
> "How human love, in varied shapes, might work
> "As glory, or as rapture, or as grace:
> "How conversancy with the books that teach,
> "The arts that help, – how, to grow good and great,
> "Rather than simply good, and bring thereby
> "Goodness to breathe and live, nor, born i' the brain,
> "Die there, – how these and many another gift
> "Of life are precious though abjured by me."

The facts revealed by the poet in Book XII then have to do with the few objective details and the written documents that shed light on the aftermath of the Franceschini murder trial; they are important not in themselves but only as they support the poet's assertion that the human condition makes suspect any single assessment of a human act. The four quoted documents, like the ten monologues, demonstrate this conclusion of the poet; the sermon teaches it explicitly, but also demonstrates it implicitly. The opinion the poet reveals

3/See, for example, William C. DeVane, *A Browning Handbook* (2nd ed. rev., 1955): "We may take these cogitations of the Augustinian brother to be Browning's own" (p. 338).

– a conviction, actually – is more significant: that the poetic act transcends the limitations of human speech by providing a means for man to evolve a single truth out of many different fallible interpretations. This exalted conception is powerfully reinforced by the linking of the poet's positive affirmation to the uncertain recognition of Fra Celestino that it may not be enough here on earth to grow *'simply good,'* that there exists the possibility of bringing *'Goodness to breathe and live,'* so that it will never die. Recognizing the possibility that man might share in some way in God's creative power, to perfect and make immortal something human, is enough to shake the friar's confidence that the religious life was the highest choice he could have made. His wording of this vision only faintly glimpsed – to make goodness *'breathe and live'* – recalls the poet's claim that *'breathing'* he could *'blow the spark'* of dead ashes to living flame, and restates the appraisal in Book I (729–34) of the artist's role.[4] Through him *'something dead may get to live again, / Something with too much life or not enough, / Which, either way imperfect, ended once.'* It is only the poet who

> *intervenes,*
> *Makes new beginning, starts the dead alive,*
> *Completes the incomplete and saves the thing.*

4/A. K. Cook, in *A Commentary upon Browning's "The Ring and the Book"* (1920), pp. 319–326, notes that in his two later editions of the poem, Browning made relatively more alterations in Book XII than in any other Book, and that a large proportion of the changes and added lines of this Book occur in the sermon of Fra Celestino. A study of Cook's tabular analysis reveals further that Browning's attention to revision centred particularly on the passage discussed here in which Celestino admits to the possibility of some lasting human achievement. All the changes were directed toward strengthening the impression of doubt in the friar's words, emphasizing his uncertainty about his choice of life, and clarifying the nature of the alternatives he now sees. For example, the line "for many a *doubt will* fain perturb my choice" originally read "for many a *dream would* fain perturb my choice"; in the second edition Browning changed "dream" to "doubt" and in the third and final edition he strengthened the line still further by changing the verb "would" to "will." The next line – "Many a dream of life spent otherwise" – did not even appear in the first edition; it serves to make the doubt more explicit. In the following line, "that human love ... might *show*" became the more positive "might *work*." The last line of this passage shows most clearly Browning's intention to stress Celestino's recognition: the original phrase was "how these and many another gift / *May well be* precious though abjured by me"; in the final version it reads "How these and many another gift / Of life *are* precious ..." (italics mine).

Chapter VII

To "Tell a Truth Obliquely": the Integrating Pattern

Books I and XII implicitly and explicitly set forth the thesis that no man can see the truth in any human event so clearly as the artist, who possesses a special gift for seeing and "evolving" truth. Limited as he is by his own human knowledge, the artist can nevertheless in his role as "resuscitator" take long-dead historical personages and restore them to life by giving them voice; in the process of their subsequent self-revelation, with the poet's own voice concealed or "withdrawn," they expose the truth gradually, each voice giving one limited, relatively reliable or distorted facet of the whole. The reader-audience shares in the poet's final vision of the truth by assuming temporarily each limited viewpoint, measuring and judging the extent of its distortion, and extracting from it whatever expression of fact and opinion is valid, if any. So says the poet-speaker of *The Ring and the Book*. At the conclusion of the series of revelatory monologues, he asserts, we should share his vision of the truth: that in the seventeenth-century Franceschini murder case the child-wife Pompilia was the innocent victim of the unreasoning hatred of her husband, the hypocritical Count Guido. This verdict on the principals in the case is not to be taken as the MEANING of the poem – the meaning has to do with the PROCESS by which the artist sees and shares his vision of truth – but the poet's explicit verdict on the principals in Book I indicates that the monologues will clearly bear out his judgment, and in so doing, will illustrate the poetic process at work.

The reader does share the poet's vision, of course; the overwhelming impression that the poem leaves is of the goodness, gentleness, and helplessness of Pompilia in the face of Guido's wily and rapacious cruelty. And yet only half the ten speakers in the poem express this view; the other half present some convincing arguments for the husband's rights in a case which is anything but clear-cut in all the details. The answer, as has been seen, lies in the fact that, on balance, the pro-Pompilia arguments carry more conviction and make a deeper impression than the pro-Guido protestations. The reasons for this unequal weight on Pompilia's side go much deeper than the mere use of sympathetic imagery by her defenders; the preceding analysis of "voice and address" in each monologue identified some of the myriad elements that combine to structure the ultimate viewpoint in each case. The speaker's personality, his general attitude, the degree of involvement or impartiality he exhibits, his characteristic speech habits and mode of address: all have a bearing on the reader's impression of the validity of his conclusions. In addition, the cumulative effect of similar opinions enters into the formation of the final impression. What effects, for example, do the monologues have on each other? that is, how do they interact and relate to the over-all design of the poem? A look at three aspects of this design – Browning's selection, arrangement, and balancing of the speakers' perspectives – will provide some answers.

The first and last books may be considered together since they constitute a kind of frame enclosing the other monologues and complementing each other. Their role and their exact relation to the other books in the poem have long been disputed, with many critics attacking their inclusion on the ground that they break down the dramatic framework of the poem, and others seeing them as evidence that Browning could not resist the temptation to harangue his readers at length on the story he was about to tell, and had to announce the verdict in his own voice without allowing the reader to decide for himself.[1] But to object thus is to see these two books as a kind of

1/Some critics expressing this view are A. K. Cook, in *A Commentary upon Browning's "The Ring and the Book"* (1920), who says that "it detracts from the claim of *The Ring and the Book* to be what Mr. Chesterton calls it ['the epic of prose exposition, included merely for the purpose of clarifying and summarizing the real poem, when in fact they both constitute poetic dramatic monologues and are an integral part of the poem's structure.[2] The analysis of "voice and address" in chapters I and VI reveals that all the elements of the speaker–environment relationship found in the other monologues are present here as well and that, in fact, Browning took great pains to establish the particularity of the locale, the audience's presence, and most especially, his dominant personality as the poet-speaker. In so doing, he conveyed the impression of the poet, not as detached, omniscient, judicious, but as excited, emotionally involved, and partial, representing one more viewpoint in the circle of monologues. The difference is that the poet has arrived at *his* viewpoint in a unique way: confirming his initial inspiration by re-creating the actors in his own mind and letting them express themselves. Putting all the resultant differing expressions together, he has evolved the truth about their motivations and now intends to demonstrate this process for his audience, letting it follow step by step through to his conclusion. Then in Book XII he reinforces the rightness of his view by presenting a brief "reprise" of certain voices heard earlier, repeating their biased and restricted views. Thus in the over-all design, Book I describes and sets the stage for

free speech'] that Browning appears as expert at the start; before he has summoned a single witness he tells us quite plainly what our 'ultimate judgment' is to be" (p. 3); Hoxie N. Fairchild, "Browning the Simple-Hearted Casuist" (1949), who objects to the "giveaway" in Book I and the way Browning "steps forward in his own person" in XII to provide the moral, seeing these books as evidence that he is "Unwilling to trust the dramatic method" and is "one of the least impersonal of English poets" (pp. 239–40); and Robert Langbaum, *The Poetry of Experience: The Dramatic Monologue in Modern Literary Tradition* (1957), who feels that Browning's poem only achieves "completeness through devices outside the scope of the dramatic monologue" (p. 157). He sees Browning "abandoning the dramatic monologue entirely – by speaking in his own voice in the first and last Books in order to establish the *right* judgments ..." (p. 158).

2/John Crowe Ransom, *The World's Body* (1938), makes a relevant point about the significance of the poetic rather than prose statement, in describing the dramatic monologue form: "First, the poet puts on the mask. It places him before his public – and in his own mind for that matter – as an anonymous person and not as himself. ... Now the mask is not actually a piece of cloth, but its equivalent for the purpose: it is the metre. For metre is an artificial language. One does not transact actual business in it, one does not appear before the Chamber of Commerce uttering metres. The poet within us is released by the adoption of a tongue whose principle is novel, and wholly irrelevant to the virtues of prose discourse." (Pp. 257–8.)

the poetic process, Books II through XI demonstrate this process dramatically, and Book XII underlines and generalizes its application. The very meaning of the poem thus dictated Browning's emphasis on his role as artistic creator in the first and last books.

The reasons for the choice of other speakers are clear. The first three obviously represent the views of onlookers, observers who have no immediate personal connection with the events of the murder and trial. They therefore supply a perspective which would be missing in the words of subordinate actors such as the Abate Paolo and the Comparini, on whose views they speculate freely. But more than this, the poet's giving them only generalized names emphasizes that each is to be taken as representative of a whole class of people: the husband's sympathizers, the wife's, and those who are uncommitted to either side. Highly individualized as these speakers are, they still stand for a considerable body of public opinion; the poet's point, further underscored by his repeated reference to each monologue as a 'sample-speech,' is that had he selected any other three onlookers from anywhere in Rome, he would have found just such a divergence of opinion, caused by just this kind of innate prejudice. Further, the anonymous three show the effects of varying backgrounds and temperaments; knowing nothing specific about them, we can still deduce from the frame of reference their words reveal that Half-Rome, with his materialistic values, is of the bourgeois class, Other Half-Rome, with his feeling for beauty in distress, perhaps represents a higher social class or at least a more compassionate temperament, and Tertium Quid, with his clever bid for advancement, is a fringe-member of the decadent aristocracy.

The selection of the next three speakers seems inevitable: Guido the murderer, Pompilia the victim, and Caponsacchi her would-be rescuer. Their emotion-charged utterances contrast sharply with the relatively detached narratives of the previous speakers and point up the depth of their involvement in the tragedy which constitutes little more than a conversation piece for others. The next triad of voices represents an even more detached view than the first three: the two lawyers are so oblivious to the respective guilt or innocence of their clients and to their fate that their speeches seem curiously irrelevant to the drama, completely separated from the throbbing world of the accused and accusers. Arcangeli and Bottini represent the dead machinery of law that grinds uselessly on, with no relation to the justice it is supposed to serve. The Pope's speech, on the other hand, though detached from the swirling emotions of the courtroom, sets off the lawyers' triviality in bold relief by the largeness and humaneness of its view: Innocent's justice represents the victory of human understanding and love over the futile exercises of the law.

The arrangement of the speeches in three groups of three suggests something of a series of triangular perspectives, with the last in each group presenting the high point between two extremes: Tertium Quid, the man superior in rank, who considers himself above taking sides in the controversy; Pompilia, who seems to speak from a plane of resignation and faith far above the defiance of Guido and the despair of Caponsacchi; and Innocent xii, whose elevated thought makes the lawyers' world mean and sordid by comparison. The triad arrangement is broken finally for the second speech of Guido, necessary to reveal the extent of his duplicity in the first monologue; and the uniqueness of its position after the public, the principals, and the law have spoken, suggests something of the isolation in which the prisoner finds himself, cut off from the world of humanity by his own choice.

Far from being the purely mechanical division that this tripartite arrangement might suggest, the "voice and address" analysis shows conclusively that the order of their occurrence accounts in no small measure for the peculiar impact of individual monologues. Each one gains something from our knowledge of the previous one, and the effectiveness of each is in turn modified by those following it. For example, Half-Rome's fulminations against the law that offers husbands no protection from betrayal become more understandable, if not more acceptable, in the light of the opinions of Other Half-Rome, who can only see the same husband as a vicious animal, trapping and torturing his helpless wife, the faultless Pompilia. The extremity of both points of view is made more pronounced by the commentary of Tertium Quid, who sees with devastating clarity the mistakes on both sides. In addition, the repetition of certain figures of speech in later monologues induces in retrospect a more complex reaction to the earlier usage. When jealous Half-Rome uses the reference to "Adam and Eve," it effectively connotes the deceit of Violante and the stupidity of Pietro in his fool's paradise; for sympathetic Other Half-Rome, this image implies the understandable weakness of the woman tempted by the serpent and makes Half-Rome's assessment seem less apt and even somewhat perverse; Tertium Quid uses the same reference both ways, to condemn and to excuse the woman who succumbs to temptation, and in so doing he exposes not only the looseness of his own moral code, but the essential emptiness of both previous arguments.

The effect of the juxtaposing of the three principals' arguments is even more significant. By coming first, immediately following Tertium Quid's elaborately impartial presentation, Guido's brilliantly conceived courtroom defence wins a distinct advantage in the struggle for sympathy. Frank and indignantly fearless, he dwells on the unfeelingness and unfairness of those who condemn him without hearing his side of the case, so that, besides illustrating effectively that there are indeed two sides to this story, his strong defence reflects unfavourably on the uncommitted limpness of Tertium Quid, whose superficially wise commentary now seems only cynical and frivolous. Guido's speech loses some of *its* effectiveness when followed by the passionate outburst of Caponsacchi, whose uncalculated, almost incoherent, outpouring of words makes Guido's highly rhetorical performance seem in retrospect over-controlled and contrived, relying too much on ingenious rationalizing. A typical example is in their contrasting attitudes toward the judges; Guido's subtle flattery, with its barely discernible edge of irony, seems daring and straightforward: (v, 917–20)

> *Your lordships are considerate at least –*
> *You order me to speak in my defence*
> *Plainly, expect no quavering tuneful trills*
> *As when you bid a singer solace you, –*

– until Caponsacchi's indignation explodes in corrosive irony that pays no heed to consequence: (vi, 105–8)

> *Men, for the last time, what do you want with me?*
> *Is it, – you acknowledge, as it were, a use,*
> *A profit in employing me? – at length*
> *I may conceivably help the august law?*

Caponsacchi's speech is in turn strengthened rather than weakened by Pompilia's story, since she not only corroborates his narrative but exhibits the same artless and spontaneous quality of lyrical expression.

The change of pace, from this high level of involuntary self-revelation by two idealists to the devious machinations of the lawyers, is swift and complete.[3] Arcangeli's feast and family boasts and

3/A less important element in the change of pace is the relief provided by the lawyers' triviality and their unconscious humour, after the intense emotion of the Caponsacchi and Pompilia speeches: they "let you breathe a little," Browning said, "before the last vial is poured out." Richard Curle, ed., *Robert Browning and Julia Wedgwood: A Broken Friendship as Revealed by Their Letters* (1937), p. 153.

Bottini's slurring references to women are particularly repugnant coming after Pompilia's deathbed blessing. Likewise, the Pope's wide and all-encompassing perspective not only seems all the more noble after the narrowness and meanness of the advocates, but it gains in power and stature even more in the light of Guido's frenzied outburst in the prison-cell: the condemned man's furious castigation of hypocritical Churchmen makes the Pope's solemn meditations on the same topic seem by comparison mild, but wisely prophetic. Innocent's last thoughts had been directed to the hopeful possibility of Guido's repentance; as if in awful answer comes the violent unmasking of the prisoner's hardened despair. The analysis of the two Guido monologues in chapter v pointed out the advantages of being able to study both voices of the man side by side, but for its full impact the second speech must come in its rightful place, after the sober and prayerful philosophizing of the Pope, whose duty it is to condemn the prisoner. The conclusion is inescapable that Browning's arrangement of the speeches is essential to the richness and complexity of our response to each. To omit or to change the position of any would be to impair the design of alternating contrast, reinforcement, and counter-balancing of tone, emotion, and tempo.

The analysis in the foregoing chapters has explored what is probably the basic element in Browning's presentation of the monologues: the detection of relative distortion which each allows, so that even before we have the advantage of other contrasting perspectives, we make an instant judgment of the speaker on the basis of his revealed motives. The close reading of each speech illuminated the role of the *time* element – the relation of the speech in time to the commission of the murder – as almost as significant as the tone and diction in accounting for the distinctive viewpoint. Half-Rome's suspicions of his wife's fidelity during the coming Carnival make his diatribes against Violante and Pompilia suspect anyway; his enjoyment of a kind of vicarious thrill in lingering about the church where Violante's corpse has just been laid out makes his attitude perverse. Other characteristics – his too-assertive manner, his vulgar colloquialisms, and his debasing *'angler'* image – increase the unpleasant effect, and we tend to dismiss his assessment of Pompilia as an extreme result of his personal situation. Other Half-Rome's bias is not so obvious; he is patently sentimental in his idealization of Pompilia as angelic, hardly human, but the knowledge that he has only just come from viewing her at Santa Anna's where she lies on her deathbed makes the exaggerated admiration more understandable. Further, his respectful, quiet manner, the uncertain, intuitive mode of his discourse, and particularly his use of delicate imagery cause us to accept much of his evaluation as the impression of a sensitive and thoughtful observer. Tertium Quid's viewpoint, while the most sophisticated and undoubtedly the most clear-eyed of the three, is so obviously aimed at impressing his audience while straddling the fence of decision – the trial has not yet begun and he is not one to commit himself recklessly – that in the end it carries little weight for or against either side, although the bias is slightly in favour of Guido.

The extent of Guido's distortion of the facts is not apparent in his first appearance. The effectiveness of this address to the court rests on its evident candour and the fact that it follows so soon after the Vigil-torture, to which he constantly alludes in a bid for sympathy. Caponsacchi and Pompilia are so intense and unself-conscious in their presentations that we find their agitated and confused narration adding to, rather than detracting from, their conviction, and the circumstance of Pompilia's imminent death intensifies their credibility. That their speeches take place on the same day – the fourth after the attack, the last of Pompilia's life – and perhaps at the same hour is another factor binding them firmly together. The lawyers' speeches carry no conviction; their unconcern with the dead girl's name and the fate of the imprisoned Guido and their fascination with their own technique highlight the emptiness of their arguments, and we dismiss them as ignorant and blind. This concern with technique, indicated in Arcangeli's view of himself as classical poet and Bottini's picturing himself as a master painter, serves to link them in their vanity with Guido, who also sees himself as a consummate artist. His only regret about his crime is that it is incomplete; he asks complacently: (XI, 1565–7)

> But, treat my act with fair unjaundiced eye,
> What was there wanting to a masterpiece
> Except the luck that lies beyond a man?

thus betraying the same kind of shallowness that the lawyers exhibited, a concern with superficial form at the expense of essential meaning. Additionally, taking place as they do some weeks after the speeches of the principals and before the Pope's decision, the lawyers' arguments seem isolated in time, as in concern, from the high points of the drama, the deaths of Pompilia and Guido.

The Pope's speech, free of any ulterior motive, carries the most weight of all; accepting him as neither omniscient nor infallible, we nevertheless feel that his perceptiveness and instinct lead him to the right decision. Coming as it does at the end of the trial and representing the prisoner's last resort, his decision attains added import from the deeply troubled and uncertain progression of thought leading to it. Finally, in Guido's climactic last speech hours before his execution, the revelation of his true motives for the murder demolishes the sympathy which the first argument had gained, and establishes Pompilia's innocence beyond doubt.

This necessarily constant evaluation of pressures and motives in listening to each speech makes it clear that the apparently even division of arguments – those of Half-Rome, Tertium Quid, Arcangeli, and the two Guidos on one side, of Other Half-Rome, Caponsacchi, Pompilia, Bottini, and the Pope on the other – is misleading. On the one side, the argument of Half-Rome is largely negative (against Pompilia rather than for Guido) and becomes progressively weaker in the light of other arguments (as, for instance, that of Bottini whose leering association of woman's beauty with dirt and evil recalls and casts further doubt on Half-Rome's similar attitude);[4] Tertium Quid and Arcangeli are almost entirely ineffective in arousing sympathy for Guido, and his own second speech destroys all that the first had built up. On the other hand, we are willing to accept, with some qualifications in most cases, all the sympathetic evaluations of Pompilia (except Bottini's, which is only superficially a '*defence*' of her).

The difference in the weight of the arguments does not depend simply on their number, either; a cumulative effect comes about from the interlocking relationships of the Pompilia arguments. The ostensibly pro-Guido speeches have little positive in common in their defence of him; on scrutiny, they turn out to be almost entirely directed against women in general, with Pompilia a more particular target. That Bottini is seen in Book XII actively engaged in destroying Pompilia's name to gain her estate merely underscores this point; his defence of her is perfunctory and half-hearted, masking an obsessive hatred of women. The pro-Pompilia speakers, on the other hand, are bound together by a common conviction of her goodness. This conviction is conveyed mainly through the "third person"

4/A small but revealing example of the links between these two is the way a phrase used casually but strikingly by Half-Rome to describe Pompilia's mother – '*The creature thus conditioned found by chance / Motherhood* like a jewel in the muck' (II, 564–5, emphasis is mine) – is employed repeatedly and significantly by Bottini.

references of their monologues and by certain shared verbal associations. Pompilia is the third person consciousness that presses so
heavily on the mind of Other Half-Rome and Caponsacchi both,
the former unable to forget the sight of her as she lay dying, the
latter wracked by the knowledge of his helplessness at this moment
– 'Pompilia is only dying while I speak!' Caponsacchi in turn becomes her "third person" as she speaks to defend him, and the two
are thus linked together by still one more strand.[5] Her third defender
is the Pope and although he speaks of her only briefly, it is in a
prayer to her as a saint in heaven, the 'single rose' of his poor garden.
These two figures, the saint and the flower, immediately recall the
respective dominant images of Other Half-Rome and Caponsacchi
and thus enrich Pompilia's memory by enveloping it in a whole
pattern of verbal associations suggesting the spiritual and beautiful.
Other motifs in the Pope's speech had recalled Pompilia: the dark–
light contrast (already linked with Caponsacchi's black–white opposition) and the belief in the superiority of intuitive response over
rationality in apprehending truth, a belief also shared by Caponsacchi. Again, Other Half-Rome's gentle-bird and sheltered-flower
images merge with those used by Pompilia and the Pope, to convey
a consistent impression of her passivity, innocence, and oneness
with nature.

What has happened is that our judgments of Pompilia and Guido
have been formed in the course of our reading of the poem, not by
their arguments alone, but by our further judgment of all the other
speakers, who are themselves in the act of rendering a verdict on
these two. We have become aware that in every case those who condemn Pompilia do so because of some blind spot in their perspective
which makes them incapable of understanding goodness. The broken
fragments of truth that they can discern consist mainly of the recognition of guilt, in the Comparini, the Church, the law, the society.
They can all assess blame, but they cannot distinguish between the
foolish mistakes of a Violante and the depravity of a Guido. In each
case, the blind spot is caused by the perversion of some naturally
good quality or emotion: Half-Rome's love for his wife turned to
fierce jealousy, Tertium Quid's neatly balanced mind sunk to moral
indifferentism; Arcangeli's domesticity and parental love deformed
into gluttony and obsessive pride, Bottini's cleverness and legal

5/Contrarily, Guido is the one speaker who has no third person consciousness; as a result he is all egotism and isolation and seems beyond the reach of
Pompilia's gentle blessing.

acumen wasted on triviality and trickery, and finally, Guido's desire for power and recognition twisted into skulking brutality. Each one, then, has condemned himself to a lifetime of half-truths and distortions because he has let a natural talent wither or a healthy emotion become an abnormality.

Those observers whose eyes are open to goodness, on the other hand, have a greater grasp of the truth, because their motives are purer, undistorted by selfishness or pride. The Pope, Pompilia, Caponsacchi, and Other Half-Rome, each in his own way and on his own level, all reach toward the truth out of some form of love, whether for the human or the divine. Although they comprehend the power of goodness and the weakness of evil, the truth for each can be no more than a light shrouded in darkness: they share a perplexity and despondence at the evidence all about them of blindness and injustice. Their light remains only a faint reflection of the brilliant white light of the poet's vision; nevertheless, it holds out for them a promise of a more complete apprehension in time. We understand that they see as much as it is given to man to see without the poet's gift of divine inspiration. And we accept their judgments, just as we rejected the others.

The pattern is clear. As a result of the operation of all integrated elements of the principle of "voice and address" functioning in each monologue and within the larger design (the selection, arrangement, and balancing of the "voices") we are left with the overwhelming impression of Pompilia as innocence and goodness personified, Guido as a kind of negative embodiment of evil – the same impression created by the poet's imagery of lamb and wolf in Book 1. Then he had only described them as such, but now we share his assessment, and with conviction, because we have taken part in the process of evolving it, step by step, piece by piece, through assuming for a time each of the differing perspectives involved, measuring and weighing its validity against that of the others, until we come at last to the conclusion the poet had pointed to.

Browning's complex technique embodied in the principle of "voice and address" thus carries out the process described in the ring metaphor of Book 1. Such a technique makes heavy demands on the reader. He must respond to each speaker in the poem with the same degree of attention and concentration, alert to every subtle signal of voice, audience, time, place, diction, motive, fact, opinion. He must note, interpret, and remember the appearance and re-appearance of myriad strands of motifs, images, concepts, attitudes, and emotions, and watch their gradual development into an intricate web of cross-references and verbal echoes, influencing and controlling his step-by-step apprehension of the truth. The demands are great, but so are the rewards: a sense of sharing in the poet's creative process, arriving at a new appreciation of the poet's skill and power, and a deeper understanding of how it is *'That Art remains the one way possible / Of speaking truth.'*[6]

6/Wayne Booth, *The Rhetoric of Fiction* (1961), describes the author-reader relationship in terms particularly applicable to *The Ring and the Book*: "The author makes his readers. If he makes them badly – that is, if he simply waits, in all purity, for the occasional reader whose perceptions and norms happen to match his own, then his conception must be lofty indeed if we are to forgive him for his bad craftsmanship. But if he makes them well – that is, makes them see what they have never seen before, moves them into a new order of perception and experience altogether – he finds his reward in the peers he has created." (Pp. 397–8.)

Chapter VIII

"And Save the Soul Beside":
the Larger Design

THE FOREGOING summary of Browning's design in his longest and most successful poem answers some important questions about his view of the nature, function, and method of the artist. But it raises some further questions as well. Helpful and even necessary as a rigorous formal analysis is in trying to apprehend a poem of such magnitude, it can clearly never be more than the first step in an approach to the poem. Impressed as we may be by the exalted concept of the poet's role so triumphantly expressed here, we are bound to wonder how Browning came to believe in it; how, one might ask, did a work of such ringing conviction come to emerge from the age of doubt and compromise, the age of *In Memoriam* and *Dover Beach*? And, having seen the intricate operation of the "voice and address" technique in the linked dramatic monologues, we want to know what brought Browning to conceive of this unique vehicle for expressing his poetic ideas, and what steps went into its development. And finally, having seen how he conveys his ideas about good and evil, we want to know why he arrived at them, what standards he used to judge the men and women he presents to us; what was the particular view of human nature, in short, that caused him to find in the sordid testimony of the old yellow book such an inspiring lesson of love and self-sacrifice? A brief look at the years that led up to the composition of his masterwork will help to put *The Ring and the Book* into perspective in these three areas: first, the development of his conception of the poet's role (as seer, re-creator, judge); second, the experimentation with various lyric and semi-dramatic forms which led to his highly organized dramatic monologue form; and third, the evolution of the moral philosophy which informed his judgments of human actions and shaped his belief in the moral function of art.[1]

For such a purpose, his poetry can be seen as falling into two phases: the earlier, extending throughout the 1830's, in which he laboured in *Pauline*, *Paracelsus*, and *Sordello* to make artistic coherence out of conflicting views of the poet's function, and the second, lasting throughout the next two decades, in which he resolved the conflict by adopting the technique of the dramatic monologue and at the same time codified his ethical standards for judging the success or failure of individual human acts. By the beginning of the 1860's, when he came upon Pompilia's story in the old yellow book, he was ready to combine all three of these ideas into a single significant statement: he would show how the poet's particular capacity for assessing human behaviour could be shared, through the medium of the dramatic monologue, with the reading audience, not only to satisfy it aesthetically but to further its moral progress.

From the very beginning of his writing career, Browning seems to have been convinced that the poet had some unique task to perform, but he was not at all clear about just what that task was to be. The work of his early years reveals how painfully he struggled to ascertain the answer. In a recent study, J. Hillis Miller has brilliantly captured the feeling of creative energy caught between the longing for stability and the thrust toward dynamic movement which marks Browning's early style: "Massive substance, a seething diffused energy, a shaping force urging the shapeless bulk toward form — these make up the initial Browningesque self and Browningesque world." The creative urge is inhibited by a division of aim: "This jelly-lump" of unrealized form is "paralyzed by a fundamental contradiction in its impulses. ... Back and forth Browning vacillates between the desire to become some one concrete thing, and the desire

---

1/See Thomas J. Collins, *Robert Browning's Moral-Aesthetic Theory 1833–1855* (1967), for a full-length study of the development of Browning's philosophy in the earlier years of his career.

to remain permanently uncommitted, and therefore the only material mirror of the infinite richness of God."[2] Although biographers and critics have been quick to label this conspicuous tension a symptom of psychological conflict in his personal life,[3] it is perhaps more to the point to see it as an artist's natural tendency to realize most intensely his own uniqueness colliding inevitably with the equally strong urge to participate, through his creative imagination, in the diversity and richness of life around him. The ultimate solution to this dilemma, suggested in the gold and alloy metaphor of *The Ring and the Book* (where the poet exercises his artistic self-consciousness to re-create in imagination a world from which he subsequently withdraws his own personality), would come to him only after years of unremitting efforts to clarify his poetic aims and then fit them to the proper medium.

The young Browning first faced the choice between individuality and diversity in an age in which pre-Darwinian speculations were in the process of demolishing the last remnants of the old static hierarchy of discrete essences in the Great Chain of Being, and he seems to have greeted with enthusiasm both the greater opportunities and the greater demands which the new world view thrust upon the artist. Although the early fluctuation between subjectivity and objectivity that Miller notes may seem to suggest that he was suffering from the same ambivalence toward the prophet's role felt by contemporaries like Tennyson and Arnold, Browning gives no evidence that he was reluctant to accept the responsibility; under the tutelage of Shelley he apparently subscribed wholeheartedly to the Romantic belief that the artist's function was no longer merely to reflect the world but to be actively creative and socially accountable. In A. O. Lovejoy's words, this new view held that "Man's high calling was to add something of his own to the creation, to enrich the sum of things, and thus, in his finite fashion, consciously to collaborate in the fulfilment of the Universal Design."[4] But even as he embraced this version of the poet's role, Browning was forced, like his Roman-

2/*The Disappearance of God: Five Nineteenth-Century Writers* (1963), p. 84.

3/See, for example, Betty Miller, *Robert Browning: A Portrait* (1952), who sees the poet's tension arising out of a clash between "the ideals of Shelley and those of Sarah Anna Browning" (p. 11); F. R. G. Duckworth, *Browning: Background and Conflict* (1931), who interprets the "conflict" as a reluctance on the poet's part to share his private life with the public; and Stewart W. Holmes, "Browning: Semantic Stutterer" (1945), who diagnoses in the poet a "feeling of guilt at his semantic impotence" (p. 237).

4/*The Great Chain of Being: A Study of the History of an Idea* (1948), p. 296.

tic predecessors, to grapple with the problem of just how the noble vision was to be translated into concrete reality. Uncertainty about the specific goal and the precise instrument it called for, then, rather than any doubts about taking up the poetic mission explains the initial vacillation. In pointing out the difficulty for the new artists, Lovejoy quotes Schiller on the tension between form and content inherent in the Romantic theory of art:

Since the *world* is spread out in time, since it is change, the complete realization of that potentiality which relates man to the world must consist in the greatest possible variability and extension. Since the *person* is that which is permanent through change, the complete realization of that potentiality which is antithetic to change must consist in the greatest possible self-sufficiency and intension.[5]

These are precisely the conflicting drives that plague the young Browning. Convinced, almost from the outset, that his destiny as a poet depended upon his solving the dilemma, upon his bridging the gap between the uniqueness and permanence of self and the plenitude and change of the universe, he set resolutely about the task of finding an artistic medium which would satisfy both demands: he would learn, on the one hand, how to be true to his own individual vision and, on the other, how to realize in his poetry all the values of the richly various material world.

In *Pauline* (1833), his first published work, the initial attempt to reconcile the individual and social impulses is clearly a failure. He begins by glorying in his singularity:

> *I am made up of an intensest life,*
> *Of a most clear idea of consciousness*
> *Of self, distinct from all its qualities,*
> *From all affections, passions, feelings, powers;*[6]

but this intense self-consciousness is linked to a '*principle of restlessness,*' the hunger to '*be all, have, see, know, taste, feel, all*' (I, 11). His imaginative power enables him to '*look and learn / Mankind, its cares, hopes, fears, its woes and joys*' (I, 16), but at the same time he is continually diverted from this task by the selfish desire to enjoy

5/*Ibid.*, p. 302.
6/*The Works of Robert Browning*, ed. F. G. Kenyon, I, 11. All quotations from Browning's poetry in this chapter are from this edition and all the quotations, including those from *The Ring and the Book*, are identified in the text by volume and page number.

his 'bright sights' in solitude, to 'let them fade / Untold' (I, 18). He despairs at ever being able to close what he calls the 'chasm / 'Twixt what I am and all I fain would be' (I, 23). At one moment he feels the need to be 'concentrated,' at the next, he delights as his soul 'Expands' (I, 27, 28). He exults in the power to immerse himself in every living thing: 'I can live all the life of plants ... I can mount with the bird ... Or like a fish breathe deep the morning air' (I, 24), and he approves the definition of the perfect bard as one 'Who chronicled the stages of all life' (I, 30). But his last plea to the 'Sun-treader,' who is Shelley, his ideal poet, is 'Thou must be ever with me' (I, 34), revealing a sense of inadequacy at the awesome task of turning the poetry of mystic intuition into inspiring prophecy. Clearly, Pauline shows that, although he has at this initial point in his career fully committed himself to the concept of the 'seer,' Browning is as yet confused and uncertain about his power to become a 'sayer' capable of sharing his dream with others.

Critics have long blamed the poem's "morbid self-consciousness" and inept confessional style on Browning's youthful thralldom to Shelley,[7] but it is perhaps more important to note that, even this early, Browning was discriminating between his idol's idealistic AIM, on the one hand, and his visionary METHOD on the other. The reiterated admission that he must depart from him, however reluctantly, points to the growing realization that the Sun-treader did not have the answer to how the poet was to satisfy the hunger to 'be all,' that in fact he was a victim of the same dilemma as his young admirer. Still unclear about exactly what the right way is, the poet of Pauline nevertheless suggests by his references to the 'bright sights' of solitude that the Shelleyan mode of introspection, leading as it does to abstraction and impractical idealism, is a dangerous habit for the prophet whose energies must be directed at the real world. What Browning DID accept from Shelley, as Pauline shows, was the lesson that, whatever the actual way out of the poetic conflict between subjectivity and objectivity, it could only be found by the poet whose motives were unselfish; that is, only that artist can realize himself fully in poetry who creates FOR THE SAKE OF OTHERS. The single clear attitude that emerges from the hero's analysis of his situation is that

7/See Park Honan, Browning's Characters: A Study in Poetic Technique (1961), pp. 11–17, for a description of the Shelleyan influence on diction and syntax in Pauline, and Frederick A. Pottle, Shelley and Browning: A Myth and Some Facts (1923), for a fuller treatment of the relationship between the two poets.

he has been guilty of egotism, and he must renounce his self-absorption in favour of the true bard's dedication; '*but now,*' he concludes, '*I shall be priest and prophet as of old*' (1, 34). His definition of the perfect bard as one '*Who chronicled the stages of all life*' is a further, if implicit, admission that the poet must participate in other lives. Browning is in fact taking as his guide, not the Shelleyan lyricism, but the Shelleyan pronouncement of *A Defence of Poetry*:

The great secret of morals is love; or a going out of our own nature, and an identification of ourselves with the beautiful which exists in thought, action, or person, not our own. A man, to be greatly good, must imagine intensely and comprehensively; he must put himself in the place of another and of many others; the pains and pleasures of his species must become his own.[8]

This ideal, of unselfish service to others, became the cornerstone of Browning's moral-aesthetic philosophy. In his next poem, *Paracelsus* (1835), he immediately began to put to work the lesson of *Pauline*, that the poet "must put himself in the place of another," in two ways: first, by adopting a new vehicle for his theme (again, the poetic search), and secondly, by arriving at some specific judgments about the causes of poetic success and failure. Not only does he substitute for the transparently autobiographical form of the earlier poem a semi-dramatic format (with a listing of dramatis personae and a division into acts), but he objectifies the two conflicting poetic drives in the characters of Paracelsus and Aprile, poets who embody opposite tendencies and results: Paracelsus, the intellectual, attains something of a victory, and Aprile, the poet of feeling, dies a failure. What both share is a Shelleyan belief in the inspired quality of the poet's vision and a conviction of the moral necessity to use this gift for others; what they differ in, significantly, is the WAY in which they choose to express the vision. Paracelsus says he answers to God '*Who summons me to be his organ*' (1, 48), but Aprile, although he shares the '*mighty aim*' to create all forms of art, insists on leaving all his beautiful works imbued with his own spirit (1, 80). Herein lies Aprile's failure; unlike Paracelsus, whose intellectual power allows him to deal with objective reality, Aprile loves mankind blindly, with a consuming passion bound to burn itself out in vaporous abstractions. He cannot separate his creations from himself. They can never have a life of their own, but remain ever as pale ghostly images of the

8/*The Complete Works of Percy Bysshe Shelley,* ed. Roger Ingpen and Walter E. Peck (1965), VII, 118.

poet. Each time he tries to single out one of the lovely shapes that crowd around him, 'to give that one, entire / In beauty, to the world' (1, 83), he finds himself distracted by all its equally beautiful companions. And 'mist-like influences, thick films, / Faint memories of the rest ... float fast' around him until he feels like one caught in 'whirling snow-drifts' (1, 83). He fails as an artist simply because his love is too ethereal, too pure, to partake of man's earthly existence.

Paracelsus, on the other hand, meets with more success, but even his victory is only partial: superior knowledge engenders in him an intellectual pride which makes him loath to stoop to the imperfect condition of struggling humanity. But at least the labelling of Paracelsus' victory as partial indicates that Browning has discovered what direction his search must take now; a new kind of poet, he says, can and must emerge, a poet who combines equally love and knowledge: 'a third / And better-tempered spirit,' who is neither an 'over-radiant' star like Aprile, too blind with love to see man's faulty reality, nor a 'dark orb' like Paracelsus, who sees man's incompleteness but is too proud to accept his part in the struggle toward perfection (1, 168). The third way will be Browning's, then; he will be the kind of poet who, avoiding excessive subjectivity and emotion, enters fully into the lives of the imperfect human beings he serves. This position represents substantially that of the poet in The Ring and the Book, although it is more tentatively expressed; Browning is not yet sure he can achieve his aim. But two basic ideas have taken shape: that the poet must learn to 'stoop' to the limitations of lesser men, and he must do it by letting his creations have a life of their own. The lesson Aprile learned too late is expressed in terms remarkably like those the poet in The Ring and the Book will use, to indicate how the poet mirrors God: 'God is the perfect poet, / Who in his person acts his own creations' (1, 85).

It is surely ironic that, having attained at such effort to what he thought was a resolution of his poetic conflict of aims, Browning should then proceed to publish the notoriously incomprehensible Sordello (1840). But even Sordello's palpable weaknesses of structure and characterization cannot obscure the fact that, with its completion, Browning had taken a considerable step forward in the struggle to find the right medium. His poetic aims satisfactorily defined, he had now to work out a method for expressing them, and Sordello is notable for the way he experiments with various techniques. Not surprisingly, he continues the course set out in Paracelsus of making his protagonist an historical character. His often-quoted

note to the edition of 1863, in which he points out that "The historical decoration was purposely of no more importance than a background requires," and that his "stress lay on the incidents in the
development of a soul" (1, 178) is somewhat misleading in its hind-
sight, since in fact the development of Sordello's soul depends almost
entirely on his particularized historical situation, a point which
Browning takes care to call to our attention frequently in the course
of the narrative. His repeated comment that the action took place
'six hundred years ago,' and his laboured explorations of the intri-
cacies of the Guelf-Ghibelline conflict (explanations which contribute in no small way to the impenetrability of the plot), prove his
determination to escape both the self-consciousness of the speaker
in *Pauline* and the insubstantiality of Aprile in *Paracelsus*, by incar-
nating the "development of a soul" in a concrete, identifiable, well-
developed situation. Additionally, he apparently feels that the use
of a narrator will help him avoid the pitfalls of confessional auto-
biography; interestingly enough, however, he uses this device with
a curious self-consciousness and awkwardness. Almost immediately
he has the speaker-poet admit to his audience that he would have
preferred letting his hero Sordello speak for himself: (1, 179)

> *Never, – I should warn you first, –*
> *Of my own choice had this, if not the worst*
> *Yet not the best expedient, served to tell*
> *A story I could body forth so well*
> *By making speak, myself kept out of view,*
> *The very man as he was wont to do,*
> *And leaving you to say the rest for him.*

Little or nothing seems to have been gained by the interposing of a
narrator between the main character and the audience;[9] in fact, the
occasional blurring of the two viewpoints (as in Book III, where the
speaker attributes to Sordello an incident in which he himself fig-
ured) merely increases the already well-nigh impassable thickets
of obscurity. What *is* significant is that, even as he chooses to try
the device of a narrator, Browning experiences the urge to keep

---

9/For some recent attempts to justify the narrator's function, see Daniel
Stempel, "Browning's Sordello: The Art of the Makers-See" (1965), which sees
the device of "dioramic narrative" giving an organic unity to the whole, and
Robert R. Columbus and Claudette Kemper, "Sordello and the Speaker: A
Problem in Identity" (1964), which reads the poem, not as Sordello's story, but
as an exploration of the speaker's identity.

himself 'out of view' and let 'The very man' speak for himself, with the audience left to join in the creative process by supplying what the poet leaves unsaid. These lines alone might suggest that Browning was already feeling his way toward the monologue form; in a later passage in the same poem he deals even more explicitly with the question of technique and makes it clear that he has rather clearly envisioned the particular poetic mode best suited to his purpose.

This passage has to do with Sordello's search for his proper role in life, a search which appears at first to be merely a repetition of that in the two earlier poems, with the familiar inability of the hero to choose between conflicting aims of withdrawal and commitment; however, there is a distinct advance, at this point, in the hero's recognition of what specific actions his artistic vocation demands. He begins by feeling himself a part of every living thing he beholds, and then is moved to invent a world of men in which to immerse himself: he wants to 'be men, now, as he used to blend / With tree and flower' (I, 202). These inventions, the narrator assures us, were only 'abortive boy's-attempt,' but nonetheless they augur well for future achievement once Sordello can find his proper medium, can, as he puts it himself, ' "acquire an instrument" / "For acting what these people act" ' and then he adds, excited at the possibility: ' "my soul" / "Hunting a body out may gain its whole" / "Desire some day!" ' (I, 203). The phrase is striking: 'soul hunting a body' is almost exactly the description of the creative process in Book 1 of *The Ring and the Book* in which the poet claims that he 'May so project his surplusage of soul / In search of body' that 'something dead may get to live again' (v, 25). Clearly, even thirty years before he wrote that description, the image had caught Browning's imagination as the perfect one for suggesting how a poet works, not by merely describing, or even inventing, a world of men, but by re-creating human life – breathing his own soul into inert forms in direct imitation of divine creation.[10]

10/Actually, the "resuscitator" image may have been in Browning's mind as early as *Pauline*. Commenting on the "curious introductory passage" from Cornelius Agrippa which he appended to *Pauline*, Maisie Ward, in her biography, *Robert Browning and His World: The Private Face (1812–1861)* (1967), adds the following interesting footnote: "Cornelius Agrippa, an occult philosopher of the sixteenth century, was also a magician reputed to be able to cause an evil spirit to enter and apparently resuscitate a corpse" (n., p. 310). The "evil spirit" is a far cry from the poet's beneficent power, of course, but it may be significant that in *The Ring and the Book* the first "resuscitator" reference is to

Browning goes even further in *Sordello* in analysing the details of the creative process. Dissecting the hero's plight – what Sordello himself calls the ' "*need become all natures, yet retain*" / "*The law of my own nature*" ' (I, 241) – the narrator reveals that there exist different types of poet, their varying levels of accomplishment dependent on the method they choose for presenting their ideas:

> For the worst of us, to say they so have seen;
> For the better, what it was they saw; the best
> Impart the gift of seeing to the rest. ... (I, 265)

The lowest form of poetry, then, seems to be that in which the poet narrates, or merely EFFUSES his private vision, the next higher, that in which the poet INTERPRETS his vision for the reader, and the highest of all, that in which the poet dramatically RENDERS his vision so that his reader can experience it with him. Poets of this last type he calls the '*Makers-see*' (I, 267). What we have here, in addition to the description of the poet's "resuscitation" method of *The Ring and the Book*, is an anticipation, in remarkably explicit terms, of the poet's need to "de-personalize" his creation in order to let the reader share his vision of truth. It is not enough that the '*seer*' become '*sayer*'; for the highest art he must be able to put aside his interpreter's role and let the reader see exactly what he himself sees.

All that is left to complete the formulation of Browning's aesthetic philosophy is the concept of poet as judge, and even that idea is adumbrated in *Sordello*. In working out the various stages of artistic development, the poet says that at first he simply paints men the way he wants his audience to see them; he can ' "*marshal you Life's elemental masque*," / "*Show Men, on evil or on good lay stress*" ' and make it clear ' "*Which sinner is, which saint*" ' (I, 319). In the next stage, however, he moves on to '*unstation*' characters, ' "*conduct*" / "*Each nature to its farthest*" ' (I, 320), so that they act out their hopes and fears and loves ' "*In presence of you all*" ' and the audience is left to decide for itself who is good, who bad. Finally, ' "*Man's inmost life shall have yet freer play*" ' as the poet is able to '*cast external things away*' entirely and actually '*decompose*' his characters' natures. Apparently Browning here foresees a stage of

an unnamed "mage" who is compared first to Faust and then to the biblical Elisha. The marked turn from black magician to Hebrew prophet might indicate that Browning was not unaware that the awesome creative powers could be used for evil as well as good. See note 23 below.

attainment for the poet where he will have so mastered a knowledge of man's moral nature that, in almost god-like fashion, he will be able to judge human beings, not on the basis of how their behaviour conforms to any objective moral standard, but out of an understanding of each man's deepest spiritual promptings. But the next lines are even more significant: here he indicates that the poet, at this last stage, will have succeeded in making his audience in effect his equals; sharing his god-like powers of penetration, they will know, AS HE KNOWS, what before they had to accept on his word. Sordello concludes his description of this third stage by exclaiming: (I, 320)

> How I rose,
> And how have you advanced! since evermore
> Yourselves effect what I was fain before
> Effect, what I supplied yourselves suggest,
> What I leave bare yourselves can now invest.

The wording reminds us of the poet's insistence in the first and last books of *The Ring and the Book* that this is how, by co-operative effort with the creator, the reader understands a speaker's motives ('*See it for yourselves!*' ... '*you have seen his act / By my power – maybe, judged it by your own*'). And once we recognize the similarity of the situations, it suddenly becomes clear that here, almost buried beneath Sordello's diffuse and often obscure theorizing on poetics, is an astonishingly accurate outline of the actual structure of Book I of *The Ring and the Book*. The three summaries of the Franceschini story, which as we saw were intended to represent the stages of the creative process, correspond precisely with the levels of achievement Sordello here describes: the first impassioned description by the poet-speaker, so concerned to convince the reader of Pompilia's innocence and Guido's guilt, represents the lowest level of creation in which the poet merely effuses his private vision, pronouncing '*Which sinner is, which saint*'; the second impersonal factual summary, after which the reader was enjoined to listen to the actors in the drama, is the equivalent of the higher stage in which the poet '*unstations*' his characters and sets them before the reader without comment; finally, the introduction of the monologues, with the withdrawal of the poet's voice, represents the direct rendering of motivations for the reader's judgment – the last and highest form of poetic achievement. What this means, simply, is that *The Ring and the Book* must be seen as the final accomplishment of a poetic design that had crystallized in Browning's mind three decades before; little wonder, then, that he makes the poet-speaker there so exultant about his achievement.

Despite the blow that the obscurity of *Sordello* delivered to Browning's burgeoning reputation, then, the poem's importance in the evolution of his aesthetic philosophy cannot be overestimated.[11] Its completion left him with a firm grasp of what the creative process entailed: he needed substantial human characters, located in an identifiable historical situation; he must portray them in all their incomplete efforts to perfect themselves; he must render the struggle dramatically and yet let the characters reveal themselves in their own words. Above all, he must make the revelation as direct as possible. In Sordello's words: (1, 320–1)

> "Leave the mere rude
> "Explicit details! 'tis but brother's speech
> "We need, speech where an accent's change gives each
> "The other's soul –. ..."

Not surprisingly, Browning thought to find in the drama the mode best suited for this direct rendering of thought, but he was to find instead that the demands of plot advancement proved a hindrance to what he now saw as his main task, the revelation of character. Since what mattered to him was not the choice of action but the reasons behind the choice, more and more he turned to use of the soliloquy to let his characters explain, defend, and justify themselves. Eventually it became clear to him that it was just this form, detached from the external conflict of drama, that would allow him to "give a man's soul" directly to another. The single, compressed, semi-private utterance, growing solely out of the interaction between speaker and audience, could be used to expose concerns and attitudes of which even the speaker might not be aware. Of equal importance, the reader could be drawn into the creative process by being made to experience the sensation of complete, if momentary, identification with the viewpoint of another person. The process, to which Browning now turned his full attention, involved not only a mastery of the literary

---

11/See Thomas J. Collins, *Robert Browning's Moral-Aesthetic Theory 1833–1855* (1967), pp. 61–70, for a detailed examination of the developing aesthetic ideas in *Sordello*. Collins finds them pointing to Browning's feeling for the inadequacy of language: the poet's thought can never be fully communicated "because language, especially at the extremity to which Sordello – and Browning – would like to take it, becomes ineffectual ..." (p. 70).

form, but an understanding of the psychological responses from the speaker AND the reader of the defensive argument.

Audience reaction to the first-person argument has long concerned literary critics. Even Plato dealt with it; foreseeing the possibility that an actor might identify too closely with his assumed personality, he warned that dramatic recitations ought to be restricted to "appropriate types of character" and any characterizations that are "mean or dishonorable" avoided, lest the actors voicing the opinions become "infected with the reality."[12] From another point of view, that of the epistolary novel, modern critic Wayne Booth has taken note of the singular capacity for persuasion inherent in use of the first-person argument; recalling Samuel Richardson's distress at learning that his "case-hardened sinner, Lovelace" had won some readers' admiration, Booth observes that

> once Lovelace has been given a chance to speak for himself ... our reaction to him even at the moment when we fear for Clarissa most intensely is likely to be double-edged. Unlike our reaction to villains presented only from the outside, our feeling is a combination of natural detestation and natural fellow feeling: bad as he is, he is made of the same stuff we are. It is not surprising that Richardson's intentions have often been counteracted by this effect.[13]

This "double-edged" reaction is what Robert Langbaum, in his study of the dramatic monologue, calls "the effect created by the tension between sympathy and moral judgment." Using *My Last Duchess* as an example, he points to the way we suspend our moral judgment in responding to the speaker in order the better to appreciate his extraordinary qualities; we are in fact less interested in the "utter outrageousness" of his behaviour than we are interested in his "immense attractiveness."[14] The question of Browning's intention in this poem arises, however. It is quite true that in this case we do not feel called on to make a moral judgment of the speaker, but it is somewhat misleading to see the reason as a willingness "to understand the duke, even to sympathize with him." We are under no illusion that we are being given any intimate revelation of the duke's secret motivations; clearly, we are merely being treated to a good

12/*The Republic of Plato* (III. 395), trans. Francis MacDonald Cornford (1945), p. 85.

13/Wayne Booth, *The Rhetoric of Fiction* (1961), p. 323.

14/Robert Langbaum, *The Poetry of Experience: The Dramatic Monologue in Modern Literary Tradition* (1957), pp. 82, 85.

show. For all his elegance, poise, intelligence – the admirable qualities that Langbaum and other critics point to – what we feel most over-whelmingly about him is his CONTROL, of the situation, of the envoy, even of us the readers. One critic has noted something of a reversal of roles between speaker and reader: "the reader, like the envoy, feels that he, and not the Duke, is being inspected."[15] The duke has assumed the role of a theatrical impresario, artfully manipulating his properties and audience for maximum dramatic effect: *'Will't please you sit and look at her? (... none puts by / The curtain I have drawn for you, but I) ... Will't please you rise? ... we'll go / Together down, Sir'* (III, 265–6). The carefully spaced *'Sirs,'* the directing of the envoy's attention (*'There she stands ... Notice Neptune'*), the re-minders of the duke's management (*'I said / "Frà Pandolf" by de-sign ... I repeat'*) – all emphasize that every nuance and gesture of the performance has been carefully staged with an eye to the effect on the audience. (Even the use of the rhymed couplets subtly con-tributes to the over-all sense of calculation: the enjambment ensures an uninterrupted flow, but the measured recurrence of rhyme builds up, almost without our being aware of it, the effect of controlling design.) We become passive spectators in the presence of a master craftsman, admiring not what he does, but the style in which he does it. We have, in fact, taken the same role as the envoy and – this is the point – we find no occasion to "identify ourselves with the duke." His manner ensures that we are kept at a distance from him, are relegated to the role of observers only.

In other words, "sympathy" and "natural fellow feeling" are not of concern in Browning's portrait of the Duke of Ferrara. One of the earliest and briefest of his dramatic monologues, it belongs to that period, concurrent with his writing of plays, when he was still work-ing out his standards of morality for judging characters. In other monologues of this period, like *Johannes Agricola in Meditation* and *Porphyria's Lover*, he shows a similar willingness to portray an extraordinary moral position without arousing the reader to make a moral response. By the time of his next series of "dramatic lyrics," however, he is clearly intent on making moral distinctions about the attitudes of his characters; furthermore, he insists, through the manipulation of the speaker–audience relationship within the poem,

15/W. David Shaw, "Browning's Duke as Theatrical Producer" (1966). Shaw goes on to diagnose in the Duke a Freudian "obsessional neurosis" and con-cludes, somewhat surprisingly, "Thus to see Browning's Duke as a theatrical producer is not to suspend our moral judgment of him" (p. 22).

that we the readers share his conclusions. An example of this new attitude is *The Bishop Orders His Tomb at St. Praxed's Church.* I cannot agree with Langbaum's conclusion that in this case "our judgment is mainly historicized," that is, we can read the poem simply as a portrait of the age, "our moral judgment of the Bishop depending on our moral judgment of the age."[16] Rather, the care with which Browning directs our response to the Bishop indicates, I think, his condemnation of him, not just as a representative of the "predilections of the Italian Renaissance," but as a human being. The Duke of Ferrara, from what we could see of him, was a man who deliberately chose a course of action, whatever its morality; the Bishop of St. Praxed's is a man who has refused to make a clear-cut choice – for Browning, the greatest sin of all. He shares many of the duke's characteristics – worldliness, pride, aesthetic taste – but whereas in the duke's portrait they could be accepted as admirable qualities, in the Bishop they have been unmistakably reduced to baseness: greed, lust, jealousy, blindness. The perversion has taken place because of the Bishop's refusal to commit himself frankly to either of his two worlds, the life of the senses or the life of the spirit. He has insisted instead on playing at the role of ecclesiastic; had he accepted his natural impulses he might have been a great creator or patron of art, rather than the petty hoarder he is, ludicrously pretending to a moral authority he has never earned. The Duke of Ferrara may have been playing a role, too, but his theatrical performance is so well executed we accept the role as appropriate – we have no way of measuring how far it may be from his real personality. We do know the discrepancy between the Bishop's real self and his pose, however. To ensure that we know it, Browning here calls into play in full power all the various elements of the dramatic monologue that he was to make use of so successfully in *The Ring and the Book*: the highly individualized speaker, his immediate audience (*'Nephews – sons mine'*), the "third person" presence (*'Old Gandolf with his paltry onion-stone'*), the interaction between these elements producing the speaker's motives (his jealousy of Gandolf, his distrust of his auditors, his awareness of his powerlessness) – all work together to structure our response to him.

The diction and imagery are perhaps the most telling elements in the Bishop's portrayal and suggest how far Browning has advanced in the technique of voice and address. The blurring of distinctions in the dying man's speech – between the sacred and the profane, the

16/Robert Langbaum, *The Poetry of Experience*, p. 97.

significant and the trivial, the real and the unreal – perfectly reflects
the habitual lack of discrimination in his life. As he did not understand what life was about, he does not grasp the meaning of death:
'Do I live, am I dead?' (IV, 125) he asks. Even the dividing line between time and eternity is for him indeterminate and indistinct. His
essential character traits, self-love without self-knowledge and the
desire to escape into illusion by role-playing, are conveyed in a
single image: (IV, 127)

> Dying in state and by such slow degrees,
> I fold my arms as if they clasped a crook,
> And stretch my feet forth straight as stone can point,
> And let the bedclothes, for a mortcloth, drop
> Into great laps and folds of sculptor's work. ...

In the Bishop's total unawareness of the terrible variance between
the pose and the reality, between what he claims to be and what he
is, we feel the full force of Browning's assessment of the man – and
are made to share it.

What he is doing is particularly remarkable in the light of the
"doubled-edged" effect inherent in the use of the first-person argument: he is using the natural sympathy we have for the speaker, our
tendency to identify with him, as a way of making us assess him. We
have to weigh, measure, and, if need be, condemn the speaker's
defence of himself, as all the while his first-person argument reminds
us of our "natural fellow feeling" for him, that "he is made of the
same stuff we are." We are acutely aware of his shortcomings because they are so like our own, but we cannot palliate them as we
might wish, because Browning holds constantly before us the possibility of an alternative to these actions. The speaker's own words
always provide a measuring-rod of what he might have become, they
always imply the direction in which his potential for growth might
have been realized. What we have here, in short, is a situation where,
as in The Ring and the Book, any subordination of judgment to
sympathy would simply vitiate the poet's purpose. We must condemn the Bishop's perversion of values because he himself reveals,
by such graphic images as that of his "good shepherd" pose, that he
well understands what he might and should have been.

From this time on, Browning is concerned to elicit an increasingly
complex response to his dramatic monologues, as witnessed by the
lengthy, casuistical arguments he begins to introduce in the volumes
of the decade immediately preceding The Ring and the Book. They

show how he was constantly refining both his moral and his aesthetic theories along the lines already laid down. In *How It Strikes a Contemporary* and *Fra Lippo Lippi*, he dramatizes the artist's role as an intermediary between man and God, using his insights into men's lives as an instrument of moral good – '*God uses us to help each other so / Lending our minds out*' (IV, 113). In poems like *The Statue and the Bust, "Childe Roland to the Dark Tower Came,"* and *A Grammarian's Funeral,* he stresses the ideal of commitment for the ordinary man, regardless of the world's estimate of the goal. But he lavishes most of his time and care on a new exercise – preaching this same lesson through the mouths of reprehensible characters, frauds, and failures like Bishop Blougram and Andrea del Sarto and Sludge the Medium. That these speakers, all clearly objects of Browning's scorn, voice some of his own most cherished beliefs provides a further complication to the question of sympathy versus judgment. The complaint is commonly made that he has by this time become so enamoured with the play of intellect that he lets his characters run wild with ideas, leaving us no clear criterion for separating valid ideas from invalid or for determining what he is condemning from what he is condoning. As W. O. Raymond has admitted, somewhat ruefully, "It is difficult to avoid the conclusion that Browning's casuists are never really routed from the standpoint of reason."[17] And this is the main point about the casuists, of course – there is nothing logically wrong with their arguments. Their ideas for the most part correspond exactly with Browning's own. But we do not hesitate to label these speakers "casuists" (a name we would never apply to the Pope in *The Ring and the Book,* who also voices many of Browning's own opinions), simply because, in spite of our difficulties with their line of reasoning, we recognize somehow that they are misusing ideas, perverting noble concepts for ignoble ends. Once again, in other words, what counts is not what the speaker says, but what motives he has for saying it.

The real motives of the casuists, however, are much more difficult to identify than those of the speakers in the earlier poems like *The Bishop Orders His Tomb,* and in this way they foreshadow the more subtle advocates of *The Ring and the Book.* In these longer poems, the situation is usually less critical, the audience less clearly defined, the speaker at once more expansive and less revealing about himself, choosing his words with a careful eye to effect. To find what makes

17/William O. Raymond, *The Infinite Moment and Other Essays in Robert Browning* (1950), p. 133.

this kind of speaker call true things by wrong names we have to look beyond his present situation to the circumstances that shaped the habitual mental attitudes he now displays. The most disconcerting element is the speaker's candour; we are disarmed in our attempt to pass judgment on one who has such a clear-eyed view of his own limitations. Each one makes the same basic case for himself, that he is only acting "as God made him." Blougram defends his worldliness and scepticism in just these terms: *"My business is not to remake myself, / But make the absolute best of what God made'* (IV, 139). Andrea reasons in similar fashion: (IV, 118)

> *we are in God's hand.*
> *How strange now, looks the life he makes us lead;*
> *So free we seem, so fettered fast we are!*
> *I feel he laid the fetter: let it lie!*

Sludge accepts his shortcomings with equal equanimity: *'Man's still man, / Still meant for a poor blundering piece of work / When all's done'* (IV, 348). And this is the key to their failure, of course. As they talk this way, we discover that their apparent humility is in fact a deadly complacency, their frank acceptance of limitation actually a rejection of their potential for growth. Lest we miss the point, Browning has each one of them at some point acknowledge the possibility that his talent might have led to greatness in some other course: Blougram in politics (*'There's power in me and will to dominate / Which I must exercise'*) (IV, 138), Andrea in art (*'I can do with my pencil what I know, / What I see, what at bottom of my heart / I wish for'*) (IV, 118), Sludge in religion, or even in poetry (*'I was born with flesh so sensitive, / Soul so alert, that ... I guess what's going on outside the veil'*) (IV, 355).

These are all men, then, who have committed the unpardonable sin in Browning's eyes: in their impervious egoism they have turned their backs on human progress. Worse than this, they have refused to admit the evasion; not only is each a hypocrite, playing a role before the world (faithful believer, self-sacrificing lover, "medium"), but he is self-deluded, playing a role for himself – by using his uniquely human faculty of reason to justify his fraud and to shift the blame for his failure to God. Self-love, illusion, evasion of responsibility: the symptoms of thwarted growth are always the same. To them need be added only one more element to complete the lowest rung on Browning's scale of perverted humanity: when self-knowledge is finally forced upon the deluded egoist, it flashes forth as murderous hatred – like that of Count Guido Franceschini.

In the character of Guido, Browning presents his final estimate of the nature and consequences of sin. Like the other casuists who perverted reason out of a complacent self-love, the Count can argue his case before the court with confidence and consummate artistry as a man who did only what honour demanded, but in his prison speech he falls back on the same defence that the other casuists all use, that he is only "as God made him." Pompilia had said this of him; giving up the attempt to understand his inexplicable behaviour, she had meant it to excuse him, but instead she is unwittingly pointing to the source of his evil. Whenever he uses this argument to justify himself, that he is not responsible for the way he is, he remembers that Pompilia had anticipated it, and the memory rankles: (VI, 251)

> *What shall I say to God?*
> *This, if I find the tongue and keep the mind –*
> *"Do Thou wipe out the being of me, and smear*
> *"This soul from off Thy white of things, I blot!*
> *"I am one huge and sheer mistake, – whose fault?*
> *"Not mine at least, who did not make myself!"*
> *Someone declares my wife excused me so!*
> *Perhaps she knew what argument to use.*

Again, he cries: 'So am I made, "*who did not make myself*": / (*How dared she rob my own lip of the word?*') (VI, 286). His defensiveness in using this excuse is a tacit admission that he knows indeed how different he could have been.

When he considers explicitly the alternative possibilities his life offered, however, he again evades the truth about himself. Typical of the casuist, he even plays a role in private, deluding himself even up to his last moments that he possesses the boldness and fierceness of the ravening wolf, that he was meant to be magnificent in evil. What he really hates about Pompilia is her strength, which exposes the hollowness of his claim. In the midst of his raving against her pallidness and meekness – when what he needed was a '*Borgia*' to match himself – he slips into the admission that although Pompilia was '*cold and pale and mute as stone*' she was '*Strong as stone also*' and that '*same stone strength*' gave her a '*self-possession*' almost like the '*terrible patience*' of God (VI, 262–4). His last tormented cry – '*Pompilia, will you let them murder me?*' (VI, 295) – is his ultimate

206 / BROWNING'S VOICES

acknowledgment of her power and his weakness. He has tried to play the wolf, to hide his skulking cowardice behind a facade of ferocity, but the mask falls and exposes the grotesque stunting of his moral nature.[18] In a telling image, the Pope suggests the discrepancy between what he should have been and what he is: (VI, 173)

> Cased thus in a coat of proof,
> Mailed like a man-at-arms, though all the while
> A puny starveling, – does the breast pant big,
> The limb swell to the limit, emptiness
> Strive to become solidity indeed?
> Rather, he shrinks up like the ambiguous fish. ...

Instead of growing, Guido 'shrinks up' like a fish: his rejection of the natural law of development has resulted in a regression, a sliding back in the scale of life to some lower, barely defined state of existence. This is in fact what Guido had sought when he rejected his humanity in favour of a fiercer animal existence, crying 'Let me turn wolf ... Grow out of man, / Glut the wolf-nature' (VI, 284). He had thought such a transformation would win for him the fear and dread he had never been able to inspire; instead it has made him a nullity – in Caponsacchi's words, doomed to 'absolute nothingness' (V, 315). Unable finally to distinguish between his assumed wolf disguise and his natural sheep-like cowardice, he can only cling with blind egoism to the hollow core of self: he pictures himself in the next life, in some new form of existence, but, he adds, 'With something changeless at the heart of me' (VI, 294). He needs 'some nucleus' that is himself because his very sense of selfhood is disintegrating. What Browning is showing here is the final, devastating loss of identity that befalls the man who betrays his nature; because he refuses to grow, he

18/For an entirely different interpretation of the effect assuming a disguise has on a Browning character, see Charles Edwin Nelson, "Role-Playing in The Ring and the Book" (1966), which sees role-playing as a therapeutic psychological device for discovering one's real identity: Caponsacchi, for example, in seeking his true personality, reluctantly disguises himself as St. George only to discover that the role "fits him rather well" (p. 92). Nelson finds, however, that Guido employs disguises to hide from his real self; unaccountably, he demurs at a suggestion made by Professor Morse Peckham that Guido's wolf aspect is a guise too. Nelson concludes nevertheless that evil holds out no possibility of integration for Guido's personality, which I think is the basic point – that for Browning the choice of evil is a rejection of natural order which can only result in the destruction of self.

ceases to be. Hence, Caponsacchi's terrible judgment of him is right:
(v, 314–15)

> I think he will be found ...
> Not to die so much as slide out of life,
> Pushed by the general horror and common hate.
> Low, lower, – left o' the very ledge of things,
> I seem to see him catch convulsively
> One by one at all honest forms of life,
> At reason, order, decency and use – ...
> And thus I see him slowly and surely edged
> Off all the table-land whence life upsprings
> Aspiring to be immortality. ...

Several points bearing on the completion of Browning's moral-aesthetic theory emerge from this examination of the nature of Guido's evil. One is that, although Guido is by far the blackest of all the villains Browning ever conceived, his guilt is different only in degree, not in kind, from that of the other casuists. All the characteristics that marked the failure of the Bishop of St. Praxed's, Blougram, Andrea del Sarto, and Sludge the Medium are here: egoism, hypocrisy, stunted growth. What is more, they are recognizably, in darker hue, the same characteristics that marked all the anti-Pompilia speakers of *The Ring and the Book*. This means that Browning had been consistently hardening his moral judgments, moving from the comparatively distant perspective of *My Last Duchess* to the harsher condemnation of the charlatan Sludge; now as he prepared to portray the ultimate failure in Guido, he recognized that he could strengthen even further his theory of moral responsibility by repeating the pattern of casuistic behaviour in a single work. By showing, in Half-Rome, in Tertium Quid, in the lawyers, how uncontrolled egoism *invariably* degenerates into blindness and grotesque deformity, he could at once foreshadow Guido's ruinous course, uncover the root causes of his villainy, and prepare the reader to accept in his portrait what might otherwise appear inexplicable depravity. What is more, he could, by the very act of linking a series of monologues about a central incident, reinforce and universalize his conclusions about human motivations, without sacrificing any of the intensity of the first-person argument. What led him to this discovery is not clear: perhaps the experience of paralleling major motifs in the sub-plot of a play, or the experiment in *Pippa Passes* of repeating a pattern of behaviour in several separate incidents. At any rate, he saw that his old yellow book materials called for a wider scope than the single viewpoint could provide and that the linked monologues gave him just this scope: they allowed him to demonstrate the partiality of the individual human perspective and they allowed him at the same time to transcend that partiality to evolve a single all-encompassing truth.

Where this pattern of repeated behaviour is of even more direct service to his purpose is in the pro-Pompilia speeches, where he develops the obverse of the casuists' lesson and shows why *these* speakers are capable of grasping truth as the egoists were not. We saw how Other Half-Rome, Caponsacchi, and the Pope, by sharing the same "third person" consciousness and using the same kind of images (of "helpless bird" and "sheltered flower"), were character- ized, like Pompilia, as observers concerned more with others than themselves and therefore free to make the commitment that leads to growth and an apprehension of truth. All refuse to play the escapist role that opportunity offers; even Caponsacchi, diverted into acting a false role for a time, has resumed his natural bearing as a man of action when we first hear him. More important, all reveal that capa- city for creativity that is only released by selflessness. Although each justifies his actions by recourse to "nature" or "instinct" (in con- trast to the casuists who are as one in falling back on social institu- tions or customs, such as "law" or "honour"[19]), this justification is never in terms of the need for self-fulfilment but rather in terms of the need to meet a responsibility toward someone else. Similarly, each attributes his new-found ability to grow, or "rise," to the inspiring example provided by another, a point of view conveyed by the "guiding star" image used by all four speakers. Browning is doing two things in emphasizing the parallels in their attitudes and

19/Robert Langbaum, in an important chapter in *The Poetry of Experience*, sees this as one of Browning's major points, that "all social and moral abso- lutes" are inadequate to man's understanding of the truth. Calling *The Ring and the Book* a "relativist" poem, he points out that Pompilia's case "presented a challenge which the instituted machinery showed itself unable to meet" (p. 123), and it is just this recognition, shown by their rejection of "official morality," that distinguishes the actions of Caponsacchi, Pompilia, and the Pope from those of the casuists who cling blindly to the outmoded machinery. See also E. D. H. Johnson, *The Alien Vision of Victorian Poetry: Sources of the Poetic Imagina- tion in Tennyson, Browning, and Arnold* (1952), for a similar exploration of the "anti-social" implications of Browning's exalting of intuition over institutions.

the consequences of these attitudes (self-knowledge, concern for others, growth): he is repeating, in positive form, the lesson taught by the casuists' fate – the absolute necessity for man to break out of the shell of self-love if he would grow to completeness – and he is also, indirectly, pointing to the way the poet follows the same pattern (the poet who is in this poem, it should be remembered, the last of the pro-Pompilia speakers): he serves man by rescuing from obscurity and misunderstanding the God-given example, in Pompilia's story, 'Of love without a limit' (VI, 200) and preserving it as an inspiration for generations to come.

These conclusions, about the larger design of the linked monologues of *The Ring and the Book*, show how at this point in his career, Browning's moral philosophy, his belief about what moral choices are required of man, and his aesthetic philosophy, his belief about what artistic choices are required of the poet, have coalesced in a single dominating conviction. When we see how he consistently views human activity in terms of contrasting basic patterns of behaviour, that of egoism which leads to destruction and of selflessness which leads to creativity, we recognize that the original poetic conflict of "intension" versus "extension" that marked his earliest works, such as *Pauline* and *Paracelsus*, had finally been triumphantly resolved. The struggle to find the proper medium for sharing his artistic vision had yielded up the answer, that man and artist both serve best when they enter most fully into the life of another, and their highest service is to inspire others in turn to selfless action.

All this proves that Browning had indeed come a long way from his poetic beginnings. If it were true, as a writer like J. Hillis Miller contends, that the truth *The Ring and the Book* reveals is only a "momentary and evanescent perception," that we learn from it nothing but "the transcendence of God and the impossibility of joining finite and infinite," that, in fact, in his life-long poetic search, Browning "has not advanced at all from his starting point,"[20] then

20/*The Disappearance of God: Five Nineteenth-Century Writers* (1963), pp. 152, 153. Robert Langbaum, in *The Poetry of Experience*, comes to a somewhat similar conclusion about the limited nature of the truth Browning reveals: "What we arrive at in the end is not *the* truth, but truth as the worthiest characters of the poem see it" (p. 122). Although he brilliantly analyses the way truth is "psychologized" through our judgments of the speakers' motives, he somewhat surprisingly finds it a fault that "Our judgment is forced from the beginning" (p. 135). A. K. Cook, too, in his *Commentary upon Browning's "The Ring and the Book"* (1920), is uncertain about what or how much truth Browning is finally revealing; he seems to accept Lord Morley's assessment that the

well may one ask, 'Why take the artistic way to prove so much?' (VI, 321). Browning himself agreed that if the original Franceschini documents which proved to his satisfaction that Pompilia was innocent could convince the world of her innocence, then there would be no need of his services as poet; he might toss the old yellow book into the fire and there would be no loss. But all the evidence shows that the world cannot disentangle the confused and contradictory threads of testimony in the mass of lifeless 'fact' and, without the poetic intercession, the glorious truth God provided for man would continue to lie hidden as it has for two hundred years. Because he has, through years of unremitting effort, forged the precise instrument necessary to make the truth apprehensible, this poet can now use the dead fact to teach a universal, a lasting, truth: the possibility of the humblest human being acting as redemptive agent for mankind, by providing a model of love and self-sacrifice amidst overwhelming odds. This is the meaning of Pompilia's story as he makes us see it; not just that she was innocent, or that she suffered unjustly, but that she to whom it was not given 'to know much, / Speak much, to write a book, to move mankind' could become a blazing star for those still struggling on earth. She could become this only because the poet, to whom it is given to write a book and move mankind, makes her live again and lets us see how good can overcome evil. In this, he is doing God's work, completing the incomplete, saving the good from oblivion, teaching the lesson of how man is to 'love in turn and be beloved, / Creative and self-sacrificing too, / And thus eventually God-like' (VI, 200).

'Creative,' 'self-sacrificing,' 'God-like' – the words are strikingly like those used in Book 1 to describe the artistic process; they recall the stages (predicted in Sordello) of imaginative re-creation of the vision, of immolation of self in the created objects, and of resultant 'glory' in repeating 'God's process.' The analogy between human and divine love in The Ring and the Book is thus finally linked to the analogy already made between the poetic method and divine creation. As the poet mirrors God, doing His work on earth and making Him apprehensible to man, he stands as the connecting link between time and eternity, drawing the finite and the infinite ever more closely together.[21]

poem is a "parable of the feeble and half-hopeless struggle which truth has to make against the ways of the world" (p. 260).

21/In this connection, many critics see the Incarnation, as symbol of the ulti-

Unquestionably, the claim is a high one, but the tone and theme of Book XII prove that Browning believed that he had fulfilled it. Why then the common critical assumption, as expressed by Miller's complaint about the "evanescent" quality of the poem's perception, that he had achieved no such apprehension in *The Ring and the Book*? Much of the blame, I think, can be placed on the misunderstandings that have attached to his statements about his use of '*fact*' in the poem.[22] Browning's repeated assurances that he had been absolutely faithful to the original sources have ironically led many readers to feel that he was reducing the role of creative imagination and making the poet a mere reporter and interpreter, instead of the seer, re-creator, and judge that he describes. Outside the poem, as well as within it, he constantly emphasizes his adherence to the facts as he

mate union of the finite and infinite, playing a central role in Browning's work; for a full-length study of this theme see William Whitla, *The Central Truth: The Incarnation in Robert Browning's Poetry* (1963). Thomas J. Collins, *Robert Browning's Moral-Aesthetic Theory 1833–1855* (1967), sees the Incarnation image in the final version of *Saul* suggesting the link between the subjective and objective poets, and as such it represents the "epitome of Browning's moral-aesthetic philosophy" (p. 126). William O. Raymond, *The Infinite Moment*, sees the concept of the Incarnation as pivotal even in *Pauline* and *Paracelsus*, where Browning's acceptance of the paradox of man as "a being in whom the claims and purposes of the finite and infinite meet" accounts for his rejection of romantic egoism (p. 163).

22/Critics have generally recognized the importance of Browning's emphasis on fact, but have disagreed about how to interpret it. The question has been argued at length in journals even recently; see Paul A. Cundiff, "Robert Browning: 'Our Human Speech'" (1959) and "Robert Browning: 'Indisputably Fact'" (1960), which stress the poet's distrust of distorted, as opposed to demonstrable, fact; Donald Smalley, "Browning's View of Fact in *The Ring and the Book*" (1959), which rejects, on the evidence of all his poetic output, the idea that the poet was "scuttling knowledge" and sees him instead characteristically reading his own ideas into facts; and Robert Langbaum, "The Importance of Fact in *The Ring and the Book*" (1960), which holds that Browning does indeed change the facts, not arbitrarily, but solely to reveal the truth which will otherwise remain hidden in them. In a different approach, Morse Peckham, in *Beyond the Tragic Vision: The Quest for Identity in the Nineteenth Century* (1962), explains Browning's conception of art as a moral instrument by describing it as an "illusion," a "lie," but a *way to truth*, because it breaks up our orientations and re-structures them, releasing us to attain a new apprehension and "do a significant act" (p. 276). I think both Langbaum and Peckham are correct about what Browning thought he was doing with fact: artistically re-ordering it, by imaginative re-creation and dramatization, to let the ordinary reader "do a significant act" in seeing a truth otherwise denied him.

found them: "the minutest circumstance that denotes character is true," he insisted, "the black is so much – the white, no more."[23]

But this is the point: these are the facts as *he* found them – he, the poet, with his God-given gift for penetrating beneath the surface confusions and contradictions of the written record. He could not have misread the record; to do so would be to deny the infallibility of the poet's intuitive grasp of the truth.[24] Others could misread it, of course, had indeed misread it, and part of his task was to demonstrate how that had happened and would continue to happen whenever the ordinary reader tried to deal with the court testimony as set down in the old yellow book. If the knowledge of Pompilia's innocence was God's gift to HIM, the poet, our knowledge of Pompilia's innocence is the poet's gift to US. In *The Ring and the Book* he shows how the knowledge is imparted in each case: his truth flashing forth on the first reading of the record in an instantaneous revelation, ours worked out only gradually in the step-by-step process of weighing the speeches he renders for us. But the important point, as the gold and alloy metaphor reminds us, is that, although the process of rendering will require some modification, by dramatization, of the original vision in order to make it comprehensible to others, the poet

23/Richard Curle, ed., *Robert Browning and Julia Wedgwood: A Broken Friendship as Revealed by Their Letters* (1937), p. 144. In another letter, Browning describes the way he feels driven to tell "the *truth*" in his poetry and wonders if it is really for his readers' sake or just by the working of "natural law" (p. 34). An interesting sidelight on his attitude toward the poetic gift of insight into truth is provided by Isobel Armstrong in "Browning's *Mr. Sludge, 'The Medium'*" (1964), in which she sees him exploring, with courage and profundity, the "inherent possibility of corruption" that the artist's powers carry with them (p. 8); Browning, then, is here facing the fact that Sludge's charlatanism is actually a perversion of his own high gift of seeing "outside the veil."

24/Critics who have compared the poem with the original source are unanimous in agreeing that Browning did in fact misread it, and the original Pompilia was at least partly guilty. See, for example, A. K. Cook, *A Commentary upon Browning's "The Ring and the Book"* (1920); Beatrice Corrigan, ed., *Curious Annals: New Documents Relating to Browning's Roman Murder Story* (1956); J. M. Gest, *The Old Yellow Book, Source of Browning's "The Ring and the Book"* (1925); and J. E. Shaw, "The 'Donna Angelicata' in *The Ring and the Book*" (1926). See also Donald Smalley, ed., *Browning's Essay on Chatterton* (1948) for evidence that Browning interpreted Chatterton's actions on the basis of what he thought were his motives, and not on the basis of documented fact. None of these accusations of misreading would have impressed Browning at all, of course, except to confirm his conviction that he was the only one who could find the real significance of motive behind the apparent significance of act.

is not free to compromise or dilute the truth in any way: the process merely involves a willingness on his part to stoop to the level of ordinary man, to offer him, 'No dose of purer truth than man digests, / But Truth with falsehood, milk that feeds him now' (v, 28). As one critic has said of Browning's attitude: "He is willing to adapt his manner to the world's capacity, but his matter is in higher keeping."[25]

The painstaking resuscitation of the actors is the poet's act of "stooping" in that it requires sacrificing some of the splendour and intensity of the original vision to the limitations of the human condition, the "stooping" that the hero of Pauline and the poets of Paracelsus were not capable of. Rather than give himself up to the delights of contemplating the 'pure white light' (as had Aprile in his failure), Browning commits himself to the arduous task of diffracting the light's brilliance, through his own person, so that the various rays composing it can be viewed by eyes too weak to see it in its full strength – the rays of 'Red, green and blue that whirl into a white.' Once the reader has seen the deflected rays in 'The variance now,' he too will experience the 'eventual unity' of the white light of truth (v, 44), because of the poet's freely offered sacrifice of his perfect private vision. The image is essentially that of Shelley's "dome of many-coloured glass" which "Stains the white radiance of Eternity," but Browning sees the glass, not as an obstacle to viewing the divine truth beyond, but rather as an instrument for making that truth visible to the human eye. The results of his "stooping" to let man rise, he feels, justify the price; he has reached as high as a human can aspire in repeating 'God's process in man's due degree' (v, 24).

But the victory is not only his. The poet's exultant tone in the first and last books conveys a sense of satisfaction that he has made us see what we had never seen before, made us know what only he knew before. It is as if Browning agrees that, as Wayne Booth has said of the author-reader relationship, the author "finds his rewards in the peers he has created." We experience, as a result of the poem, a sense of having moved into "a new order of perception and experience altogether,"[26] rising to a different, wider viewpoint in much the same way as all the truth-seekers of the poem: through a greater knowledge of self and through the good example of another to a completer apprehension of the truth. So in the end we become "pro-Pompilia" also, not because we have been told of her innocence, but

25/E. D. H. Johnson, The Alien Vision of Victorian Poetry, p. 135.
26/Wayne Booth, The Rhetoric of Fiction (1961), pp. 397–8.

because we have seen it demonstrated to our own satisfaction; we know it to be true, because the poet has imparted *'the gift of seeing'* to us. This is the final significance of the "voice and address" method of the poem. The complex and elaborately developed technique is not just a means to an end; it is means and end at once, WHAT we know finally as well as the WAY we know it. Only by understanding its operation and function can we fully appreciate the loftiness of Browning's aim in *The Ring and the Book* or the impressiveness of his accomplishment: to write a book that means *'beyond the facts,'* a book that can *'suffice the eye'* with its artistry, and can *'save the soul beside,'* by providing an inspiring demonstration of an artist's dedication to his moral and aesthetic ideals.

WORKS CITED

ABBREVIATIONS USED IN WORKS CITED

CE   College English
ELH   Journal of English Literary History
MLN   Modern Language Notes
PMLA   Publications of the Modern Language Association of
        America
SEL   Studies in English Literature, 1500–1900
SP   Studies in Philology
UTQ   University of Toronto Quarterly
VN   Victorian Newsletter
VP   Victorian Poetry
YR   Yale Review

Works Cited

ARMSTRONG, ISOBEL. "Browning's *Mr. Sludge, 'The Medium,'* " *VP*, II (Winter 1964), 1–9.

BOOTH, WAYNE. *The Rhetoric of Fiction.* Chicago, 1961.

BROWNING, ROBERT. *The Complete Works of Robert Browning*, ed. Charlotte Porter and Helen A. Clarke. 12 vols. New York, 1898.

————— *The Works of Robert Browning*, ed. Frederick G. Kenyon. 10 vols. London, 1912.

COLLINS, THOMAS J. *Robert Browning's Moral-Aesthetic Theory 1833–1855.* Lincoln, 1967.

COLUMBUS, ROBERT R. and CLAUDETTE KEMPER. "Sordello and the Speaker: A Problem in Identity," *VP*, II (Autumn 1964), 251–67.

COOK, A. K. *A Commentary upon Browning's "The Ring and the Book."* London, 1920.

CORRIGAN, BEATRICE, tr. and ed. *Curious Annals: New Documents Relating to Browning's Roman Murder Story.* Toronto, 1956.

COYLE, WILLIAM. "Molinos: 'The Subject of the Day' in *The Ring and the Book*," *PMLA*, LXVII (June 1952), 308–14.

CUNDIFF, PAUL A. "Robert Browning: 'Indisputably Fact,' " *VN*, no. 17 (Spring 1960), 7–11.

———— "Robert Browning: 'Our Human Speech,'" *VN*, no. 15 (Spring 1959), 1–9.

———— "The Clarity of Browning's Ring Metaphor," *PMLA*, LXIII (December 1948), 1276–82.

CURLE, RICHARD, ed. *Robert Browning and Julia Wedgwood: A Broken Friendship as Revealed by their Letters.* New York, 1937.

DEVANE, WILLIAM C. *A Browning Handbook.* 2nd ed. revised. New York, 1955.

———— "The Virgin and the Dragon," *YR*, XXXVII (1947), 33–46.

DRACHMANN, A. G. "Alloy and Gold," *SP*, XXII (July 1925), 418–24.

DUCKWORTH, F. R. G. *Browning: Background and Conflict.* London, 1931.

FAIRCHILD, HOXIE N. "Browning the Simple-Hearted Casuist," *UTQ*, XVIII (April 1949), 234–40.

FRIEDMAN, BARTON R. "To Tell the Sun from the Druid Fire: Imagery of Good and Evil in *The Ring and the Book*," *SEL*, VI (Autumn 1966), 693–708.

GEST, JOHN MARSHALL. *The Old Yellow Book, Source of Browning's "The Ring and the Book."* Boston, 1925.

HODELL, CHARLES W. "A Literary Mosaic," *PMLA*, XXIII [New Series XVI] (1908), 510–19.

———— *The Old Yellow Book: Source of Robert Browning's "The Ring and the Book."* New York, 1911.

HOLMES, STEWART W. "Browning: Semantic Stutterer," *PMLA*, LX (March 1945), 231–55.

HONAN, PARK. *Browning's Characters: A Study in Poetic Technique.* New Haven, 1961.

HOOD, THURMAN L., ed. *Letters of Robert Browning Collected by Thomas J. Wise.* New Haven, 1933.

JAMES, HENRY. *Notes on Novelists with Some Other Notes.* New York, 1914.

JOHNSON, E. D. H. *The Alien Vision of Victorian Poetry: Sources of the Poetic Imagination in Tennyson, Browning, and Arnold.* Princeton, 1952.

KING, ROMA A., Jr. *The Bow and the Lyre.* Ann Arbor, 1957.

LADRIÈRE, JAMES C. "Voice and Address," *Dictionary of World Literature*, ed. Joseph T. Shipley. 2nd ed. revised. New York, 1953. (Pp. 441–4.)

LANGBAUM, ROBERT. "The Importance of Fact in *The Ring and the Book*," *VN*, no. 17 (Spring 1960), 11–17.

—— *The Poetry of Experience: The Dramatic Monologue in Modern Literary Tradition.* New York, 1957.

LOVEJOY, ARTHUR O. *The Great Chain of Being: A Study of the History of an Idea.* Cambridge, Mass., 1948.

McELDERRY, B. R., Jr. "Victorian Evaluation of *The Ring and the Book*," *RSSCW*, VII (June 1939), 75–89.

—— "The Narrative Structure of Browning's *The Ring and the Book*," *Research Studies of the State College of Washington*, XI (September 1943), 193–233.

MILLER, BETTY. *Robert Browning: A Portrait.* New York, 1952.

MILLER, J. HILLIS. *The Disappearance of God: Five Nineteenth-Century Writers.* Cambridge, Mass., 1963.

NELSON, CHARLES EDWIN. "Role-Playing in *The Ring and the Book*," *VP*, IV (Spring 1966), 91–8.

PECKHAM, MORSE. *Beyond the Tragic Vision: The Quest for Identity in the Nineteenth Century.* New York, 1962.

PLATO. *The Republic of Plato*, trans. Francis MacDonald Cornford. New York, 1945.

POTTLE, FREDERICK A. *Shelley and Browning: A Myth and Some Facts.* Chicago, 1923.

RANSOM, JOHN CROWE. *The World's Body.* New York, 1938.

RAYMOND, WILLIAM O. *The Infinite Moment and Other Essays in Robert Browning.* Toronto, 1st ed. 1950, 2nd ed. rev. 1965.

SANTAYANA, GEORGE. *Interpretations of Poetry and Religion.* New York, 1927.

SHAW, J. E. "The 'Donna Angelicata' in *The Ring and the Book*," *PMLA*, XLI (March 1926), 55–81.

SHAW, W. DAVID. "Browning's Duke as Theatrical Producer," *VN*, no. 29 (Spring 1966), 18–22.

SHELLEY, PERCY B. *The Complete Works of Percy Bysshe Shelley*, ed. Roger Ingpen and Walter E. Peck. 10 vols. London, 1965.

SMALLEY, DONALD, ed. *Browning's Essay on Chatterton.* Cambridge, Mass., 1948.

—— "Browning's View of Fact in *The Ring and the Book*," *VN*, no. 16 (Fall 1959), 1–9.

SMITH, C. WILLARD. *Browning's Star-Imagery: The Study of a Detail in Poetic Design.* Princeton, 1941.

STEMPEL, DANIEL. "Browning's *Sordello*: The Art of the Makers-See," *PMLA*, LXXX (December 1965), 554–61.

SYMONS, ARTHUR. *An Introduction to the Study of Browning.* 2nd ed. revised. New York, 1906.

WARD, MAISIE. *Robert Browning and His World: The Private Face (1812–1861).* New York, 1967.

WASSERMAN, GEORGE R. "The Meaning of Browning's Ring-Figure," *MLN,* LXXVI (May 1961), 420–6.

WHITLA, WILLIAM. *The Central Truth: The Incarnation in Robert Browning's Poetry.* Toronto, 1963.

Index

This book

was designed by

ALLAN FLEMING

with the assistance of

ANTJE LINGNER

and was printed by

University of

Toronto

Press